DATE DUE

TRADE IN THE ANCIENT ECONOMY

Edited by

PETER GARNSEY, KEITH HOPKINS
and C. R. WHITTAKER

UNIVERSITY OF
CALIFORNIA PRESS
BERKELEY AND LOS ANGELES

Published in 1983 by
University of California Press
Berkeley and Los Angeles

LIBRARY OF CONGRESS CATALOGING
IN PUBLICATION DATA
Main entry under title.

Trade in the ancient economy.

Bibliography: p.
Includes index.
1. Greece — Commerce — History — Addresses, essays,
lectures. 2. Rome — Commerce — History — Addresses,
essays, lectures. I. Garnsey, Peter. II. Hopkins,
Keith, 1934– . III. Whittaker, C. R.
HF375.T73 1983 382′.093 82-13652
ISBN 0-520-04803-2

Phototypeset in Linotron Palatino by
Wyvern Typesetting Ltd, Bristol

Printed in Great Britain by
Redwood Burn Ltd.,
Trowbridge, Wiltshire

Contents

To MOSES

Introduction
by KEITH HOPKINS

The ancient economy is an academic battleground. The contestants campaign under various colours – apologists, marxists, modernizers, primitivists. Since academics are individuals, well-disciplined but not all marching to the same music, these categories are neither mutually exclusive, nor internally united. Even within schools, there are sects. Besides, new strategies, new alliances, new compromises are repeatedly devised. Fresh contingents of scholars arrive; new tactics (such as under-water archaeology) are developed.

The disputed territory is enormous. In space, it covers the whole of the Mediterranean basin and beyond, northwards to Britain, and eastwards to the Black Sea and the Red Sea. In time, our period runs roughly from the eighth century BC to the fifth century AD when the Roman empire in the West collapsed. The other dimensions of the ancient economy, indeed its very existence as an autonomous entity, are disputed. As in all battles, there are innocent by-standers, who do not want to get involved, such as the conventional political historians, or the philologically oriented sub-specialists of ancient history – epigraphers, papyrologists, pot-cataloguers. Their pacifism (in this battle) has its defensive ideology and rhetoric; their focus, or so they claim, is on the 'evidence', the 'facts', and on 'what really happened'. Finally, there are the non-combatant workers, such as the field archaeologists, who continually mine for ancient artefacts, and so provide the standing armies of scholars with their only new weapons. But no new weapon is lethal; and none of the battles is finally decisive. The war continues. Its underlying causes? They are difficult to discover. But professional love of polemic, deep differences in beliefs and values, and irremediable ignorance about the classical world all contribute.

This book is part of that extended intellectual debate. In order to understand the ancient economy, we need to know the part played in it by trade and traders; in order to understand the role of trade and traders, we need to hold some view of the ancient economy. Even to state that trade was an important element in the ancient economy is contentious. But this is not the place for another history, even of recent intellectual battles. Excellent accounts exist.[1] Instead, I thought that it would be worthwhile in this introduction to outline some of the theoretical problems which provide the framework within which much of the debate about trade in the ancient economy has been conducted.

Production and consumption are the two poles of routine economic analysis. Between them, trade provides a vital link. Through trade, consumers can get a wide variety of products, which they do not grow or make themselves. The distribution of goods through trade allows the specialization of labour, within a region or between regions. Trade makes possible the growth of towns and an increase in the number of townsfolk, who are freed by trade from the need to grow or make all that they need for themselves.

But here we face some difficulties. Trade is not the only mechanism for distributing varied produce to consumers. In a pre-industrial economy, distribution can also be effected by means of taxation and by the imposition of rents, provided that they are levied in labour or in kind (if they are levied in money, then trade is implied). Distribution can also be administered by the state, for example, through officials or priests, who receive 'gifts' and then re-cycle them to their followers. And finally, cult objects can be moved from one district to another, sometimes at great expense and in large quantities (as A. M. Snodgrass shows in his contribution), by believers who erect or dedicate their gifts at distant shrines.

We cannot simply assume that all the produce distributed in the ancient world or that all the fragments discovered by modern archaeologists were moved by trade. Instead, we have to ask what proportion was moved by trade, and what proportion was moved by other means. We have to ask to what extent did these proportions change in the long period covered by this book, and why did these changes take place. In sum, trade competed with other means of distributing food, goods and metals in the ancient world. In order to estimate the relative importance of trade, we have to make some judgements about the ancient economy.

A sketch of the ancient economy

The ancient economy was primarily agricultural. Most producers in all periods worked primarily on the land, and they consumed the bulk of their own produce. This is, I think, now commonly agreed. But we do not know, and there is much dispute about, how much was produced, and distributed, in any period, by way of surplus, over and above the needs of minimum subsistence. That is the main theoretical problem of this book. Until recently, scholars often used to write about the commercial foreign policies of small Greek states, and about the large industrial centres of the ancient world. These modernizing terms assumed a correspondingly high level of commercial and industrial activity, which now seems completely unjustified. They also simply assumed that modern economic concepts and institutions, such as investment, banks, freedom of trade, economic policy were easily applicable to the ancient world. In short, they assumed that there was an ancient economy, which was in some sense autonomous and which, like the economies of modern states, could plausibly be treated for most analytical purposes as separate from the polity and from society as a whole.

Over the last twenty years or so, a new orthodoxy has become dominant. It has been masterminded by A. H. M. Jones and Sir Moses Finley, successively professors of ancient history at Cambridge. It may be helpful, although it is obviously rash, to outline their views, or rather my understanding of them. The new orthodoxy stresses the cellular self-sufficiency of the ancient economy; each farm, each district, each region grew and made nearly all that it needed. The main basis of wealth was agriculture. The vast majority of the population in most areas of the ancient world was primarily occupied with growing food. To be sure, there were exceptions (such as classical Athens and the city of Rome), but they were exceptions and should be treated as such. Most small towns were the residence of local large-landowners, centres of government and of religious cult; they also provided market-places for the exchange of local produce and a convenient location for local craftsmen making goods predominantly for local consumption. The scale of inter-regional trade was very small. Overland transport was too expensive, except for the cartage of luxury goods. And even by sea, trade constituted only a very small proportion of gross product. That was partly because each region in the Mediterranean basin had a roughly similar climate and so grew similar crops. The low level of long-distance trade was also due to the fact that neither economies of scale nor investment in productive techniques ever reduced unit production costs sufficiently to compensate for high transport costs. Therefore, no region or town could specialize in the manufacture of cheaper goods; it could export only prestige goods, even overseas. And finally, the market for such prestige goods was necessarily limited by the poverty of most city-dwellers and peasants.

Several associated points can now be made. Just as the volume of trade was small, so the status of traders was generally low. And when the state required an exceptionally large amount of food or goods, for example, to supply the city of Rome or the Roman frontier armies, it relied primarily for their supply on the administrative system, via taxation in kind, rather than on traders or on purchase in the open market. The market was not stable enough or large enough, and the traders were not big enough, to be able to guarantee supplies in the necessary volume. Traders were typically small-fry. As with traders, so with craftsmen. Most of their units of production were small, family workshops with an apprentice perhaps or a handful of slaves, making goods mostly on demand and for the local market. Their generally low status reflected their low total output. Manufacture and commerce were rarely sources of considerable wealth, and if by chance they were, that wealth was rapidly transferred from trade to land. A. H. M. Jones put the case very clearly:

> Trade and manufacture played a very minor part in the economy of the Roman empire. The basic industry was agriculture; the vast majority of the inhabitants of the empire were peasants, and the wealth of the upper classes was in the main derived from rent. Fortunes might be made in trade, or more commonly in government service or in the more lucrative professions, such as rhetoric, but they were invested in land, the only form of stable capital. ((1974) 30)

Admittedly, there were some important ports and towns which acted as entrepôts for exported foods, goods and metals. But even in these towns (such as Carthage, Aquileia, Alexandria), local leaders were more likely to derive their wealth from the ownership of land than from active participation in manufacture or even commerce. Commerçants occasionally became prosperous town-councillors, although known instances are quite rare, while some town-councillors and even some aristocrats dabbled in commerce; they probably made money out of it. But practically all the wealthy Greeks and Romans we know about were, above all else, owners of agricultural land. Admittedly, they sold the produce of the farms which they managed directly, but that did not make them traders, any more than the leasing out of clay-pits for brick-making made them building contractors. In Greek and Roman society as a whole, commerce was always a side-issue compared with land-owning.

Ancient towns were typically centres of consumption, rather than centres of manufacture or commerce (Finley (1977)). They were consumption cities in the sense of Sombart's ideal type: 'By a consumption city, I mean one which pays for its maintenance . . . not with its own products, because it does not need to. It derives its maintenance rather on the basis of a legal claim, such as taxes or rents, without having to deliver return values.'[2] In this view, the scale and direction of petty commodity production in classical towns were fixed by the agricultural land-owners resident in the towns, not by commercial pressures to produce for external markets. Of course, this is an ideal type. It by no means excludes the fact that some Greek and Roman towns were also centres of administration or garrison towns. Nor does it ignore petty commodity production. Finley's intention here, I think, was that we should not automatically assume that the high level of Graeco-Roman urbanization was an index of its high economic development, just because urbanization was an index of economic development in post-mediaeval Europe. In the classical world, urbanization was more a reflection of a cultural pattern than of economic growth; it was a reflection of where rich agricultural land-owners chose to live and of their culturally induced patterns of conspicuous consumption.

Economic activity reflects both economic structure and cultural values. In the ancient economic structure, land and labour were the two most important factors in production. That was why the ownership of land, supplemented by the ownership of slaves or by the control over tenants, brought such high status; and that was partly why high status depended upon landed wealth. But high status in the Graeco-Roman world also brought with it specific obligations and cultural values about how money was to be acquired (and how it was seen to be acquired), and how it was to be spent. In other words, status dictated both methods of acquisition and patterns of consumption. Professor Finley's elevation of status (*The Ancient Economy*, Chapter II) at the expense of class has drawn the fire of those Marxists who are still trying to milk the rhetoric of class struggle and the dominant mode of production. The stress on status was no doubt intended to be polemical. But it was also a rare attempt to assimilate cultural value into economic analysis. It was an attempt to recognize a problem: classical man did not behave like economic man. There was in ancient society no moral reinforcement for productive investment, nor for profit maximization; no heavenly salvation was promised to the puritanical saver. Instead, high status involved competitive and ostentatious expenditure, whether in the service of the state, or in the local community, or in the pursuit of purely personal political glory. Vulgar acquisition was ideally left to underlings. If they succeeded, they were rapidly absorbed into the dominant spendthrift culture. In sum, among the rich in ancient societies, greater value was attached to conspicuous consumption than to increased production, or to the painful acquisition of more wealth.

These are the bare bones of the Finley model of the ancient economy. It is by far the best model available. It provides a matrix of coherent proposals about the structure, character and operation of the ancient economy. It provides a theoretical framework within which individual surviving fragments of evidence and individual case studies can be lodged. Alternatively, individual case studies can test the limits of the model and its applicability to different periods and regions of the classical world. In short, the Finley model provides a theoretical context for all the contributions to this book, whether they are in full agreement or in marginal dispute. But this is not surprising, since the book grew out of a series of seminars, most of which Sir Moses himself attended, at which we thrashed out, or more often went in circles round, areas of agreement and disagreement. Both the seminars and the book were designed as yet another recognition of Sir Moses Finley's charismatic and influential contributions to ancient history.

Economic Growth

A model of the ancient economy has a lot to cope with. It must cover the considerable diversity which existed within the Mediterranean basin, and it must take account of the considerable political changes which occurred in the period 1000 BC–AD 500 (Finley (1973) 29). The price we pay for having a single model to cover such diversity is that it may appear too uniform, almost static in composition. And paradoxically for a theory which proposes that the ancient economy was embedded in the polity, it seems to underestimate the impact of political changes. In short, I want to suggest an elaboration of the Finley model to accommodate modest economic growth and subsequent decline.

In my view, the size of the surplus produced in the Mediterranean basin during the last millennium BC and the first two centuries AD gradually increased. The upward trend was gradual, not very large but significant, and with many oscillations either way. The growth in the surplus produced and extracted was largely the result of two factors, political change and the spread of technical and social innovations. By political change, I mean here growth in the size and power of political systems, as previously autonomous tribes and independent city-states succumbed to successive conquering empires (Athenian, Alexandrian, Carthaginian, Roman). I shall argue in a moment that the exaction of taxes by these states forced an increase in the size of the surplus produced. But economic growth was also the result of the diffusion of technical innovations and social institutions throughout the whole Mediterranean basin. The axis of this diffusion was, generally speaking, from the south-east Mediterranean towards north-eastern Europe. Among narrowly technical aids to improved production, I include iron tools, iron knives, screw presses, rotary mills, even water mills. But social innovations probably had even more impact: silver and bronze coins, money taxes, chattel slavery, writing, schools, written contracts, commercial loans, technical handbooks, large sailing ships, shared risk investment, absentee landlordism – these are only some of the social innovations which spread throughout the Mediterranean world in the last millennium BC and the first few centuries AD. Let me stress that what matters here is not where or when they were first invented or first attested. What matters is the increase in their use and the impact which their widespread use had on a) production, b) consumption and c) trade.

The proposition that there was a general trend throughout much of classical antiquity towards the production of larger surplus is difficult, perhaps impossible, to prove or to disprove. It is also more complicated than it may appear at first sight. The complications become apparent when the proposition is broken down into components. For the sake of clarity, I shall present these components in a very strong form (i.e. without all the appropriate qualifications) in seven clauses.

First, total agricultural production rose during classical antiquity, as more land in the Graeco-Roman world as a whole was brought under arable cultivation. Settlement patterns and pollen counts provide illustrative evidence of increased agricultural production, just as they indicate a decline in arable area and settlements during the third and fourth centuries AD. But the coverage of such evidence is slight compared with the total area under consideration.

Secondly, the population of the Roman world in the first and second centuries AD was greater than the population of the same area a) 1,000 years earlier and b) 500 years later. Thirdly, the proportion of the total population engaged in non-agricultural production and services increased. Most craftsmen and petty traders probably lived in towns, but many continued to live in villages. Therefore the increase in urban populations which occurred in classical antiquity (witness the increase in the built-up area of towns) is only a very crude index of this change. However, additional corroboration can be found in the sophisticated division of labour for which there is incomplete evidence, for example, in Pompeii (85 known occupations), Corycus (110 known occupations) and the city of Rome (264 known occupations).

Fourth, because of the increased division of labour, total non-agricultural product rose. One crude index of this increase is the common archaeological observation, at least in the western provinces of the Roman empire, that more artefacts are found at Roman than at pre-Roman levels: more coins, more pots, lamps, iron tools, carved stones, ornaments. Material culture in the first two centuries AD reached a higher level in a wider area of the Mediterranean than it was to reach again for centuries. Archaeological finds comprise not just luxury objects made of gold or ivory, but also, for example, simple glazed table-ware, relatively expensive blown-glass bowls, sophisticated medical instruments, and everyday items like padlocks and iron nails. But we have to be careful, because these residues were deposited over a long period of time. They may also represent accumulation through intensified exploitation (see below clause six) rather than increased total production.

Fifth, average productivity *per capita*, the average amount produced by each person engaged in agriculture and in non-agricultural production, rose. The increase in average agricultural productivity is relatively unproblematic, since it is implied by clause three; in the first two centuries AD, proportionally fewer food-producers were growing more food than ever before for more non-agricultural producers. At this stage, I should enter a qualification; much of this increase in average agricultural productivity achieved by the first century AD resulted from the diffusion of standards of productivity which has been achieved much earlier in several parts of the eastern Mediterranean. But I suspect that by the first century AD, there were also increases in average agricultural productivity, compared with classical Athens (for reasons which I outline below). Such increases in average productivity were very modest and are impossible to prove. But illustrative corroboration for generally increased productivity can be found in the wider use of iron tools, in some improvements in agricultural implements (e.g. screw presses), and in the mere existence of agricultural handbooks, which were symptoms of attempts to rationalize the use of labour, particularly slave labour. Agricultural productivity increased, above all because of the increased pressure of exploitation. Two types of exploitation need to be distinguished. First, agricultural slaves were forced to work longer than free men and were given, on average, more land to work than many free peasants could afford to own. Secondly, free peasants and owners of slaves were forced to work harder in order to produce taxes for the state, and in a significant minority of cases, in order to produce rent for the legal owners of the land which they worked.

The increase in non-agricultural productivity, that is in the average produced by each person engaged in handicrafts (the word manufacture is preferable but tends to be misleading) and in commerce and other services is much more problematic. Clearly, there was no basic shift. Any overall change was modest in its impact on the total economy. Human and animal muscles remained the main motive power. Muscle power was supplemented by levers, pulleys and ratchets, by fire, by water (for mills in late antiquity and for mineral washing), by wind (for ship-sails not mills), and by technical competence. Roman engineering works are understandably famous; to take one modest example, at Lincoln, fresh water was brought to the town and was pumped uphill in a pipeline sealed in concrete (a Roman invention) to withstand pressure. There were some technical advances (e.g. rotary mills, and methods for improving the air flow in iron smelting), and there were increases in common unit size of production and transport. Once again, part of this improvement involved the diffusion of practices known earlier in the eastern Mediterranean. After all, the largest 'factory' known from the ancient world was in Athens in the fourth century BC; it employed 120 slaves in the manufacture of shields. Yet is seems reasonable to suppose that there were more large units of production (such as potteries employing sixty slaves), just as there were larger ships (ships of 400 tonnes burden were common; ships of up to 1,000 tonnes burden were built but rare) in the first two centuries AD if only because huge consumer markets existed. The city of Rome had perhaps almost one million inhabitants, while Alexandria, Antioch and Carthage, each with a population of several hundred thousand, needed to be supplied not merely with food, but also with consumer goods, cloth, timber, pots, bricks, dies and luxuries. The sceptic may argue that few of these alleged larger units (except ships and potteries) existed, and even if they did exist, they did not necessarily deliver greater productivity; large ships carried proportionately larger crews, without effecting improvements in safety or speed. Then why were they built?

Three other stimuli to improved productivity in handiwork and commerce deserve to be mentioned: institutional innovations, slavery and peace. Under the rubric, institutional innovations, I include the diffusion of business practices, stretching from small business partnerships to commercial loans, from banks to associations for sharing risks in large investments. Cato the Elder, for example, is said to have participated in maritime loans only on a share basis; he combined fifty ships, fifty borrowers and fifty lenders, then took one share in the total risk (Plutarch, *Cato the Elder* XXI). Roman associations (*societates*) for investing in tax-farming are notorious, but there were also similar associations engaged in silver-, gold- and salt-mining (*Digest* III 4.1). Roman mining enterprises, to judge from slag heaps of twenty to thirty million tonnes in southern Spain, were sometimes on a very large scale. And it seems reasonable to suppose that co-operative capital investment was profitable because large scale enterprises increased productivity. Many men working together produced more on average than men working alone or in small family enterprises. If not, why invest?

A similar argument applies to slavery. The mere fact that many slaves were bought to produce or sell goods presupposes that slaves could be forced or encouraged to work hard enough to yield a profit on the capital which the slave owner had invested. How was that profit to be achieved except by increased productivity? The sceptic may object that the potteries at Arezzo, worked by slaves, lasted only a short period and were replaced by equally large potteries in southern and central Gaul, worked by free labour; the slave status of workers did not create a price advantage in production which outweighed other costs of production and transport. A trenchant point. But in so far as slaves were used as workers in crafts and commerce, their capital cost probably stimulated economies of scale and organization which were subsequently copied. The organization of lamp-making at central, and later at branch factories, is a case in point.[3] Slave organization and economies could be imitated by employers of free labour, and at lower capital cost (for an example of free wage labour contracted in mines, see *F.I.R.A.* III 150).

Finally, peace. For more than two centuries, the Roman peace more or less freed the inhabitants of the Roman world from major military disturbances; the Mediterranean was free of pirates, major roads were usually clear of brigands; tax burdens were by and large predictable. I do not want to eulogize the grandeur of the Roman empire. But it seems likely that these conditions allowed the gradual accumulation of capital. In agriculture, the construction of retaining walls, terraces, ditches and drains, in commerce, freedom from piracy, the construction of larger ships, the building and repair of roads and bridges, the predictability of markets, the acquisition of tools and the recoverability of loans, all may have contributed to substantial increases in productivity in some pockets of the ancient economy, and perhaps to marginal increases in average productivity overall.

My sixth clause or sub-proposition is that a) the total amount and b) the proportion of total production extracted from primary producers in taxes and in rent increased. In other words, the screws of exploitation tightened. As the size and power of states increased in classical antiquity, the state exacted more for itself in order to support the superstructure of professional, regularly paid military defenders, an administrative infrastructure of paid officials and clerks, and an expensive imperial Court. In addition, the state permitted, indeed it supported, the extraction of a greater surplus by rich landowners from tenants who paid rent. As a system of production, slavery set the benchmark for the degree of exploitation condoned. In that sense, slavery 'dominated' the ancient economy. But it was prevalent only in the heartlands of empire, in Attica and in Roman Italy, and there it was a major factor in forcing up productivity. In Roman Italy, slave-owners earnt a return on their capital investment in the purchase of labour by making slaves work harder than free men wanted to and on larger estates than free families could work with their own labour. Slavery thus provided economies of scale and by the displacement of free peasants (whether to the city of Rome or to distant colonies) forced an economically rationalizing reallocation of the two prime factors in ancient production, land and labour. That said, in terms of volume, slavery was by no means the most important mechanism for stimulating the production of a larger surplus. That was done by the Roman state's universal exaction of tax on agricultural land. Particularly, in the western provinces, these exactions by the Roman state forced peasants to produce a surplus which either they had previously consumed themselves or more probably which they had not produced before. In addition, the extension of Roman law legitimated the exaction of rent from tenants who worked land 'owned' by others. Conquest by Rome involved support for the superstructure of the state and for the competitive, consumptive life-style of local, provincial and metropolitan aristocrats.

Finally, the seventh clause. In the first and second centuries AD the Roman state exacted a large amount of taxes in money and then spent them, predominantly along the frontiers where the armies were stationed and in the city of Rome where the emperor normally kept

Court. The expenditure of taxes (and similarly of money rents paid to absentee landlords) at some distance from where they were raised stimulated a large volume of long-distance trade, as tax-payers secured money with which to pay taxes in successive years by the sale of produce (for detailed arguments, see Hopkins (1980)). In this scheme, towns played a vital role, as centres in which local craftsmen converted the locally produced surplus into higher value, lower volume goods for transport and sale to distant markets. There is no intention here to underrate the amount of taxes raised in kind, or the extent of trade which was stimulated by other factors, such as reciprocal needs and market forces. It is an attempt to suggest the consequences of the fact that Romans raised considerable taxes in money in core provinces and spent them elsewhere. How else did tax-paying peasants find the money with which to pay their taxes? The same question, *mutatis mutandis*, has to be asked and answered about the exaction of rents by absentee landowners, who lived in provincial capitals or in the city of Rome. In sum, the thickened network of Roman trade provided an underpinning for the state's capacity to exact its money taxes and then spend them in distant locations.

It is often argued that the high cost of transport overland precluded large-volume overland trade. Land transport cost roughly sixty times as much as sea transport and ten times as much as transport by river downstream (there was obviously a lot of variation around these means). But the pattern of archaeological survivals suggests that goods were transported far and wide overland and by river; see for example the striking evidence provided by A. Tchernia in this book. According to Diocletian's *Edict on Maximum Prices* (AD 301), the cheapest wool could be transported 300 km by mule for only a 10 per cent increase in price (*Edict* 1, 17 and 25). And comparable evidence from the Middle Ages suggests that although sea-routes from Venice or Genoa to northern Europe were used, the land-routes from northern Italy to northern Europe continued in use also; they were more expensive, but safer and quicker.

Finally, money. The use of money percolated deep into the Roman economy, witness price lists at inns and huge amounts of small change; even in Egyptian villages, as many surviving scraps of papyri show, labour contracts and contracts for rents and loans were usually in money. Between 157 and 80 BC, the volume of Roman silver coins in circulation increased tenfold (Hopkins (1980) 109). And all impressions suggest that in the Roman empire as a whole, in the first two centuries AD, the volume of silver and bronze coinage increased enormously.

Increased monetization suggests increased trade: more transactions by producers selling food, goods and metals to unspecified customers, with money as the medium of exchange. A Rabbi Isaac in the second century AD advised: 'A man should always divide his money: one third in land, one third in trade, and keep one third in hand' (*Bava Mezia* 42a). It was advice which not many could follow, but in the beginning of the ancient economy, such advice would have been meaningless.

These seven clauses taken together imply that overall in the first two centuries AD, total production, consumption and trade were greater than they had been in the previous centuries or were in subsequent centuries. In my view, the Finley model of the ancient economy is sufficiently flexible to incorporate this modest dynamic, without undermining its basic primitivism. In closing this section, let me stress again, that the proposals outlined above cannot be proved, nor can they be easily disproved. Some scholars simply take them for granted. Others dismiss them out of hand. But then, one of the excitements and disadvantages of ancient history is that even fundamental points are disagreed.

Problems and Issues

Whatever the theoretical framework, important substantive and technical problems remain to be solved or discussed. These problems form both the explicit and the hidden agenda of this book. Above all, we need to know the volume and the value of trade in the classical world. We need to know what was traded and the routes along which food, goods and metals flowed. How much did the volume, value, content and direction of trade change over time and between regions during classical antiquity? What was the status of traders, and how much did their status reflect, or affect the scale of trade, or the size of the trading units involved (e.g. the size of ships and of partnerships)?

These questions are difficult enough. But trade was a bridge between production and consumption. Once we acknowledge that, then the list of necessary questions inevitably grows longer. We need to know to what extent variations in the system of production (from free peasants to slaves to tied tenants, for example) affected the size of the surplus produced or extracted, and the volume of trade. We need to know how far political changes, for example, the development of empires in Athens and Rome, also created consumer markets in the capital cities, and the extent to which these consumers were supplied by trade or by requisition. And finally, we need to know the extent to which ancient states, consciously or unintentionally, pursued policies which encouraged trade, and the extent to which states circumscribed trade by fostering other mechanisms of distribution, such as taxation in kind. In sum, trade and its alternatives bring us to the heart of the ancient political economy. They were its arteries and veins.

One obvious reason why it is so difficult to answer these questions is the fragmentary quality of our surviving evidence. Modern economic historians use official trade figures, price series, state budgets, routinely as tools of their trade. Historians of antiquity, by contrast, have no such ready-made statistics. Instead, most analysis of the ancient economy is painfully built up from fragments. The fragments are sometimes numerous, as the reader will see, but they are still fragments. Repeatedly, therefore, throughout this book, we face three interconnected technical problems of interpretation: the problem of the unknown universe, the problem of representativeness or bias, and what I shall call the problem of proxies. Let me deal briefly with each. First, scholars often try to reconstitute the universe from which the surviving fragments come. From surviving sculptured statues, can we estimate how many statues were set up in Greece throughout the whole Archaic period? Or how much trade in wine is implied by the tens of thousands of clay wine jars dug up in southern France? Secondly, there is the well-known problem of bias. For example, how much is our picture of the pattern of trade affected by regional differences in the activities, practices and interests of archaeologists? Are distribution maps of artefacts therefore more maps of archaeological activity than of ancient trade? The third problem, the problem of proxies, is closely related. Pots survive better than cloth or wood, bronze survives better than iron. Can we validly use surviving pots as proxies, or as tracers for items which have long perished? Moving from wine containers to the wine trade is plausible enough. But, for example, would the distribution map for the ancient wool trade look like recent maps for the distribution of ancient pots? The answer to this question is surprisingly critical for the study of the ancient economy.

The thirteen essays in this book are written by leading archaeologists and historians from four different countries (England, France, Italy and Holland) and from varied intellectual traditions. Although I cannot here summarize their individual arguments, nor indeed would it be particularly useful since different readers will have different interests in them, nevertheless it might be useful to touch on elements in their arguments which concern the theoretical, substantive and technical problems which I have just outlined.

The first five pieces (by Cartledge, Snodgrass, Garlan, Millett, Mossé) deal with Greece in the archaic and classical periods, from the eighth to the fourth century BC. They are all, I think, firmly primitivist in emphasis. Snodgrass, for example, argues that the very large number of heavy marble statues found throughout the Greek world from the archaic period were not items of trade, but religious objects, commissioned by powerful patrons. By the sixth century BC, there was an increase in trade; witness the existence of a port called Emporion and the construction of purpose-built merchantships. But any talk of a 'commercial' aristocracy or of a 'commercial' policy is unrealistically inflated and anachronistic. Even in classical Athens, where the existence in the fourth century BC of special law-courts to try commercial cases indicates sophisticated development, trade was predominantly small-scale. Some elite members dabbled in trade, usually through lower status intermediaries; but all depended upon agriculture for their basic wealth and social standing. Professional traders did not belong to the political elite; there was no significant commercial representation in politics. Again, the existence of banks and of maritime loans in Athens has often been taken to imply sophisticated commercial credit. But much is unknown; there is no evidence even that Athenian banks paid interest on deposits. Besides, most borrowers borrowed from family, not from banks. The typical size of shipping loans was small; we do not even know how usual they were. The vast majority of loans, excluding maritime loans, were used to pay for extra consumption, not for increased production or trade. And most were the results of chronic underfunding. Millett argues, by association, that maritime loans were not a sophisticated means of splitting risk, nor even a type of insurance policy, but rather a reflection of the small-scale and chronic underfunding of Athenian trade.

A second block of contributions (by Goudineau, Tchernia, Pucci and Carandini) are concerned with pots (containers and tableware) and with trade in high volume. Even from the narrow case study of Marseilles, we can trace the rapid growth of Roman wine imports during the last two centuries BC. And in southern France, as a whole, a spectacular number of Roman winejars datable to the period 130–20/10 BC, have been found. For example, 24,000 were found at one river site, and those were only a fraction of what could have been dredged up. The export of Italian wine to Gaul seems to have been principally connected with the import of

Gallic slaves into Italy, though at the probable rate of exchange, the volume of wine traded was only a small proportion of all that was then produced in Italy. Even so, there can be no doubt that here we are faced with trade in significant volume, even if the exchange of wine for human slaves was more a reflection of unequal power than of developed trade, at least among the Gauls. Whatever the difficulties of interpretation, the sheer volume of Italian pots exported cannot be argued away. Compared with ancient literary comment, that is hard evidence. The scale of total production was large; the units of production were also large, employing perhaps up to sixty slaves in one 'factory'. The decline of the potteries at Arezzo in the early first century AD and their replacement by provincial potteries worked by non-slaves is very difficult to explain (especially for those who consider that the juridical status of workers is crucial). Yet we are not primarily concerned with pots as and for themselves – they were only a minor item in gross product. We are more concerned here with pots as tracers for other items of trade, now vanished. In this light, the study of African pottery is very important. From the late first century AD, Italian ware was no longer exported to northern Africa, and north African pottery, principally from modern Tunisia, was exported in increasing volume to Italy. In the second century AD, north African ware (much of it olive oil containers) predominated at Rome; and so we must deduce large scale traffic in olive oil from north Africa to Rome in that period. From the third century AD, African ware was spread widely throughout the Mediterranean basin, and continued to be widely diffused, especially in the eastern Mediterranean until the fifth century AD. I must stress that no figures are available to compare with those given by Tchernia for southern France, but even so we get the strong impression of widespread and relatively large volume trade. What else could account for the dispersion of so many African pots?

A third set of papers (by Thompson, Garnsey, Pleket and Whittaker) deals with distributions in kind effected by state requisition rather than by trade, and with the status of traders. The supply of food to capitals (Alexandria, when it was capital of Egypt, and Rome) was politically too sensitive an issue to be left to the rough play of market forces. The cities were large, 500,000 to a million people; the city of Rome required perhaps 200,000 tonnes of wheat per year. Much of that was provided by tax in kind, but it was brought to Rome at least until the third century AD by private shippers, who were usually freeborn substantial property-owners and traders, of well below aristocratic or knightly status. The mere size of Roman merchant ships (350–400 tonnes burden was quite common) indicates the scale of Roman trade and the large sums of capital invested and at risk in it. But there is considerable debate as to who the investors were. Were they aristocrats investing through slave and ex-slave intermediaries, or knights and town-councillors, that is landed property-owners with strong but subsidiary commercial interests? Or were they ex-slaves who had to some extent shaken off ties with their former owners and who then acted independently and often with substantial capital of their own? Or were these investors freeborn respectables of intermediate status with only modest capital resources? The answer is probably a mixture of all four categories, with exact specification of relative importance impossible. And, as Pleket stresses, the exact status of traders may not be critical for determining the volume of trade. All the more so because the total volume of transfers in kind executed by the state, or by private landowners (and later by the Church), is completely unknown. In the final essay, Whittaker argues the revolutionary hypothesis that increased state exactions in kind in the late Empire (fourth to sixth centuries AD) and the effective decommercialization of the economy reflected a reorganization of the means of exchange rather than economic decline. There was, he maintains, no fall in production or exchange, only a decline in the entrepreneurial commodity market.

Much is unknown, much disputed. The contributors to this book do not all agree with each other, even about fundamental elements in the ancient economy. But then controversy and debate seem a suitable tribute to Sir Moses Finley, to whom this book is dedicated.

[1]

'Trade and Politics' revisited: Archaic Greece

by PAUL CARTLEDGE

' "Shades of Hasebroek", the reader will exclaim.' So began one review of the published proceedings of the Second International Conference of Economic History (ancient section).[1] That of course was the intention of the section organizer, M. I. Finley, implicit in the title chosen for the section. For Johannes Hasebroek's two books were, as Finley observed, 'the most controversial twentieth-century works in Greek economic history'; and though in his own contribution to the conference Finley did not aim to 'defend the whole Hasebroek position, and least of all to re-open the *oikos* controversy', he did wish to underline the truth and fruitfulness of Hasebroek's 'fundamental distinction between an import interest and a commercial interest'.[2]

Hasebroek's 'bombshell' (de Ste. Croix's word) did not drop out of a clear blue sky of serene research into ancient Greek economic history. Finley's short-hand reference to 'the *oikos* controversy' locates Hasebroek's contribution within the wider 'Bücher-Meyer controversy',[3] which in turn links it to the (also mainly German) nineteenth-century debate concerning the periodization of world economic development. This latter debate has been summarized adequately for our purposes by Edouard Will (1954) and need not concern us further; but Will's article is of more than passing interest. For it sought to define the chief lineaments of 'three quarters of a century of research on the ancient Greek economy' in relation to the great debate between the 'modernizers' (Eduard Meyer and his followers) and the 'primitivists' (Bücher and his followers). This debate, Will commented, was then nearly a century old and not yet closed. A quarter of a century on, it has if anything acquired fresh vitality, thanks partly to its transplantation into economic anthropology, in part to the pace of recent archaeological discoveries.

It is not my aim in this position paper to update Will, but these pages may be seen as a contribution towards that useful task. For the quantity and quality of the work published on archaic Greece since 1954 are remarkable.[4] All this work bears directly or indirectly on the problem selected for renewed discussion here; but no less remarkable has been the recent response, whether conscious or not, to the suggestions for further research proposed by Finley ((1965) 33–5) and de Ste. Croix.[5] The time therefore seems propitious, after half a century of productive labours, for a *mise au point* on 'the Hasebroek problem'.

I express the problem this way deliberately. Mele, whose brief monograph (1979) is the most detailed discussion to date of the mechanics of archaic Greek trade and its relation to politics, fails even to mention Hasebroek; while Murray, whose general account of the archaic period is probably the most widely used by English-speaking students, is of the opinion that 'the old controversy on the role of trade in early Greece . . . has been largely outmoded by archaeological discoveries and the changes in our conception of political history'.[6] This studied neglect is, I believe, unjustified and I begin with a full synopsis of Hasebroek's position on 'trade and politics' in archaic Greece.[7]

II

What inspired Hasebroek's counterblasts was the modernizing of ancient history, which he traced back to Mommsen's *Römische Geschichte*. According to the modernizers, the economic development of the ancient world more or less closely prefigured that of the modern in all essentials, the differences being of degree rather than kind. It was therefore in order, indeed obligatory, to project modern economic concepts onto the ancient Greek world. The clearest expression of this outlook was presented in the anti-Bücher polemics of Eduard Meyer, who believed quite literally that the seventh and sixth centuries BC in Greece corresponded to the fourteenth and fifteenth centuries in the development of 'die Neuzeit', the fifth BC to the sixteenth AD.[8]

To such modernizers Hasebroek objected on general grounds that ancient economic history was still in its infancy, that the evidence particularly for archaic Greece was insufficient to support bold reconstructions, but that the little contemporary evidence there was told against their pictures. For even in classical Greece the structure of the Greek economy as a whole was 'primitive' or relatively so, and the onus was on the modernizers to disprove the *a fortiori* argument that in the archaic period it had been more primitive still. Clearly, much turns on what Hasebroek understood and implied by 'primitive': was the distinction he drew between the ancient and modern worlds one of quality or quantity?

In making his positive case Hasebroek argued his interpretation of archaic and classical Greece on consciously Weberian lines. Max Weber had characterized 'the ancient citizen' (Bürger) as a *homo politicus*, thereby both distinguishing him from the ideal-typical *homo economicus* of the modern world and insisting that ancient economic activity had to be situated for purposes of analysis within the peculiar matrix of the ancient city (cf. Finley (1981)). Thus, whereas in medieval trading cities 'the decisive motivations . . . were the elimination of bothersome competitors, the domination of the trade routes or their liberation from tolls, and the gaining of trade monopolies and staple rights', in the ancient Greek city 'the economic policy . . . was dominated by direct provision for grain supplies', 'an employment and output policy oriented around independent craft producers never appeared as a significant element', in short 'nowhere were the politics of an ancient city dominated by . . . producer interests'.[9]

Or, in the words of Hasebroek ((1933) vii), 'the interests of national production, or of a class of producers, never determined the policy of the autonomous Greek state . . . The so-called commercial policy of the ancient state was not concerned with trade, but with the supply of necessities, such as grain and timber, and with the enrichment of the treasury by means of tolls and duties.'

Within this overall institutional framework Hasebroek combated what he took to be the misconceptions of the modernizers and substituted his own picture. In detail, he vigorously attacked the view that in archaic cities like Miletus, Aegina, Corinth and Marseilles 'a brilliant new commercial aristocracy at first intermingled with and ultimately displaced and overthrew the old landed gentry' ((1933) 45). For although the aristocratic-oligarchic governing classes of such archaic states had overall control of commercial intercourse, as did the rulers and headmen in all primitive societies, this control 'did not make them traders or the basis of their power commercial' ((1933) 16). Rather, the conception of the Greek ruling classes as commercial was mistaken twice over: it overlooked the real sources of their wealth, that is agriculture, pasturage, piracy and plunder; and it failed to grasp that direct involvement in commerce was incompatible both with Greek notions of aristocracy and citizenship and with the dominant psychological attitude to labour. In revealing contrast, the aristocracies of late medieval Venice, Holland and the Hansa towns might properly be characterized as commercial, since there, trade was 'imbued with the aristocratic spirit' ((1933) 21).

Trade and manufacture, Hasebroek somewhat reluctantly conceded, did increase in importance between the eighth and sixth centuries BC. But nowhere in pre-hellenistic Greece did there develop large-scale industry, factories or an export industry involving the distribution of mass-produced commodities for mass consumption. Peaceful trade did gradually become differentiated from piracy and voyages of adventure and discovery, just as the specialized wind-powered merchantman became functionally separated from the oared warship and pirate cutter. But still in the sixth century there is no evidence for the regular, inter-regional exchange of items of everyday need. Trade was conducted in special articles of high value, and the wide distribution of Corinthian and Attic luxury ceramics was compatible with small-scale production in cottage industries, like that of Chinese porcelain and Persian carpets in more modern times.

As to the personnel involved, very few full citizens of archaic Greek states were in Hasebroek's view traders or craftsmen. Such professional commerce as came to be taken over by Greeks from the Phoenicians was typically in the hands of an impoverished and deracinated proletariat, for whom this occupation was very much a *pis aller*. Some, perhaps many, of these proletarians might in favourable circumstances enrich themselves. For the absence of permanent markets and of price-equivalence, together with the physical difficulties and dangers of trading (bad weather, piracy, reprisals, warfare: cf. Knorringa ((1926) 32–4), could make for high profit margins in archaic Greece. However, a successful trader would quickly cease to trade in person and would devote his windfall profits to the purchase or rental of land.

In so far as archaic nobles could be said to trade at all, they travelled – like Sappho's brother, Charaxus, and perhaps Solon and Pindar's Aeginetan patrons – to dispose of the surplus produce of their estates. Typically, though, their economic activity took the form of 'pure physical force' and brutality, a point which Hasebroek labours ((1933) vii, 17, 103, 110, 136, 139). Hence the rudimentary level of Greek economic thinking even in the classical period, which was reflected in the primitive character of Greek economic organization: no state budgets, no state money economies. Instead of 'geschlossene Handelsgebiete' we find 'politische Machtgebiete' ((1931) 272): ancient imperialism, the limiting case, was the handmaiden of necessary supplies for rentier citizens not an economic system set up to secure advantages for citizen merchants or producers. In short, Miletus and the rest were not commercial cities with merchant citizen bodies; if trade played a more important role in these than in the average archaic Greek city, this was because they were focal points of trade, emporia where tolls levied on goods in transit served the 'exchequer' as a means of 'fiskalischer Ausbeutung' ((1931) 273).

III

For Hasebroek, then, with whose general picture I am in complete sympathy, the distinction in economic development between the ancient Greek and the modern worlds was both quantitative and qualitative; but for polemical reasons he had primarily emphasized the former. Moreover, in his eagerness to hammer the lid shut on the coffin of modernizing theories he had inevitably bent a few nails. It was not difficult for hostile critics to challenge such views as that practically all archaic trade and manufacture was in the hands of non-citizens, that security and stability are indispensable to the flourishing of a commercial civilization, and that Attic and Corinthian fine pottery was not certainly made in fixed centres of production by full-time potters and painters. In a celebrated essay A. W. Gomme ((1937) 57 n.1) scornfully recommended: 'Let anyone who is still taken in by Hasebroek's pretentions read his (A. Blakeway's) articles, and learn what scholarship means.'

This dismissive attitude was not perhaps as scholarly and disinterested as it may appear, since modernizing theories 'débouchaient souvent sur une apologie du système d'exploitation capitaliste'.[10] But in any case Hasebroek's empirical deficiencies were taken by those who shared this attitude to disqualify his theoretical schema from serious attention. Gomme, for example, simply ignored the institutional framework within which Hasebroek had been careful to couch his discussion and referred his readers to the work on archaic trade of a thoroughgoing modernizer. He thereby succeeded in overlooking what Will ((1954) 13) in some ways correctly regarded as Hasebroek's main achievement, to have removed 'the analysis from the plane of the forms of economic activity to the plane of the relation between these forms and political life within the framework – unique in history – of the *polis*'. Hasebroek, though, had not gone far enough.

On the one hand, he had not insisted sufficiently clearly and firmly that what we call, rather misleadingly, 'the economy' was not in fact, and therefore was not conceptualized as, a differentiated, quasi-autonomous sphere of social activity in archaic and classical Greece. On the other hand, he had not adequately brought out the fact that ancient Greece belongs to the class of pre-capitalist economic formations, in which the distribution and exchange of commodities take quite different forms from those current in the modern world, most relevantly because of the absence of a system of interconnected price-fixing markets. Both these points had been fully grasped in the mid-nineteenth century by Marx, but the rough drafts in which his insights were contained, the so-called *Grundrisse*, were not published until 1939, not widely available until 1953, and not fully absorbed into the mainstream of critical economic theory and history until the 1960s.[11] It was chiefly due to the influence of Karl Polanyi, who was himself influenced not by Marx but by R. Thurnwald, that similar insights were first brought to bear on archaic Greece.[12]

Briefly, the burden of Polanyi's critique of current thinking in anthropology paralleled that of Hasebroek's polemic against the modernizing of ancient history. Instead of employing concepts appropriate if at all to developed systems of market exchange Polanyi preferred to point to the substantive institutions through which the economic process was conducted in 'primitive' and 'archaic' societies (1957, 1968, 1977).[13] These substantive institutions or modes of 'interaction between man and his environment' Polanyi broadly categorized as three 'patterns of integration': reciprocity, redistribution and market exchange. Each generic pattern comprised several species and sub-species;[14] and typically any society employed more than one of the patterns. Trade Polanyi defined institutionally as 'a method of acquiring goods that are not available on the spot' or 'the mutual appropriative movement of goods between hands', and again he distinguished broadly three main types of trade: gift trade, administered or treaty trade, and market trade. Each of these too could be further analysed in accordance with the personnel and goods involved, and with the aims and context of the transactions.

There seem to me several flaws in 'Polanyism' as a self-sufficient theory of economic history, principally the absence of a concept of exploitation, an economic analysis based on patterns of allocation rather than relations of production, and the stress on integration at the cost of disregarding conflict and competition.[15] Besides, Polanyi's own first-hand knowledge of the ancient Greek world was far more limited than that of Hasebroek. Yet, so far as 'trade and politics' in archaic Greece is concerned, Polanyi's work does share a signal merit of Hasebroek's: it compels us to rethink or rather to think away concepts appropriate only to the capitalist market economy. Moreover, unlike Hasebroek, Polanyi did also develop a detailed set of alternative concepts specifically designed to account for the peculiar features of non-market exchange.[16]

IV

The two recent contributions to the study of archaic Greek trade on which I propose to concentrate are by Bravo (1977) and Mele (1979), who take as their points of departure respectively the positions reached by Hasebroek and Polanyi.[17] Neither makes much, if any, use of archaeology, and both rely heavily on a philological approach, Bravo's being stimulated initially by the recent publication of a business letter from Berezan written on lead around 500 BC (Austin/Vidal-Naquet (1977) no.41), Mele's consisting in a thorough backcombing of Homer and Hesiod's *Works and Days*.

Bravo begins by summarizing the conclusions of his detailed study of the Berezan letter (1974); the remainder of his long article expands rather than revises these conclusions. He emphasizes – necessarily, given the evidence – that most of his views on archaic trade must be hypothetical and that his hypotheses have their origin in the Weber–Hasebroek ideal type described above. But he aims to modify this model while retaining its essential intention. Thus he accepts that the production and exchange of commodities constituted a very restricted sector of the Greek economy, that it is justified to use the *a fortiori* argument from the level of development of commerce attained in classical Athens to that of archaic Greece, and that the concept of a 'commercial aristocracy' in archaic Greece is entirely false. However, he is appreciably readier than was Hasebroek to soil the hands of the archaic nobility with the taint of commerce, though, as we shall see, he does not go so far in this direction as Mele.

On Bravo's modified hypothesis the great landowners of archaic Greece, the opulent nobles, exported and imported 'merchandise', not just their surplus agricultural produce but also manufactured goods. Indeed, from the second half of the eighth century Greek maritime commerce was a 'mass phenomenon', which rested on the ever-increasing number of colonial foundations. Middling landed proprietors, such as Hesiod had in mind, might trade their own produce. But this comprised but a small proportion of total archaic commerce, the bulk of which consisted in the transport of merchandise by men who stood in a relation of personal dependence, if not of belonging, to the great noble landowners. At one end of the social scale these agent-traders might be impoverished nobles, in whom Bravo identifies the most 'entrepreneurial' element of a society characterized by 'extraordinary creative dynamism'. At the other end, they might be either slaves or 'between free men and slaves' or free dependants of the big men.

Did the big men themselves personally undertake trade? Bravo rightly says that there are no sure proofs that they did and counter-indications that normally they would not. At any rate, he takes the Homeric evidence (especially *Od.* VIII 158–64) to show that wealthy nobles could not perform an economic function in such a way that their social status was defined by that function. This is surely correct.[18] Their role in trade would therefore broadly have been twofold: either they sent their dependants abroad to trade in commodities they owned, both manufactures and *naturalia*; or they made maritime loans on the security of land to impoverished nobles. In any case, the large merchantmen on which more than one trader conducted business (hence *emporos*, originally just a passenger on a ship, comes to mean foreign trader, a usage first encountered in the later seventh century: Semonides fr. 16 West) could clearly belong only to the wealthy nobles.

There seem to me several weaknesses in Bravo's admittedly hypothetical discussion. He exaggerates generally the extent of exchange properly to be labelled 'trade' or 'commerce'. He pays insufficient regard to archaeological evidence, preferring a too minute and not always relevant philological approach. His interpretation of Theognis 1197–1202 to give the required contemporary evidence for archaic maritime loans is forced and unconvincing.[19] Conversely, his use of Isocrates VII 31–2 as proof that dependent traders were still the norm in late fifth-century Athens shows insufficient critical reserve towards this tendentious source. Finally, despite his nods towards Hasebroek, Bravo has in effect abandoned Hasebroek's framework of analysis by concentrating on 'trade' to the exclusion of 'politics'. This last weakness is fully exposed by Mele, who besides takes Bravo to task for his incomplete account of the articulation of archaic Greek trade.

Mele's monograph is not long, but it is exceptionally dense and hard to summarize. The main thesis, though, is clear enough. It is that the history of archaic Greece of the eighth and seventh centuries (the sixth is largely ignored) is the history of the political crisis of the aristocracy and that commerce (Italian, like French, seems to lack a word for 'trade' as opposed to 'commerce') cannot but have been an integral factor in this crisis. Given this essentially Hasebroekian problematic, it seems curious at first sight that Mele should not even have mentioned Hasebroek. On closer inspection perhaps this is chiefly because Mele's conception of the relationship between trade and politics is so radically at odds with Hasebroek's.

Mele's two main authorities (the word should be given its full weight) are Homer and Hesiod, the latter above all. Their evidentiary value is held to lie in the fact that they composed for oral recitation in public so that the content of their work was socially controlled. Moreover, Mele argues, Hesiod should not be dismissed as a parochial Boeotian, isolated from the main currents of socio-economic development, since thanks to his father his purview extended through Aeolian Cyme to the area of Milesian, Pontic, Thracian, Adriatic and western influences. 'Homer' is not explicitly dated by Mele, but he seems to assume a world of Homer preceding that of Hesiod, whom he places in the years around 700 BC.

So to their testimony on archaic commerce. Homer's *prexis* commerce is judged to parallel Hesiod's *ergon* commerce in that Homer's use of *prexis* (literally 'activity') to mean private commerce represents commerce as one *prexis* among many, just as Hesiod treats commerce as one *ergon* among many. The Hesiodic ideal or model of commerce is characterized by absolute organizational autarky and perfect integration in the total field of *erga*. The production of the goods, the ship, the crew, the transport and sale of the goods are all managed by one man, and the disposal abroad by sea occurs during the fifty days after the summer solstice in the dead season of the agricultural year. This Hesiodic ideal is realized by the examples of what Mele describes as aristocratic commerce attested in Homer, so that there is a line of continuity, a relation of direct descent, binding Homeric *prexis* commerce to Hesiodic *ergon* commerce.[20]

However, both Homer and Hesiod also bear witness to another type of commerce, that of professional traders. Mele traces a hypothetical evolution in the usage of the word *prexis* from a general sense (private or public business of any kind) through the Homeric sense (above) to the sense of commerce par excellence. The final stage, he argues, had been reached in *Od.* VIII 162, the famous (and neologistic) passage where Odysseus is reviled on Phaeacia for looking not at all like an (aristocratic) athlete but on the contrary like nothing so much as an *archos* of *prekteres* (leader of traders). As for Hesiod, he roundly condemns what he calls *emporie*, external maritime trade, for three reasons: it is motivated and structured by a positive desire for gain: it is specialized and so contradicts his autarkic model of surplus-disposal; and it conflicts with the agricultural cycle, since the summer sailing season coincides with the harvest and the threshing and storage of grain.

In Mele's view both Homer and Hesiod are here acting as mouthpieces for the aristocrats, attempting to combat in words the growth of specialized, non-aristocratic commerce. For their part the aristocrats sought to maintain the Homeric tradition of *prexis* commerce in an ultimately vain effort to counter the specialists. Post-Homeric *prexis* commerce is commerce in *biotos*, that is cereals, wine, slaves, and metals, and it may alternate with piracy, for which the penteconter was equally adapted. But when piracy is hampered, this *prexis* commerce is oriented towards fixed places of trade and guaranteed by relations of guest-friendship and respect for the sanctity of the stranger's gods. It is a commerce born of the possession of a surplus, of ships and a crew. In short, it is aristocratic commerce of a high economic level.

Various examples of such aristocratic *prexis*-merchants are given, both individuals and entire ruling aristocracies: Damaratus the Bacchiad; Colaeus of Samos; Protis, oikist of Marseilles, and Pholus, both Phocaean; Charaxus; Solon; Sostratus of Aegina; the Hippobotae of Chalcis; the Ploutis of Miletus. Nor does Mele shrink from associating aristocratic commerce with aristocratic politics, as when he makes Colaeus the begetter of the 'great friendships' between Thera, Cyrene and Samos. Indeed, Mele boldly characterizes the Milesian Ploutis as 'un' aristocrazia commerciale'. I hear the shade of Hasebroek squeaking piteously somewhere in the ancient historians' patch of Hades: not only is there very little evidence available for this tissue of reconstruction, but what there is – for example, Herodotus on Colaeus – does not establish a causal connection between commerce and aristocratic politics.

Finally, Mele's picture of the crisis of old-style aristocratic *prexis* commerce. Here his hypotheses do significantly rejoin those of Bravo. For the development of specialized *emporie*, conducted by *naukleroi* who man and equip a ship and *emporoi* who possess a cargo to trade and the means to hire space on someone else's ship, is attributed pre-eminently to impoverished aristocrats and *kakoi* of one kind and another. This specialized *emporie* had appeared indirectly in Homer, as an external phenomenon associated with the Phoenicians. Hesiod's polemic had confirmed its extraneous origins, extraneous that is to the *prexis-ergon* world of commerce. The ambience within which it had incubated was above all East Greece, and the critical period for its development, when it had become locked in a life-and-death struggle with aristocratic commerce, was the last quarter of the seventh century.

The outward and visible sign of the new *emporie* is taken to be the foundation of *emporia*, ports of trade, such as Emporion, Gravisca, Naucratis and Berezan.[21] The great novelty of these, or at least of Naucratis and those in the Pontic region, is that their primary purpose was to serve as ports of exchange for cereals against decorated pottery. This new *emporie*, in other words, reflects the development and the activity of classes separated from the local aristocratic surplus, and it is conducted to satisfy their needs, not those of the old aristocracies. This process, Mele holds, was greatly fostered by the sumptuary legislation of tyrants, especially in Corinth and East Greece, which struck at the roots of the old aristocratic commerce in slaves, gold ornaments, female attire and so on. The aristocrats fought back, most conspicuously the Phocaeans and Solon (Mele can even speak of 'questa arcaica emporía foceo-soloniana'!); but by 550 they had essentially lost a war waged against overwhelming political and social odds. The adoption of the purpose-built merchantman symbolized their demise.

No one can say that Mele's intellectual enterprise is a modest one. Hesiod's *Works and Days* has surely not previously been subjected to so searching an interrogation for purposes of economic history, and Mele's reading of Homer and Hesiod as polemicists against specialized commerce is ingenious to say the least. However, his main thesis (summarized above) left me cold – or rather fired me with renewed respect for Hasebroek, on all sorts of counts.

It is true that Mele does not speak of 'trade leagues' or 'flourishing mercantile cities' in the old modernizing mode; but he does describe the ruling class of archaic Miletus as a 'commercial aristocracy' and speak of Solon and Protis 'devoting themselves to commerce'.[22] The aristocrats of the eighth to sixth centuries, in other words, are represented as not merely financing trade (Bravo's picture) but as personally and regularly engaged in the conduct of commerce, valuing it so greatly as to take vigorous steps to combat the rise of specialized, non-aristocratic commerce. Indeed, commerce in general is rated so highly by Mele that he locates the source of the aristocrats' political demise essentially in the commercial sphere.

Against this it must be stressed that in pre-industrial Europe international trade is reckoned, on far better evidence, to have accounted for but a small part of total economic activity, no more than two per cent of G.N.P.

Moreover, a sharp economic and social distinction should be made between, on the one hand, irregular aristocratic surplus- and gift-exchange interspersed with piracy aimed at securing goods to consume and *keimelia* to thesaurize and, on the other hand, commerce properly so called. As for the impoverished aristocrats and non-aristocrats who are plausibly said to conduct the specialized commerce, at times they are made by Mele to look uncannily like the late and unlamented 'commercial middle classes' conjured up in the fantasies of P. N. Ure and others.

V

In one important respect, too, Mele is vulnerable to precisely the charge of incompleteness he levels against Bravo: he makes inadequate use of archaeological evidence. Besides, what archaeological material he does take into account, that is pottery, he uses improperly. For if one thing is clear about the economic significance of Greek ceramics, it is that the decorated pottery exported would not by itself have paid for bulk imports of grain.[23] In any case, even if Scythian princes did have a taste for Greek fine pottery, that is not true of the Egyptian elite who controlled and principally benefited from the trade through the treaty-port of Naucratis (Austin (1970)). It therefore seems worthwhile to conclude this survey of recent work on archaic Greek trade by considering some archaeological approaches.

I fully accept the main conclusion of A. M. Snodgrass' chapter in this collection on heavy freight in archaic Greece. There is perhaps still room for argument over the date at which the purpose-built, sail-powered merchantman emerged in the Greek sphere, but he has adequately undermined any notion of organized commercial enterprise in the freight of heavy materials such as marble and iron ore. That chapter thus forms a useful supplement to his admirable discussion of 'Economic realities' in his general essay on archaic Greece ((1980) ch. 4). There, without referring explicitly to the great debate discussed in my introduction, he heavily weights his argument in favour of the 'primitivist' side. The 'positivist fallacy', according to which the importance of a class of evidence in antiquity is directly correlated with the quantity of it surviving today, is thoroughly exposed in connexion with the distribution of painted pottery. Trade and manufacture, Snodgrass contends, were of far less economic moment in archaic Greece than agriculture, warfare (especially booty-raiding) and religious cult. In short, 'It is indeed to the economic life of Greece generally that the word "archaic", with all the force of its implications, seems to apply most closely.'

Since Snodgrass wrote those words, the proceedings of a valuable Naples conference he refers to in a note have been published: *Les céramiques de la Grèce de l'est et leur diffusion en occident* (1978). Most of the papers were devoted to problems of characterization (and terminology) and chronology, but here and there primarily historical contributions crop out among the art-historical strata. I single out just one topic for consideration, the extent of long-distance trade in East Greek pottery.

In an intervention J. Boardman recorded his impression that much of the export and distribution of East Greek wares in the west 'may have been casual, with the possible exception of the Ionic cups, though even here I believe we can still underestimate the extent of local production'. Ionic cups are one of the three classes of East Greek pottery conventionally held to be the most frequently exported westwards, the others being banded plain ware and grey monochrome. However, the results reported to the conference of scientific analysis of grey monochrome from the south of France also pointed very strongly in the direction indicated by Boardman for the Ionic cups – so strongly, indeed, that J.-P. Morel was prepared virtually to rule out trade in such ware. In other words, although Phocaeans may well have traded in silver, tin, copper, iron, red ochre and alum (cf. Morel (1975) 856), the most abundant kind of archaeological evidence usually taken to document their presence in the west can no longer be confidently so used.

This diminuendo regarding the importance of pottery in trade is maintained in Johnston (1979). Towards the end of the seventh century merchant-marks began to be painted (later they were scratched) under the feet of vases carried for themselves rather than their contents by Corinthian and East Greek traders; the earliest known are Corinthian of about the 620s. Johnston can see 'no very obvious explanation' for the beginnings of this practice, but he does note that it coincides with the earliest Greek finds from Naucratis. Mele, who (unlike Hasebroek) fails to cite the marks, might use this as support for his picture of the development of specialized trading. Corinthian too is the earliest batchmark, of about 580.

Some 2,500 underfoot marks are known from the seventh to fourth centuries, mostly on Attic pots and chiefly perhaps the work of traders visiting the Ceramicus to place orders direct with the potteries. Etruria was a major recipient of marked ware: in the later sixth century 'much of the black-figure production at Athens seems to have been aimed directly at Etruscan tomb-furnishing'. But Johnston finds 'extremely little evidence for discrimination among Etrurian destinations on the part of individual traders'. Nor, thanks to the hazards of survival and recovery (Johnston reckons that 'no large proportion of vases has yet been discovered'), can we gain any clear impression of the scale of operation of any of these 'main-line', Etrurian traders. Even these, however, Johnston believes are more likely to have been general merchants than specialist traders in pots. For vases, though luxury articles, commanded modest prices by comparison with those asked for bronzework, and probably as a rule comprised only a small proportion of their total cargoes.

Johnston's general conclusion is justly pessimistic: 'ceramic footnotes often do not elucidate but complicate questions concerning Greek trade'. Yet more to the point, what he says of his special study – 'I fear that no neat picture of the mechanics and development of the vase trade emerges' – will also serve only too well as a general valediction to this summary of some recent work on archaic Greek trade.

VI

In conclusion I return from 'trade' to 'politics'. There can be no question of talking about archaic Greek politics in the sense that we can talk about, say, Athenian politics in the mid-fourth century BC. By 'politics' here is meant the policy or policies pursued by states, rather than the processes that lie behind their adoption. In our modern world the connexion between trade and politics in this sense is fairly straightforward; at least it is undeniable that there is a direct causal connexion between them. A good example is the Suez crisis of 1956, when the British government sent in the troops to prevent Nasser from stifling and ruining 'our trade'. In the archaic Greek world they ordered these matters differently, or so I believe.

The note of caution is required, for two reasons. First, our sources for the history of that world are normally scrappy, discontinuous and variously slanted. Second, since there were no governments or political parties in our sense, it is often impossible and never simple to explain confidently a particular foreign policy decision taken by an archaic Greek state. To illustrate, let me summarize the issues involved in one such foreign policy decision, that of the Spartans in 524 BC to restore some aristocratic Samian exiles to power by overthrowing the usurping tyrant Polycrates.[24]

Herodotus says that according to 'the Spartans', that is all or some of his Spartan informants, the Spartans were motivated by a desire for revenge for two acts of Samian piracy. But 'the Samians' told Herodotus that the Spartans wished to repay a favour done them by the Samians in one or other of the Messenian Wars. Revenge and reciprocity, then, are the alternative explanations offered by our one usable literary source. Yet they have been rejected almost unanimously by modern scholars as pretexts for deeper motives such as fear of Persian expansion, principled hostility to tyranny, imperialist aggression and even concern to restore trade-contacts.

Quite apart from the question of method, this rather cavalier attitude to Herodotus struck me as dubiously anachronistic. For revenge and reciprocity are thoroughly appropriate, because quintessentially archaic, motives for action, and this was a period when interstate relations typically boiled down to personal relations between ruling aristocrats. I therefore concluded guardedly that, although broader geopolitical and ideological considerations may well have weighed with the Spartans, what could have tipped the balance in favour of an undertaking without precedent or parallel in archaic Spartan history were the personal relationships between leading Spartans and members of the expelled Samian landholding aristocracy.

I would not wish to claim any general applicability for this tentative explanation of one particular archaic Greek foreign policy decision. But I do feel that it exemplifies neatly the problems involved in accounting for archaic Greek politics, quite independently of any putative connexion between politics and trade. So far as the latter goes, I hope my discussion of recent work has sufficiently shown that modernizing views either misprise its character or exaggerate its importance.

One final positive observation. In the archaic period the two major economic problems facing the governing classes of the Greek states were food supply and the procurement of useful metals, above all for use in war. The former could as a last resort be solved by colonization, the export of surplus mouths, and that was normally a centrally directed, state-sponsored enterprise. But the procurement of metals depended, apart from booty-raiding, on importation, often from afar and from non-Greek lands; and from the seventh century the metals trade was in private hands (Finley (1970) 603–4). How precisely the trade was conducted we do not know; but so far as its implications for archaic Greek 'politics' are concerned, we must once again insist on Hasebroek's 'fundamental distinction' – between an import interest and a commercial interest.

[2]

Heavy freight in Archaic Greece

by A. M. SNODGRASS

The larger aim of this paper is to convince historians that archaeological evidence can truly be brought to bear on problems that are of central concern to them, and that it can be perilous to ignore it. In public, of course, most historians would indignantly deny that they needed any such convincing; but in the heat of discussion a deeper stratum of scepticism and downright mistrust sometimes comes to the surface. I choose the topic of sea-borne freight as just such a central problem, omitting land-transport, partly because it has been effectively dealt with by Burford (1960), partly because the inherent advantages of sea- over land-transport in the ancient world must have been further enhanced when it was a question of carrying heavy loads, sometimes (as in the case of marble) in the form of large indivisible units. In archaic times, especially, one suspects that the provision of good roads was such as to widen rather than narrow the gap.

This brings us, however, to the question of the facilities for maritime transport in archaic Greece, and above all to the ships. The author of the most interesting recent paper on archaic sea-trade, Bravo (1977), disclaims such knowledge of archaeology as would enable him to make use of its evidence; nor does the later work of Mele (1979) set out to fill this particular gap. But I shall be taking as a working hypothesis Bravo's intriguing theory of rich, land-holding ship-owners and of 'agents', who either did not belong to the land-owning class or else were merely not rich, undertaking the actual voyages; coupling this with Humphreys' gloss that the ships used for these enterprises in the archaic period were, in the main, not purpose-built merchantmen but dual-purpose galleys, often pentekontors (Humphreys (1978) 166–8 and n.13). There is in fact supporting evidence for this hypothesis which has not been used.

Herodotus tells us (I 163.2) that the Phocaeans used pentekontors, not merchantmen, for long-distance trade. Plutarch (*Pericles* XXVI 3–4) ascribes an origin in sixth-century Samos to the type of ship called *Samaina*, a kind of super-pentekontor enlarged to take bigger cargoes. If two of the most prominent archaic trading states at least sometimes preferred oared galleys, then the burden of proof is on those who believe that purpose-built, sail-driven merchantmen were the norm elsewhere at this period. The archaeological evidence will not support them. The vase-paintings for a long time depict only oared vessels (cf. Morrison and Williams (1968)); this could be explained in terms of the greater social prestige of such ships, but the explanation wears thin when it is applied to the Corinthian votive plaques dedicated to Poseidon in his sanctuary on Pentescuphia (Acrocorinth), presumably on successful completion of a voyage – especially since one plaque shows a cargo of pots loaded on a vessel of a type indistinguishable from the war-galleys on other plaques.[1] A Samian coin of *c.*490 BC (Morrison and Williams (1968), 111, pl. 20(e)) shows the bows of what must be a *Samaina*, to judge from its close correspondence with Plutarch's description and inferences therefrom. It looks very like the Corinthian ships on the plaques; we are reminded of Thucydides I 13.2 on the naval links between these two states.

The pentekontor was a fair-sized vessel with a length to beam ratio of about 10:1. Casson (1971) 54–5 estimates its length at 38 m, its beam at 3.95 m; Landels (1978) 142 at 30.4 m and 3.04 m respectively. But nobody seems to have taken account of the 'Schiffsfundament' at the Samian Heraion, a row of nine parallel oblong stone blocks with the shortest ones at the ends and the longest one in the middle;[2] these acted as supports for a complete dedicated ship and were set up around 600 BC. No part of the ship was found, but the approximate dimensions given appear rather smaller than the above estimates, about 21.9 m long and 2.1 m in the beam. The German excavators[3] did however also find a series of wooden miniature dedications and once again they are all of war-galley type, though one might expect at least some of these Samian sanctuary-dedications to commemorate merchant enterprises rather than sea-battles. When in the last quarter of the sixth century pictures of sail-driven 'round ships' at last begin to appear on Athenian vases, there continue to be pictures of what are clearly oared merchantmen too (see Casson (1971) 66, Fig. 91). The significance of all this is that a galley required a crew of 50 (or more: Humphreys (1978) 300, n.10) trained oarsmen who had either to be paid or to take a share in the profits of a venture. Humphreys (1978) 168 notes the telling point that in Herodotus II 152.4 the *whole* crew of the ship of Colaeus of Samos makes the dedication of the tithe.

Now I turn to the question of the cargoes carried. Trade nowadays is usually quantified in terms of the value of goods exchanged (e.g. in balance of payments calculations), but even for the best-documented periods of antiquity this type of calculation is hardly an imaginable possibility: the more so for archaic times when it would have to be estimated in man-hours of labour as a proportion of the total labour input. But the next most significant index of trade is perhaps that of tonnage (as in wartime shipping losses), and for antiquity this is not quite such a hopeless proposition. We can make some progress by isolating the heaviest and bulkiest commodities which we know to have been exported and imported, and thus try to reach conclusions about a fairly substantial sample of the total volume of overseas exchanges. Here I believe that *marble* and *metal ores* between them must have composed an important part of the tonnage of archaic sea-transport in the archaic world. This would seem to be particularly true of the earlier archaic period, when the import of grain had barely entered the picture and when the necessary supplies of timber, though certainly large, may still have been mainly met from local resources. As for the slave-trade, even if we do not follow Starr in his restricted view ((1977) 91) of the scope of industrial and especially of agrarian slavery in archaic Greece, the fact remains that slaves could walk, and might therefore, unlike inanimate cargoes, be more economically moved overland in many cases. Anyway, I would observe that a block for a single life-sized archaic marble statue weighed as much as about 12 slaves.

With marble, we have to reckon with two main uses, in sculpture from about 650 BC and in marble building-stone from about 550; both become increasingly common down to the very late archaic period, when for sculpture marble begins to give way to bronze. The problem now arises of distinguishing the provenances of Aegean marbles with a sufficient degree of precision: as we were reminded a few years ago by the rather sharp exchange which took place in the pages of the *Annual* of the British School at Athens (Renfrew and Peacey (1968), Ashmole (1970), Wycherley (1973)). Most younger archaeologists felt a fervent sympathy with Renfrew's scientific approach in that debate, but time has reinforced Ashmole's argument that no scientific test is yet capable of yielding results that are definite. Even the prospects of isotope identification as a method seem to have dimmed in the last year or two (see Germann *et al.* (1980), Lazzarini *et al.* (1980)). Further, it was a serious defect of the original case that no account was taken of ancient documentary and epigraphical evidence for the origin of marbles in buildings which still survive (as Wycherley observed for the Periclean buildings in Athens). Even for the archaic period, we have a few precious pieces of evidence of this kind: Herodotus states flatly (V 62.3) that in the years after 513 BC exiled Athenian aristocrats built a temple at Delphi with extensive use of Parian marble. Two earlier buildings at Delphi are also built of marble, the Treasuries of Cnidos (*c.*560–50) and of Siphnos (*c.*525); classicists call this 'Parian' marble too, partly because it is very like that of the temple, partly (in the latter case) because Herodotus again clearly tells us (III 57.4) that the people of Siphnos, at the time when they were building their treasury, also fitted out the meeting-place and town-hall of their native island with Parian marble. More generally, the plain fact is that there are many regions of Greece which lack marble deposits, especially those of the fine white marbles which were increasingly demanded; and that many important sites for sculpture and architecture (and this means above all sanctuaries) lie within such regions. So that although a degree of scepticism is proper, I do not think that this can prevent us from concluding that marble often had to be shipped.

With sculptural marble, the epigraphic evidence throws some important light, not indeed on the provenance of the marbles used for the statues, but on an allied question: the origins of the artists who carved them. They show that beyond any doubt it was a frequent occurrence in the archaic period for a statue in city A to be carved by a sculptor from city B. On its own, this may not appear to prove very much; theoretically this could happen without the sculptor travelling, as he could simply have the finished statue shipped from B to A. Luckily, however, we can call on much written testimony to show that archaic sculptors often did travel: we read of Cretans in Arcadia, the Argolid, Sicyon and Aetolia; Corinthian exiles in Etruria; an Ionian in Sparta; Spartans at Olympia; an Athenian in Ionia; a Sicyonian in Miletus.[4] In all these cases, either we are told in so many words that the artist travelled to carry out the commission, or the size and elaboration of the work were such as to make execution on the spot essential. There are anyway the common-sense arguments that a fully-finished marble statue of any size would be a fragile thing to transport, and that ascertaining the client's desires and securing his approval would be much easier if the artist travelled. In the case of archaic temple-building, where the presence of the architect was essential, there is also a high incidence of non-native architects in the surviving accounts. To return to sculpture, it would be valuable to establish that not only was a statue at A made by a sculptor from B, but also that it was carved out of *marble* from B. This we can seldom do with complete certainty but we can get close: there is for example in Taranto an unfinished female statue in imported (presumably Greek) marble, and the workmanship does not look local.[5] But when we put together the copious archaeological evidence of imported marbles with the frequent literary attestation of travelling sculptors it is I think a fair conclusion that many archaic statues were finished *in situ* by the sculptor or his apprentices. So we have the artists fairly firmly pinned down at one end – that of the destination – of the archaic marble-shipping process.

Interestingly enough, we also have some evidence to pin them down at the other end as well. At three sites on Naxos and on Mt Pentelikon in Attica, there are unfinished archaic statues in or near ancient quarry sites, in some cases still attached to the living rock. The extraordinary thing about them is the degree to which they have been worked: in one case on Naxos, it is possible to detect the stage of anatomical knowledge which the statue reflects, and therefore its probable date.[6] This must mean, either that the sculptor himself roughed out the statue in the quarry, or that he briefed the quarryman in some detail to do so. In either case, he would have to spend time at the quarry; and anyway we know from Renaissance and later evidence that sculptors like to pick out their block in the quarry. From all this, the likeliest reconstruction of the process of creation of an archaic statue emerges as follows:

(i) client commissions artist
(ii) artist goes to marble source
(iii) artist pays quarry-owner and contractor for extracting marble
(iv) artist pays for land and sea transport of part-worked statue
(v) client pays artist's and assistants' maintenance for period of work (which would be up to a year for a life-sized statue)

The artist will of course try to ensure that the payment under (v) exceeds the sum of those under (ii), (iii) and (iv).

We can perhaps use the analogy of the fourth-century architectural and sculptural work at Epidaurus (Burford (1969)) to throw some light on the last three stages of the sequence. To take (iii), the transaction at the quarry, first: Burford reasonably asks (172) – Did quarrystone cost anything? Her answer for Epidaurus is that the intrinsic value of the stone cannot have been a major factor compared with the cost of labour and transport. This means that it is not very important whether quarries belonged more often to the state or to private individuals; what really counted were the other costs, and the evidence from Naxos and Mt Pentelikon (see above, p. 4) again suggests that the sculptor will have paid any charges at this stage, no doubt with an advance from the client. For building-stone, the picture at Epidaurus is different, but even more clear: a third party, the private contractor who had tendered for supplying each lot of stone, had to cover all stages from the quarry to the building-site (in this instance anything up to 80 km, partly by sea). There were swingeing fines for late delivery (e.g. Burford (1969) 149). At Epidaurus it is clear that, of our stages (iii) and (iv), the former was the more costly: for Corinthian limestone, which had to be brought about 48 km by land, sea and then land again, the ratio of quarrying costs to transport costs was nevertheless between 2:1 and 3:1 (cf. Burford (1969) 189–91, 193–4 and n.3 for example). To return to sculpture and to our stage (v): we should look for an all-inclusive and therefore high payment here: Epidaurus shows that the sculptors, like the building-stone contractors, accepted an 'all-in' contract which in most cases required a guarantor.

With sculptural marble we can make some attempt, however crude, at overall quantification. In her catalogue of the commonest type of archaic statue, the *kouros*, Richter lists about 177 works in stone. Nineteen of these come from one particular sanctuary, that of Apollo on Mt Ptoön in Boeotia. But another and much more detailed study[7] has been made of the sculpture from this same sanctuary; and once all the fragmentary evidence, too insubstantial to be included in Richter's book, has been taken into account, the number of *kouroi* which can be shown to have been dedicated here is at least 120, a number greater by a factor of 6½ than the figure in Richter. If this increase is typical, we can infer that traces of about 1,120 *kouroi* from the archaic period have actually been found. What proportion of the original total are these likely to represent? Here we really enter the realm of surmise, but allowing for incomplete excavation, and for the ravages of the lime-kiln over 2,500 years, I would doubt whether they represent as much as 5 per cent: a study of a particular form of clay vessel of this period, the Panathenaic amphora, has suggested that the surviving proportion is only about ¼ of 1 per cent (Cook (1959) 120). We can therefore safely multiply by twenty to give an original total of well over 20,000 archaic *kouroi*. What proportion of archaic stone sculpture is represented by *kouroi*? Very roughly, one-third, since the corresponding female statues appear to be only slightly less numerous, while other types are individually rarer but collectively would amount to a similar quantity. So there would be at least 60,000 '*kouros*-units' to reckon with. How heavy was the average *kouros*? Our very earliest life-sized marble statue, around 650 BC, is actually female, and its simplified form helps to keep its weight down to about $\frac{1}{4}$ of a ton: but by about 600, we begin to have over-life-sized statues, such as the Sounion *kouros* which weighs about 2 tons even after carving. One gigantic example on Delos, most of which has now vanished, will have weighed some 23 tons, while its surviving base (of which more below) is 34 tons.[8] It will not be excessive to work on a mean figure of three-quarters of a ton per life-sized statue, at least before final carving. Archaic marble sculpture covers a span of about 170 years. A fair guess might be that in any single year of the archaic period, an absolute minimum of 270 tons (350 '*kouros*-units') of sculptural marble would be travelling round the Aegean: the great bulk of this tonnage would have to do most of its travelling by sea, if only because the island marbles were the most favoured at this time. Inscriptions show that the Cyclades were also a major source of sculptural talent, though the sculptors did most of their work away from home. On to this sculptural total, we have to add the marble used for building-operations in the later part of the period; this would be required on fewer occasions, but of course in much larger quantities: the fragmentary inscriptions which happen to survive for the Temple of Asclepius at Epidaurus show that this modest-sized building required, for part of its cella alone, enough Pentelic marble (about 160 cubic metres) for over 500 life-sized *kouroi*.

So marble was a commodity that made big demands on archaic shipping resources. The biggest archaic marble block which we know to have been shipped (*pace* Renfrew and Peacey) is the base of the Colossus of the Naxians on Delos, mentioned above; it appears to be of Naxian marble (as its own boastful inscription perhaps hints), and it dates to about 600 BC.[9] It is 5.14 m by 3.47 m by 0.71 m and, given the measurements for oared galleys on page 17, I can see no way that it could have been safely carried on one of these; so here is perhaps an instance where either a specially-built raft or a merchant 'round ship' must be inferred in earlier archaic times. But our average statue-block, 1.83 m by 0.61 m by 0.3 m or so, weighing three-quarters of a ton, could most certainly be loaded on a pentekontor. We even have a documented case of this happening with finished statues: Hdt. I 164.3 (the flight of the Phocaeans).[10] When local stone (even local marble) was involved, Coulton's table shows that archaic architects were prepared to move around blocks of up to 73 tons.

It is time to turn to the transport of metals. Beyond saying that the quantities of iron transported must have been very large, while those of copper would have been somewhat smaller but would have to travel much longer distances on average, I shrink from attempting any quantification. There is, however, some useful evidence for the *stage* at which metal-shipments took place. Theoretically, three stages of transportation could be involved:

(i) from the point of extraction to the smelting-location
(ii) from smelting-location to craftsman's shop
(iii) from workshop, perhaps *via* a middleman, to the ultimate owner.

What the archaic Greek evidence however shows is that stage (ii) was regularly eliminated; in other words, that smelting and forging, casting or working took place at the same site (and in passing one may note that there is evidence from late bronze age Kea to suggest that the same may have been true in prehistoric Greece). Our two best examples involve island-sites with no metal sources of their own. At Pithecusae in Ischia (Buchner (1970) 97–8) quantities of iron slag, together with half-finished iron artefacts, tuyères and other iron-foundry debris, tell their own story; what is more, the slag when analysed proved to be traceable to one particular vein of ore from Elba, which lies about 400 km away to the north-west. This is interesting not least because it flatly contradicts the literary evidence, at least for a later period, of Diodorus (V 13. 1–2), who describes how the ore was smelted more or less *in situ* on Elba and then exported in the form of 'sponge' iron (blooms) to Puteoli and elsewhere, where it was marketed: a clear instance of the discrepancy between archaic and classical practice. The smaller island of Motya produced traces of iron-smelting on the spot, as well as numerous iron artefacts.[11] Equally striking in a different way is the evidence from the sanctuary of Apollo at Bassae, which lies over 1,000 m up in the mountains of Arcadia but nevertheless showed proof of iron-smelting on the site – presumably for the production of objects for the pilgrims to dedicate.[12]

What does all this suggest? Clearly, that for preference, in archaic times, iron was often transported in the form of ore, either over sea-voyages up to 400 km in length, or by arduous uphill portages on land. A few years ago, I found this a surprising conclusion, and was rash enough to say so, only to fall prey to a reviewer who described himself as 'a former sailor in the Swedish ore trade'.[13] Where I had thought that iron ore was an 'extravagant and bulky' medium for transport, he assured his readers that it was 'the embodiment of non-bulkiness', and we must take his word for it. Clearly, in the archaic period it was a frequent practice for base metals to be shipped, for the bulk of the distance over which they had to travel, in ore form; and in fact I know of no really strong evidence to the contrary at this period.

But what about stage (iii) of our theoretical model of transmission of metalwork? There is a certain amount of evidence that it was often a short and relatively trivial undertaking, and that the spectacular distances over which archaic Greek artefacts sometimes travelled were covered *after* the objects entered their final owners' possession. This is certainly true of one of the most famous cases, the gigantic bronze cauldron found in a princess' tomb at Vix in Burgundy, which was made to order and probably assembled at its destination by a craftsman who travelled there with it. Other similar cases – the Greek helmet from a river in south-western Spain, the harness-plate in the shape of a fish from northern Germany – are probably susceptible of a similar explanation (see Boardman (1981) 221 figs. 261–2; 214 fig. 254; 262 fig. 306). Within Greece, the great bulk of 'internal imports' of metalwork are found at sanctuaries, where it is far easier to believe that they have been dedicated by pilgrims from elsewhere in Greece, than that they have been imported in bulk and sold to local customers: thus, there are many dedications of bronzes from the Italian colonies at Olympia and of Cretan ones at Delphi, and in both cases we know that visitors from the areas in question were frequent. Only in rare cases does a commercial interpretation appear to force itself on us: for instance, at Samos where the excavators found 132 Egyptian bronzes in the sanctuary of Hera (Jantzen (1972)). Since there is no evidence at all for Egyptian visitors to Samos, and since we know that Samians were prominent among the Greeks who were using the *emporium* of Naucratis in the Nile delta at the period in question, it is only sensible to conclude that these are the offerings of Samians returning from mercantile ventures in Egypt. But even here, the evidence is indirect: the actual *objects* will not have got there by commerce – they merely reflect commercial activity on the part of their owners (and without written evidence we could not even know that much).

Returning to the sites that were mentioned earlier (see above p. 23), we can be pretty sure that at Bassae, the journey from craftsman to ultimate owner – stage (iii) in our model – was just a few yards long, from the forge to the nearby temple. No one would carry iron ore up to a 1,000 m mountaintop just for the sake of the favourable breeze for the smelting-furnace, and then bring it down again! There are numerous iron dedications in the archaic temple-deposits to confirm the natural interpretation. On the small islands of Ischia and Motya, in default of evidence to the contrary, we can likewise assume that the smelting and forging activities were, to a considerable extent, for the benefit of local customers: on Ischia, at least, the installations are of a size more appropriate for this than for servicing an overseas trade in finished artefacts.

The common feature of these two case-studies is their bearing on archaic Greek trade as a whole. I have suggested that, in terms of tonnage, metal ores and marble between them represented a very substantial slice of archaic sea-borne exchanges in Greece. In the case of iron ores, three particular factors will have tended to increase the tonnage shipped: the first is simply the very heavy dependence on iron as a practical metal at this period; the second is the fact that (unlike bronze) iron cannot be effectively re-worked, so that a constant supply of new ore is needed; the third, again pointing a contrast with copper and tin, is that iron ore is much less wasteful in that it yields a much higher proportional weight of usable metal (see above, p. 23), so that there was less of a deterrent to shipping it before smelting. Yet in the whole process of transmission from the mining of the ore to the sale of the finished artefact, only this ore-shipping operation could even potentially be classed as long-distance trade. In many cases, too, there would be a factor to counteract the three maximizing factors just listed: if a major centre of metal-production lay close to the metal sources (and Chalcis and Eretria in Euboea are well-known examples), then the services of the ore-shipper, the most 'commercial' of the participants in the process, would not after all be needed. Whether they were or not, however, the location of a network of foundries to serve the needs of their immediate localities was a feature of archaic Greece which, among other things, had the effect of cutting down to a minimum the operation of commerce in the field of metals. Iron ore must have been vastly cheaper, per unit of weight, than finished metalwork. If this was to any degree a deliberate policy, then we may see a possible motivation for it in the very limited resources of contemporary merchant shipping, for which I argued in the first part of this paper. As in so many aspects of the archaic economy, the practice – whether or not it corresponded to a conscious aim – was to support oneself as far as was feasible from internal resources, of labour if not of materials.

With sculptural marble, the case is even more clear-cut. There is no single stage in the process summarized on page 20 which can be classed as a 'marble trade'. The marble block is paid for at the quarry in the same way, whether it is for subsequent export or not. If it is to travel overseas at all, it does so (we have inferred) as the property of the sculptor who is travelling with it. If he has paid for it with an advance from the client, then this and his other subsequent payments, a large part of which will in any case consist of maintenance, are unlikely to be 'repatriated' if his practice is to travel further to find another commission.

If 'trade' is defined in the narrow sense of the purchase and movement of goods without the knowledge or identification of a further purchaser, then it seems that a substantial component of archaic Greek maritime shipments could not be classified as trade. How far such a conclusion could be extended to other cultures of the period, I leave it to others to judge; but let us not forget that even the most obvious counter-example, the Phoenicians, could turn into agriculturalists at the drop of a habitat, as at Carthage. I have the feeling, too, that other categories of the traditional archaeological evidence for 'trade' in archaic Greece will, when scrutinized more closely, begin to evaporate; the 'commercial export' of painted pottery is one such element which already shows signs of doing so (cf. Snodgrass (1980) 128–9, 224).[14]

[3]

Greek amphorae and trade

by YVON GARLAN

In contrast with the majority of other archaeological evidence which can contribute to the study of commercial relations in the Greek world of the classical or Hellenistic eras, amphorae offer us the *direct* reflexion of transactions involving goods consumed on a large scale (wine especially and oil, in uncertain proportions, as well as other foodstuffs such as olives, salted foods etc.).[1] As their value lay in their contents rather than themselves, and as their manufacture should not generally have presented difficulties, they had little chance of being transported empty for long distances from their place of origin.[2] The hope thus emerges of reconstructing a network of exchanges which, we may suppose, will often contrast with the pictures that are drawn from fine-ware distribution or monetary circulation.

Thanks to the patient efforts of a handful of specialists, the majority of whom have worked under the influence of the Soviet scholar B. N. Grakov[3] or of the American V. Grace,[4] we have considerably increased in the last half century our knowledge of this material, notably of the stamps, which were sometimes added before firing; but this has not always enabled us to define sources and dates,[5] nor to be confident of taking fully into account the enormous mass of discoveries[6] and of disseminating widely the mass of information which has been collected in card-indexes.[7]

Historians of the ancient economy have felt the immediate attraction of data which lend themselves readily to statistical treatment, but have not always made judicious use of them. It thus seems useful to me to consider here the precautions that need to be taken in this area, as well as the direction of any conclusions we can draw. My intention is to respond to two very pressing needs of ancient history, often underlined by M. I. Finley:[8] to bridge the gap which tends to exist between historical thought and specialist scholarly studies, and to look for more solid and more refined interpretations of archaeological data – needs which are the more strongly felt in the West, where Greek 'amphorology' (in contrast with its Latin counterpart) generally remains the private pursuit of 'antiquarians', who continue to live in blissful ignorance of the historical problems raised on the subject by Slavic-speaking scholars.[9]

From the catalogues of stamps established by specialists for a given site, historians have sometimes only taken the gross total of examples from particular centres of production and translated these hastily into economic terms, making use of texts which cannot be treated in this way or arguments of simple probability that are easily reversible.

In denouncing this 'bad' use of amphora evidence, J.-Y. Empereur[10] has recently made a just criticism of various interpretations of the Alexandrian and Delian data advanced by M. Rostovtzeff, P. M. Fraser or Cl. Nicolet. How can one speculate on the relative importance of the commerce of Thasos, Rhodes, Cnidos and the Latin West without taking account of the dating of series which overlap only partly or not at all? Or without taking account of the distortion in the data brought about by the limited nature of archaeological research in particular sectors or levels of human occupation (the last few years, for example, of Hellenistic Delos where Cnidian and Latin stamps are dominant)? Or, finally, without taking account for each centre of production of the percentage of stamps relative to amphorae, which alone allows us to have a true picture of the volume of exchange?

This last question is complex and demands attention. A clear answer can be given only in the case of Rhodian amphorae of the third-to-first centuries, which were almost all stamped and on both handles: thus it is easy to obtain, by dividing by two, a roughly exact assessment (reached by default) of the number of amphorae. But the problem is more difficult to resolve in the case of the other series, whether they carry two or, more frequently, only one stamp (and the rule may have varied with time in a single series, as with Thasian amphorae, which initially received two stamps, then usually one). The practice of stamping, outside Rhodes, was more or less widespread, although information on the subject is as yet limited. For the exported amphorae of Heraclea, Sinope, Chersonesos and Thasos found in the Black Sea, it would seem that only a fifth or sixth of the amphorae were stamped (all periods together), according to I. B. Brashinsky.[11] On the other hand, at Thasos in the second half of the fourth century and at the start of the third, 45 per cent of amphorae in the workshop of Kalonero were stamped,[12] 50 per cent in that of Koukos,[13] and up to 80 per cent in the town rubbish dump of the Gate of Zeus.[14] At Cos only a small minority seem to have been stamped, with the consequence that the 1,480-odd Coan stamps found at Alexandria might attest import on the same scale as is indicated by 80,000 Rhodian stamps.[15] There remain a number of still more problematic examples. How is this difficulty to be remedied? Evidently by counting systematically both stamped and unstamped amphorae (taking account of stamps and bases) in series that are chronologically well defined[16] – both as found on the sites of local or foreign consumers and in the dumps of workshops which produced them – so that gradually we would acquire corrective coefficients. These will certainly vary appreciably, not only according to city of origin, but also according to period – but undoubtedly much less according to findspots than might be imagined (because there is no suggestion that exported amphorae were more frequently stamped than those used in the territory of the producer city).[17]

Taking my lead from Soviet works which have long raised just this type of problem,[18] I would add that historians must introduce into their calculations a further coefficient taking account of the (average) capacity of the various series of amphorae: this can vary from one unit to ten times as much – say from 4 to 40 litres. Not to mention also the fact that since certain handles break more easily than others (those of Sinope, for example, in comparison with those of Rhodes), they will be over-represented in catalogued findings.

Thus even taking no account of the incompleteness of archaeological research (which nevertheless does not have to be exhaustive to be significant)[19] as well as some uncertainties which still bear on the identification and dating of Greek amphorae and their stamps, we have a long way to go before we are in a position to draw conclusions that are both reliable and precise on the absolute, or even relative, importance of different commercial currents and on the historical causes of their fluctuations. On this last point it has to be said that scepticism often follows the reading of the best documented works. A whole empirically established series of different arguments is used and abused ('concurrence', commercial 'monopolies', geographic situation, significant events, etc.) from which authors take their pick without any theoretical basis, according to the needs of the moment: it is amazing, in these conditions, that some recalcitrant examples are still found, escaping all explanation – such as the complete absence in third-century Tanaïs of any Heracleote or Thasian amphorae.[20] A closer collaboration between historians and archaeologists is certainly needed in this area where nothing seems decisive in itself or unequivocal: neither the domination by the League of Delos of the cities of Chios, Samos, Thasos or Heraclea, nor the siege of Sinope by Mithridates III in 220 and its integration in 183 into the kingdom of Pontus,[21] nor even the famous 'coup' delivered in 167 to the Rhodians by the opening of the free port of Delos.[22]

Without wishing to discredit these quantitative researches, I would like nevertheless to stress (or rather point out, so little known does this aspect of the matter appear to me to be) that the same material can lend itself to a different, qualitative approach to commercial exchanges.

I would cite for example the recent book of I. B. Brashinsky (1980), where the ceramic finds of Elizavetovskoe are published.[23] The abundance of amphorae on this site – mainly Heracleote, Thasian and Sinopian in origin – contrasts both with the apparent precariousness of the settlement and with their limited distribution in the hinterland (except, to some extent, along the rivers). This is best explained on the supposition that a large proportion of the amphorae imported to this *emporion* were thrown away there (in a sort of Monte Testaccio) after their contents had been decanted into supple containers (goatskins) which were carried by land route to the Steppe-forest of the Middle Don or of the Lower Volga – as was done in Rumania at Cetăţeni, Poiana, Coslogeni or Pietroiu, that is to say at the extremity of the Danubian network and at the departure point for the trans-Carpathian routes.[24] Thus in this region where Greek imports were previously very scarce, Elizavetovskoe came especially in the fourth and at the start of the third century to play a role of intermediary, and become an important centre for exchange (which bypassed the monetary economy almost totally, as only ten coins have been found there).

The preferences of consumers sometimes seem to emerge: since, just as at Kamenskoe on the Dnieper, the amphorae of the Tauric Chersonese are relatively numerous at Elizavetovskoe, more numerous in any case than in the neighbouring Greek cities, is it not tempting to conclude that this wine was particularly appreciated by the Scythians? In other regions, themselves producers of wine and oil, it would undoubtedly be possible to determine if foreign and local vintages had the same clientèle.

Thus by placing imports of amphorae within the whole range of archaeological data, it is possible to make out the economic, social and cultural needs that they were destined to satisfy.

Taken on their own amphorae can equally, on those occasions when they have stamps, inform us on the organization of the import trade of which they were the object. In this way I. B. Brashinsky, noting the over-representation at Elizavetovskoe of certain Heracleote, Thasian or Sinopian eponyms and, consequently, the unequal frequency of cargoes received, explains it by the 'pulsatile' nature of the commercial operations mounted in this frontier-zone by what might be termed 'merchant-adventurers': a view which is justified, providing one can be confident of handling a sample representative of the site as a whole, so that the frequency of certain names does not relate simply to the concentration of finds. From the equally apparent over-representation of certain 'manufacturers' the author deduces the existence of direct relations with the producing centres, excluding the intervention of redistributors installed, for example, in the straits of the Cimmerian Bosphorus – while D. B. Shelov infers from the similarity of imports to Tanaïs and Phanagoria that the Asiatic Bosphorus in the Hellenistic period was playing the role of intermediary in the commerce of the sea of Azov.[25] In considering the Thasian stamps of early type discovered on the west coast of the Black Sea, which often seem to be identical from Apollonia to Istria, I have often felt myself[26] to be following the tracks of Thasian *caboteurs* loaded with amphorae from two or three workshops. Similarly it is often possible to guess which port was the starting point for their redistribution into the hinterland: that Thasian products of the fourth century reached the territories of the Getae starting from Istria, while those of Heraclea preferred the land route coming from Tomis and especially from Callatis, a Heraclean colony.[27] But, in the absence of amphora-laden wrecks, such enquiries will only lead to decisive results on the day when we have satisfactory publications everywhere.

Especially when they are found in small numbers on a remote site, imported amphorae do not necessarily imply transactions related to their original contents: for they may well have travelled as reused containers, from a major importing centre. Thus, writes Herodotus (III 6–7), 'Jars full of wine are brought into Egypt throughout every year from Greece and also Phoenice: yet one might safely say there is not a single empty wine jar anywhere in the country. Where then, one might ask, are they used? This too I will say. Each demarch has the duty of gathering in all the jars from his city and taking them to Memphis, and the people of Memphis have to fill them with water and transport them to those waterless parts of Syria of which I have spoken. Thus the vessels brought to Egypt and emptied there are carried to Syria to join those already there.' Both in Egypt itself and in Hellenistic Delos re-use is equally well attested. V. Grace is therefore right to conclude that the thirty-eight stamped handles found at Nessana in Palestine 'must necessarily form a relatively scanty and ambiguous commercial record',[28] and J. H. Kent is right not to believe, on the basis of about fifteen handles, that much Cnidian and Rhodian wine was being consumed among the vineyards of Rheneia.[29]

Lastly it seems to me possible to push the exploitation of amphora evidence still further, up to the ideological level: that is, to use it to define the spirit in which the transactions of which it was the object were carried out. This at least is what emerges from recent advances in our knowledge of Thasian stamps resulting from the excavation of several workshop dumps:[30] those of Koukos, of Vamvouri Ammoudia and of Kalonero.[31]

As soon as it was proved conclusively that in the extensive series of so-called 'late' stamps (from around 340 to the middle of the Hellenistic period) the only name mentioned was that of an annual magistrate functioning as if eponymous, and that the 'manufacturer' was only represented by an emblem renewed every year, it became clear that the practice of stamping at Thasos had no aim of publicizing a particular craft or commercial enterprise.[32] As long as the opposite was believed, that 'naturally' this name was that of a master-potter or wine merchant and that the renewal of the emblem served to date the production (of the container or contents), we were led instead to think that the appearance of the name of the eponym – as in the early stamps with two names – had only a chronological significance.[33] The old question of state or private motivation in the amphora stamps of Thasos, and we may suppose in other contemporary centres,[34] is thus resolved – without recourse to arguments of pure 'probability'.

From the fact that Thasian stamps, especially in the early period (from the end of the fifth century to around 340), were sometimes printed very faintly, and that the amphorae, especially at Kalonero, were covered after firing in a creamy slip which often filled the hollow of the stamp to the point of making it illegible and almost unnoticeable, I deduce that the consumers took no account of the stamp in their choice, and in particular did not require from it an indication of date. The same explanation was suggested to I. B. Brashinsky by the placing of certain stamps of Heracleote magistrates on the feet of amphorae (and so in a barely visible position).[35]

Moreover, I do not believe that the purpose of stamping was to identify the receptacle (still less its contents) as Thasian to foreign consumers, because it seems clear, as I have mentioned above (p. 29) that we find abroad a percentage of unstamped amphorae more or less equal to that which occurs on the island of Thasos itself; because also at Thasos as elsewhere tiles which were only rarely exported might be stamped; and finally because all the Thasian stamps and all the series of stamped amphorae existing in the Greek world were far from bearing ethnic names or official devices. Thus the form itself of the amphora must have sufficed to indicate its origin (for those who were concerned about it). Amphora stamps went the same way as coins: the (eventual) mention of the ethnic name was less to identify than to authenticate.[36]

It emerges then that the 'average' consumer must have been perfectly indifferent to the presence or otherwise of a stamp on an amphora. This is a possible explanation, rather than the incompetence or ignorance of the engravers, of the presence of stamps without writing on certain Thraco-Getan imitations of Rhodian amphorae.[37] Accordingly one should not postulate that a non-explicit stamp, for example a monogram, should have a local origin on the pretext that 'a stamp of this type can only have had significance in a limited area where the meaning of the abbreviation was known'.[38] Without wishing to involve us in primitivism, this suggests a consumer psychology markedly different from that which is familiar to us, and it puts us on guard against the anachronisms which are so easy to fall into in this field.

It therefore seems to me beyond doubt that the stamping of amphorae (and of tiles) resulted from an administrative control, but one which was not concerned with their commercialization abroad: apart from the reasons already advanced, a number of cities which were well-known exporters of wine did not carry out this practice. We may prefer to suppose that it was a control exercised at the stage of manufacture. But that does not tell us exactly why amphorae were stamped in certain places and at certain dates, or more precisely why some were stamped and others not in proportions suggesting that stamping was not done simply on a sample. The generally accepted hypothesis (this also, among others, of V. Grace) that they relate to a guarantee of capacity does not fully satisfy me, because it does not seem to me proven that the variation in the capacity of stamped amphorae was less significant than in that of non-stamped amphorae,[39] because I cannot see the advantage of producing receptacles (still less tiles) whose unguaranteed dimensions were proclaimed by the absence of stamps, and also because this hypothesis seems to have too much regard for the idea of *fair trade*. At least for the time being, I prefer to leave the matter unresolved (especially while we await the measurements to be carried out on major series of amphorae, both stamped and unstamped, found recently at Thasos). We know so little of the economic control exercised by the magistrates of Greek cities that many other solutions seem possible, especially viewed from a fiscal aspect.

Finally, indirect light has been thrown on trade in Thasian amphorae because the early stamps of Kalonero gave us an idea of the personality of the owners of this workshop: namely, of Leophontos, Aristagoras and Demalkes in the probable order of succession, who feature there with a very variable number of different eponyms (2, 17 and 10, respectively). From the Thasian prosopography established by Chr. Dunant and J. Pouilloux[40] it is apparent that there existed from the fourth to the third centuries a family in which fathers and sons were called successively Demalkes and Aristagoras: it is represented by Aristagoras I Demalkes I who was theoros towards 370–365 (Catalogue I, col. 6, l. 50); by his son Demalkes II Aristagoras I who held the archonship between 345 and 315, certainly after 330 (I, no. 34, l. 9); by his grandson Aristagoras II Demalkes II who was theoros towards 290 (*I.G.* XII 8.288 l. 5) and perhaps also archon in 290–80 (no. 34, l. 45). It seems to me very possible, even very probable, that the two main manufacturers of Kalonero belonged to this aristocratic family (one should have been Aristagoras I and the other Demalkes II) and that this workshop was situated on their properties,[41] manned no doubt by slaves, and was similar to those which a number of rich Athenians possessed at the same period. These suggestions, which I put forward for consideration and comment, give rise to a whole resolutely anti-modernist conception of the Greek economy in the fourth century. They tend in effect to reabsorb commercial activities, and craft activities too, into the bosom of the *oikos*, to reduce their specificity and their autonomy in relation to agrarian structures: if my interpretation of the archaeological data is well-based, there is nothing against the idea that the great landowners of Thasos who were owners of amphora workshops proceeded themselves, or through trusted intermediaries, to commercialize their production of wine to the end of the Black Sea – according to the archaic model which was suggested to B. Bravo by a letter on lead of the early fifth century found at Bérézan.[42]

Another way of approaching this problem is to study the distribution of early and late stamps of a single manufacturer found in a particular potter's tip: their distribution not only abroad, as I have mentioned above (p. 31), but equally – and this opens a new field of archaeological research – *in the territory of Thasos itself*. Thus it would be possible to measure the constancy or inconstancy of the relations between a particular manufacturer and a particular group of consumers, and so the way in which they were affected by the role of intermediaries. From my first surface collections in the plain of Astris, in the south of the island, it has just recently become clear that the majority of stamped amphorae came there from the local workshops of Koukos and Vamvouri Ammoudia.[43]

These introductory remarks to a study of trade in Greek amphorae will perhaps seem too critical, even pessimistic. I have rejected certain 'economist', historicist or antiquarian illusions, while at the same time indicating new avenues of research. These last are not without ideological implications and, to be wholly fruitful, call for different practice in the field: amphora evidence should cease to be considered a by-product of archaeological activity and should sometimes impose on excavators a special strategy, directed towards the solution of specific problems. The main obstacle to the progress of knowledge in this area of research lies largely in the habits of thought and institutional traditions which strongly resist change.

[4]

Maritime loans and the structure of credit in fourth-century Athens

by PAUL MILLETT

I

My aim in this paper is to examine some aspects of the organization of Athenian foreign trade in the later classical period. This necessarily involves the close consideration of Hasebroek's position on trade, and I approach the question by analysing the part played by maritime loans in the twin structures of Athenian trade and credit relations. The distribution of the evidence, which is mainly from the Attic orators, effectively limits my analysis to the fourth century.

The general principles of the maritime loan are fairly straightforward.[1] In order to pay for the cargo being taken on board ship, the merchant (*emporos*) or shipowner (*naukleros*) borrowed money for the duration of the trading voyage; the voyage could be either one-way (*heteroplous*) or a return trip (*amphoteroplous*). The loan and interest were repaid out of the proceeds of the sale of the cargo only on condition that the ship arrived safely at its destination. This is the crucial point about maritime loans that makes them different from all other types of loan transaction: if as the result of shipwreck or piracy the ship and its cargo were lost, the borrower was freed from all obligation to repay the loan, and the loss was borne by the lender. Because of the high risks involved, the rates of interest charged on these voyages were high; anything from 12½ to 30 per cent, and perhaps even higher. The sums of money borrowed range from 1,000 to at least 4,500 drachmae, with a median value of 3,000 drachmae.[2] As a partial guarantee against fraud on the part of the borrower, the cargo was offered as security; if the borrower was the shipowner, the ship itself could be pledged as security. As a further safeguard against fraud, there was usually a written contract setting out in some detail the terms and conditions of the loan.

These are the characteristic elements of a typical maritime loan. In practice, the variations on this relatively simple theme are many and complex, but for the purposes of this paper they can fortunately be ignored.[3] The basic mechanism of the maritime loan survived through Hellenistic, Roman, medieval and modern times until well into the nineteenth century.

This brief description of maritime loans suggests that they are potentially valuable as providing evidence – almost the only evidence – about how trade was financed in classical Greece. It therefore comes as no surprise that they form an essential part of Hasebroek's theory about the organization of Athenian trade as set out in *Trade and politics*. Briefly, Hasebroek saw the most important division in the classical Greek state as that between citizen-*rentiers*, who lived on the proceeds of their own property and investments, and the mass of non-citizens (metics and *xenoi*), who were actively involved in trade and manufacturing (35). 'As far as trade was concerned their position (i.e., the wealthy citizens) was that of a *rentier* not an *entrepreneur*. They lent money to the merchant . . . but they themselves took no part in the merchant's activities except occasionally as a mere side line.' (17). Throughout *Trade and politics*, Hasebroek stressed this clear-cut division between citizens and non-citizen traders (22, 28, 101). He also argued that the great majority of these non-citizens were poor men, without extensive resources of their own (7–10, 36–7). it followed from this that in order to finance their trading voyages, they were heavily dependent on maritime loans. Hasebroek described these loans as: 'the typical method of financing foreign trade' (7 n.4); they formed the indispensable link between poor, non-citizen traders, and wealthy, non-trading citizens.

Recent work on trade and maritime loans has tended to concentrate on Hasebroek's distinction between citizen lenders and non-citizen borrowers, but the results are generally unhelpful and sometimes contradictory. I give as extreme examples the recent studies by Hansen (Isager and Hansen (1975) 70–4) and Erxleben (1974). Hansen and Erxleben both use the evidence of the Attic orators as a statistical test of Hasebroek's theories on the organization of trade. What follows is a summary comparison of their findings, giving Erxleben's figures in brackets. Actively engaged in trade as *naukleroi* or *emporoi* were 15 (11) Athenian citizens as opposed to 14 (—) non-citizens. Amongst the identifiable lenders in maritime loans there were 12 (28) non-citizens and 7 (41) citizens. Of these lenders, 12 (3) were either *naukleroi* or *emporoi*, and 9 (—) were not active as traders.

The conflict between these two sets of figures is complete, and they plainly support contradictory conclusions. Hansen uses his statistics as ammunition to attack Hasebroek's model. He argues that foreign trade was not completely dominated by non-citizens; that lenders were not principally citizens and borrowers lenders; and that *emporoi* and *naukleroi* were not so poor that they always had to borrow to finance their voyages – in 12 out of 21 cases they appear as lenders. But Erxleben's figures – and I stress that they are drawn from the same sources – give a totally different picture. They strongly suggest that Hasebroek got it right, and this is how they are interpreted by Erxleben (482).

Alarming as they are, the discrepancies between these two sets of statistics are easily explained. The speeches of the Attic orators are consistently vague and imprecise in their description of people's status and origins. This often makes it impossible to say with any certainty who are citizens, metics, *xenoi*, *emporoi* and *naukleroi*. Because the numbers being dealt with are so small, these dubious cases make all the difference. This is an unavoidable source of error. Less excusable is the cavalier fashion in which Erxleben manipulates his sources so as to maximize the number of citizen lenders, and minimize the number of citizen traders.[4] Taken together, the two sets of figures speak for themselves, and I hope they make it clear why I put no faith in the technique of counting heads as a method of condemning or vindicating Hasebroek. In any case, Hasebroek's insistence on the complete non-involvement of citizens in active trade is one of the more polemical points of *Trade and politics*.[5]

As an alternative approach, I intend to try and locate maritime loans within the overall structure of credit relations in fourth-century Athens. Hitherto, the tendency has been to treat these loans as an isolated institution, and their relationship to other types of credit is either ignored or misunderstood. In this respect, Hasebroek himself is not entirely blameless, and from my own point of view his treatment of credit is the least satisfactory part of his work. This is especially the case in an earlier paper on Greek banking, which has a distinctly 'modernist' flavour (Hasebroek (1920)). In this article, Hasebroek talked in terms of giro transactions between accounts within individual banks, and a clearing system between different banks to avoid unnecessary transferences of funds. In *Trade and politics*, Hasebroek modified his position on Greek banking. He withdrew his arguments in favour of a clearing system, and acknowledged that there was no conclusive evidence for giro-type transactions in any of the sources from the classical period.[6]

In spite of these modifications, Hasebroek's comments on credit in general, and on banking in particular, still cannot be reconciled with the actual evidence. He describes bankers as paying out interest on savings deposits, adding that: 'This was a recognized way in which *rentiers* invested their capital, and quite large sums were often so invested.' Hasebroek offers no evidence in support of this statement, and I am aware of no example in the classical sources. It is not even certain that Athenian bankers paid out interest on any type of deposit, savings or otherwise.[7] Equally unacceptable is Hasebroek's account of why money-lending was so widespread in classical Greece. He gives as 'the explanation' the desire of individuals to make their wealth 'invisible' in order to dodge liturgies, and as a protection against confiscation. Perhaps this was a significant factor in making people ready to lend money, but it was neither the only, nor the most important reason.

As it happens, these rather erratic comments on banking and credit are peripheral to the main themes of *Trade and politics*, so it does not matter too much that Hasebroek got some of them wrong. In the rest of this paper, I will try to show that a more realistic model of the structure of credit is fully consistent with Hasebroek's general approach to Athenian economy and society. And from this it should emerge that where it matters – on the role of maritime loans in the financing of trade – Hasebroek got it right. My discussion falls into three main sections, beginning with some general arguments in support of the importance of maritime loans in the organization of Athenian trade. This leads into a more detailed analysis of the rationale of maritime loans, divided into two subsections: why borrowers wanted the loans, and why lenders were willing to supply them.

II

In *Trade and politics*, Hasebroek relied on logic as the basis of his argument that maritime loans were the typical method of financing trading voyages. Traders were non-citizens; non-citizens were poor; therefore traders must have depended on borrowed money. But is there any independent evidence about this reliance of traders on credit? Hasebroek himself offered the subsidiary proof that all Athenian laws on trade and traders were concerned with maritime loans: 'Legislation, then, so far as it relates to foreign trade and finds expression in the emporial laws, was designed exclusively for the bottomry business . . . In fact, this legislation is the clearest possible expression of the dependence of all Greek trade upon borrowed capital' (172). There is something in what Hasebroek says, but the paragraphs of argument leading up to this conclusion are compressed to the point of obscurity, and need restating.

In the first place, it is not the case that all Athenian laws relating to foreign trade involve maritime loans. Our knowledge of these laws is incomplete, but there are at least two pieces of legislation which were not necessarily related to maritime credit. There was a law prohibiting people resident in Athens from shipping grain to any harbour other than the Peiraeus, and a law protecting traders from frivolous prosecutions by stiffening the penalties against unsuccessful plaintiffs.[8] There is also some doubt about Hasebroek's point that all the laws relating to maritime loans were designed to protect the interests of the lender and/or borrower. This was certainly the case with the laws which bound traders to stick to the terms of their contracts, and imposed the death penalty on traders who borrowed without adequate security. But a third law, somehow restricting the lending of money on return voyages, was not necessarily in the interests of either borrower or lender. The details of this law are obscure, but it seems to forbid any person resident in Athens to lend on a double voyage, unless the final destination was the Peiraeus and the ship carried certain types of cargo, including grain.[9]

Finally, there is the question of the scope of the so-called 'trading suits' (*dikai emporikai*) and their relationship to maritime credit. *Dikai emporikai* were a special category of court cases thought to be advantageous to the litigants because they gave unrestricted access to non-citizens and reached their verdicts with a minimum of delay.[10] Hasebroek seems to suggest that *dikai emporikai* were simply court cases which arose out of the 'emporial laws' on maritime loans. In fact, the scope of the *dikai emporikai* was defined independently of the laws on trade. So far as it is possible to tell, three conditions had to be fulfilled before a case could qualify as a *dike emporike*. One of the litigants had to be an *emporos* or a *naukleros*; the case must arise out of a trading voyage either to or from Athens; there had to be a written contract. Although these conditions seem to point to maritime loans as the motivation behind the creation of *dikai emporikai* as a special category, the evidence of the surviving court cases is ambiguous. Out of the four *dikai emporikai* in the corpus of the orators, three arose out of disputes over maritime credit. But the fourth has only remote connexions with a maritime loan, and this implies that the conditions restricting access to *dikai emporikai* were loosely interpreted.[11]

The conclusion I draw from this detail is that although the Athenian laws on trade and the regulations governing access to *dikai emporikai* were closely tied up with maritime loans, the relationship was not so clear-cut as Hasebroek assumed. It is certainly not final proof that all Greek trade depended on credit. Apart from the uncertainty which is inevitable in reconstructing laws from the orators, the law at best throws only an indirect light on social and economic institutions. Altogether more reliable is the direct evidence on the number of maritime loans. Although any sort of quantitative analysis is out of the question, there are strong numerical indications that maritime credit was at least a very common method of financing Athenian trade.

The evidence on Greek maritime loans is concentrated in four speeches from the Demosthenic corpus. They all date from the second half of the fourth century, and they all represent the interests of the lenders against allegedly fraudulent borrowers. Each of these court cases arose out of the failure to repay one particular loan, and they are the source of our detailed information on maritime loans as an institution.[12] But what is striking about these speeches is the number of other maritime loans that crop up quite casually as the speaker presents the facts of the case. Taken together, the four speeches contain references to at least twenty different maritime loans, all having some sort of bearing on the speakers' cases. Some of these loans were contracted outside Athens, confirming that maritime credit was known in other parts of the Greek world. Of course, a few of these loan transactions may well be rhetorical inventions designed to bolster up the litigant's case. Even so, they are still good evidence on the frequency of maritime loans; the speaker would presumably take care to mirror actual practice in order to avoid raising the suspicions of the jury.

Apart from this heavy concentration of maritime loans in the four cases that deal directly with trading voyages, there are scattered references in other speeches that have little or nothing to do with trade. In all, there are at least three references to specific loan transactions, and a further three references to persons lending money in maritime loans.[13] There are also a number of casual references to maritime loans outside the corpus of the orators. The 'Boastful Man' in Theophrastus' *Characters* brags about the amount of money that he has tied up in trading voyages, and gives details of his profits and losses; according to Diogenes Laertius, it was rumoured that the philosopher Zeno of Citium had more than a thousand talents which he lent out in maritime loans; there are a couple of references in comedy to maritime loans; finally, there is a reference in the *Poroi* to the institution of maritime credit. Xenophon argues that one of his schemes for increasing the revenues of Athens will bring in a return comparable to the profit on maritime loans (*hosper nautikon*).[14]

The allusion to maritime credit in the *Poroi* is remarkable for its brevity. Xenophon's readers were expected to grasp the significance of a two-word comparison between his own money-making scheme, and the mechanism of maritime loans. And the same goes for all the other casual references to maritime credit in the literature. Writers apparently made the assumption that the general principles of maritime loans were familiar to all Athenians. Even in the four trading speeches from the Demosthenic corpus, there is no summary account of the workings of maritime loans for the benefit of the jury. This can be contrasted with the laboured description of something resembling a letter of credit given in a speech of Isocrates (XVII 35–7). The implication is that the concept of a paper transference of funds was not familiar to the jury and needed a full explanation. This was not the case with maritime loans.

This direct evidence on the frequency and familiarity of maritime loans strengthens the overall impression that a majority of trading voyages were financed by borrowing. But it is no use trying to pretend that 'impressions' are conclusive proof. As I see it, the only way of proving Hasebroek right or wrong is by reinforcing these general indications with an examination of the rationale of maritime loans and their relationship to other types of credit transaction.

III

The easy availability of credit was essential to the smooth functioning of Athenian society; loan transactions of one type or another are a pervasive feature at all levels of Athenian private life. A few figures will help to give some idea of the scope of these credit operations. In the thirty-two private speeches of Demosthenes, there are references to at least 130 separate loan transactions; there is hardly a speech from the entire corpus of the orators without at least one mention of a debt. Even in a short text like Theophrastus' *Characters* there are almost thirty references to lending and borrowing. On the non-literary side, there are more than two hundred *horoi*, all recording some species of credit operation.

Maritime loans stand out from this mass of credit transactions because they were apparently productive. That is to say, they seem to have been contracted in order to increase the existing wealth of the borrower. Almost without exception, all other loans from the classical period were consumption loans, made for non-productive purposes (see Finley (1953) 256 and (1973) 141). I emphasize this point, because what ought long ago to have become accepted orthodoxy is still being challenged or ignored. As a recent example of ignoring the evidence, I cite Andreau's attack on Finley's *Ancient economy* (Andreau (1977) 1144–8). In this article, Andreau objected that Finley gave a false impression by using Bogaert's findings on Greek banking as evidence that money-lending in the Greek world was almost entirely unproductive (Bogaert (1968) 356–9). 'Car, si les opérations de crédit productif étaient le fait de propriétaires et d'hommes d'affaires non-banquiers . . . elles n'apparaîtrent dans le livre de R. Bogaert, qui concerne les banques de dépôt' (1145). Significantly, Andreau supplied no examples of these imaginary non-bankers making productive loans. This is not surprising. In my own catalogue of almost nine hundred loan transactions of all types, drawn from the whole of classical Greece, there are perhaps five – excluding maritime loans – which might conceivably be classed as productive. The case could hardly be clearer, and the five exceptions do serve to prove the rule that Greek credit was overwhelmingly unproductive.[15]

An alternative method of making Greek credit look productive is by redefining the terminology. This is the approach of Pleket in a review of Bogaert's *Banques et banquiers* (*Mnemosyne* 24 (1971) 433–7). Pleket comes up with the hypothetical case of a peasant borrowing money to replace broken or worn-out tools. He admits that this would not result in any increase in agricultural yield, but argues that: '. . . the ancients may well have had a production mentality, provided one gives the word "productive" a less modern and anachronistic twist' (434). An almost identical line is taken by Thompson, again in an article which has some critical things to say about Bogaert's views on banker's loans ((1979) 230–3). Thompson tries to argue that at least some of the loans made by bankers were not consumption loans, but 'commercial loans', involving merchants and traders. He also has two further sub-groups of loans: 'political loans' and 'commercial loans for productive purposes'.

Obviously, the whole business is in danger of getting out of hand, with the invention of categories to match up with the types of loans found in the sources. But once the original categories of productive and consumption loans have lost their precision, the exercise becomes pointless. As originally defined, productive credit – borrowing to increase existing wealth – is a characteristic of theoretical models of the modern, capitalist economy, and consumption credit is not.[16]

I have gone into some detail about the nature of productive credit in order to bring out the apparent uniqueness of maritime loans. As possible examples of productive borrowing in a society supposedly dominated by a profoundly unproductive mentality, they are an embarrassment. Finley bypasses the difficulty by presenting maritime loans as a type of insurance policy rather than as a form of credit, productive or otherwise. This is a possibility, because the mechanism of maritime credit gave the effect of insurance by shifting the risk of loss from the borrower to lender.[17] Although this insurance idea is an attractive way of side-stepping an awkward anomaly, it causes other difficulties. If it is accepted that maritime credit was taken out purely as an insurance policy and not as a loan, it cannot be argued that traders were forced to borrow through poverty. So the insurance argument can end up as an attack on Hasebroek's theory of poor traders having to rely on credit to finance their voyages.

There is a way out of this difficulty, and that is to reject the idea of maritime loans as a substitute for insurance, and show instead that they shared some of the characteristics of consumption credit. Apart from Hasebroek's evidence that traders were typically without resources, there are at least two objections to the insurance theory. In a majority of cases, only a part of the cargo was covered by the loan. There are indications in the sources that the value of the security in a maritime loan had to be twice the size of the sum borrowed. This meant that an *emporos* would have to bear the cost of half the cargo, and the insurance cover would only be partial ([Dem.] XXXIV 6–7; XXXV 18). A more fundamental objection is the fact that traders always sailed with their cargo. So if the ship went down, there was always a good chance that they would go down with it, making the question of insurance irrelevant.

This argument is less frivolous than it sounds. It is thought that proper marine insurance began to evolve towards the end of the thirteenth century, when Italian merchants stopped travelling with their cargoes, and became 'sedentary'. Because the merchant no longer ran the same risks as his cargo, it made sense to arrange some sort of insurance cover. At first, a hybrid form of maritime loan was developed to give protection against loss. These so-called 'insurance loans' (*Versicherungsdarlehn*) date from *c.*1290. At some date before 1350, insurance loans began to be replaced by a proper system of premium insurance. Although a parallel like this cannot be decisive, it does suggest that insurance was an effect rather than the cause of maritime credit in the Greek world.[18]

My argument that maritime loans shared common features with

consumption credit is more intricate. It depends on Hasebroek's theory that traders were for the most part poor men who were forced to borrow to earn their living. If Hasebroek is right, then traders borrowed from necessity, not from choice; and that is one of the key distinctions between consumption and productive credit. Of course, it is unrealistic to argue that every single trader was a poor man without any financial resources. The twelve money-lending *emporoi* and *naukleroi* detected by Hansen must mean something. But by setting the organization of trade in the wider context of the Athenian economy, it is possible to make sense of the evidence on maritime loans, while preserving Hasebroek's model more-or-less intact.

The nature of traders' demand for maritime loans can be clarified by drawing some comparisons with the organization of manufacturing and retailing in Athens. In both cases the units were small, and they operated at a low level of sophistication. Here, I am not referring to establishments like the slave workshops owned by the father of Demosthenes, which are amongst the largest known from the Greek world. Much more typical were the tradesmen who had shops and workplaces in or near the *agora*. The slaves owned by Demosthenes' father apparently brought in a good income, because he died a relatively wealthy man. But the artisans and retailers in the *agora* led a more precarious existence. There is slight but consistent evidence that, like traders, they were regularly forced to borrow to stay in business.

Hyperides' speech *Against Athenogenes* arose out of debts owed by a perfume seller (*myropoles*). The background to the case is too well known to need more than a brief summary.[19] Athenogenes was an Egyptian metic who owned three stalls selling perfume with a workforce of three slaves – a father and his two sons. The plaintiff, an unnamed Athenian citizen, agreed to buy up the business lock, stock, and barrel, in order to gain ownership of one of the slave boys, with whom he was in love. As a part of the deal, he agreed to take over responsibility for the debts contracted by the slaves on behalf of the business; he understood that only trifling sums were owed, which were easily covered by the stocks of raw materials. But after the sale had been completed, it turned out that the various debts came to a total of more than five talents. These debts appear to have been of two different types: money due to other retailers who provided raw materials on credit, and *eranos* contributions – small, interest free loans supplied by Athenogenes' acquaintances who frequented the stalls.

Athenogenes was lucky to get at least some of his loans without interest, but other stallholders were less fortunate. This is the implication of Theophrastus' description of 'The man suffering from moral insanity (*aponoia*)', who has all the hallmarks of a professional usurer (*Characters* VI 9):

He does not think it beneath himself to lord it over the many small traders in the *agora*. He lends them money on the spot, and charges interest of 1½ obols on every drachma each day (i.e. 25%). He goes the rounds of the hot food stalls, the fresh and salted fishmongers, collecting his interest from their takings, and putting it straight into his mouth.

Although Theophrastus' character sketches are caricatures, they are meant to be recognizable, and are in large part true to life. There are also parallels from other societies for this species of usurious lending to market traders.[20]

There is general evidence for this particular type of credit transaction in the catalogue of monthly suits (*dikai emmenoi*) given in the Aristotelian *Athenaion politeia* (LII 2). A *dike aphorme* may be brought as a monthly suit: 'if anyone borrows *aphorme* from a person because they want to carry on a business (*ergazesthai*) in the *agora*'. *Dikai aphormai* are usually described as suits brought against people who borrow capital in order to start a business in the *agora*, but this gives a misleadingly modern impression. Other uses of *aphorme* suggest that the word has a more neutral sense than 'starting capital'; a better translation would be: 'what is needed to keep something going'.[21] In the passage from *Athenaion politeia*, *aphorme* presumably refers to loans to market traders enabling them to stay in business. The Athenians thought that this branch of credit transactions was sufficiently important to deserve the privileged status of a monthly suit.

I interpret these loans made to retailers in the *agora* as broadly comparable to the maritime loans made to *emporoi* and *naukleroi*. Both groups operated at the margin without proper reserves, and for them, as for all Athenians, the natural way out of financial difficulties was by borrowing. The loans were productive only in the narrow sense that the profit made by working with the borrowed money had to cover the interest charge. The borrower was motivated by a desire, not to increase his wealth, but simply to stay in business, and I cannot see these loans as evidence for a true productive mentality. Instead, they serve to emphasize the poverty of traders, being forced to borrow to pay for their cargoes.

The other evidence on traders' lack of resources has been collected by Hasebroek, and there is little to add.[22] But equally suggestive is the absence of evidence for wealthy traders. So far as I am aware, from the whole of the classical Greek world, only two persons are known who owned more than one ship: Lampis, 'the greatest shipowner amongst the Greeks' (Dem. XXII 211), and Phormio the banker, who had his ships detained by the authorities in Byzantium (Dem. XLV 6). The smallness of trading concerns is further evidence for the non-productive attitude of Greek traders. There seems to have been no concept of ploughing back profits in order to increase the scale of operations. This explains the appearance of traders as lenders in maritime loans. If they did achieve a surplus, they preferred to lend their spare cash on another trader's voyage, rather than use it to expand their own business.

IV

So far, my analysis has focused on the demand side of maritime credit – why traders wanted maritime loans. My conclusions support Hasebroek's theory that traders depended on maritime credit because of their poverty. I now turn to an examination of the sources of supply of maritime loans, and the possible involvement of wealthy citizens as *rentiers*. Again I do this against the background of other types of credit transaction. Earlier work on the sources of maritime loans – and on the sources of credit in general – has tended to concentrate on the role of the banks; other types of money-lending have been ignored. In a way, this is understandable. According to modern economic theory, banks are the suppliers of credit *par excellence*, and because of the chance survival of a group of law-court speeches, we are comparatively well informed about Athenian banking.[23] But the attention that has been paid to Athenian banks as providers of credit is out of all proportion to the surviving evidence on bankers' loans. Despite the mass of detail on banking operations preserved in the orators, there are references to only eleven loans made by bankers, and none of them is a maritime loan.[24]

The detailed evidence of the orators shows that the bulk of loans were supplied not by bankers, but by the family, friends, and neighbours of the borrower. Obviously, this is related to the fact that people typically borrowed because of financial distress, and there was a strong ethical obligation to help relatives and friends who were in difficulties. On a wider scale, this obligation operated between fellow citizens through the institution of *eranos* loans. Citizens who were in need went the rounds of other citizens in the expectation of raising voluntary contributions. It goes without saying that these loans were interest-free, and almost always without security. The result was a complex system of credit transactions, creating a corresponding network of reciprocal obligations.

There is a good illustration of how the system worked in the pseudo-Demosthenic speech *Against Nicostratus* ([LIII] 4–13). Apollodorus (the plaintiff) and Nicostratus were friends and neighbours who often helped each other out with favours. On a journey to recapture a runaway slave, Nicostratus was captured by pirates, and himself sold as a slave. He was ransomed by some *xenoi*, but was obliged to pay over to them the price of his freedom (2,600 drachmae) within thirty days, or be indebted for double the amount. Because he was desperately short of funds, he appealed to his friend Apollodorus for a loan. Apollodorus made him an outright gift of 1,000 drachmae and, because he was himself short of ready cash, he raised the balance by borrowing. He took out a loan of 1,600 drachmae at 1⅓ per cent interest per month, offering a lodging house as security. Apollodorus handed over this money as an interest-free loan for one year, on the understanding that Nicostratus would pay him off by raising an *eranos* loan. The trouble started when Nicostratus refused to pay up. There is no obligation to believe that everything happened exactly as Apollodorus claimed, but the speech presumably reflects common practices in Athenian society.

Of course, this lending to friends and relatives is a different world from that of maritime credit; nevertheless, it is an essential preliminary, because it defined and conditioned people's attitudes towards money-lending in general. Most important of all, it explains the underdevelopment of institutional sources of credit through bankers and other professional lenders. There are two reasons for this. In the first place, there were plenty of non-institutional sources of interest-free credit, which could be tapped in preference to professional money-lenders who would charge interest and demand security. Secondly, the emphasis on consumption credit encouraged the attitude that lending to those in distress was a moral obligation, and it was considered despicable to make a financial gain out of other people's misfortunes by taking interest. This explains the expressions of hatred for professional money-lenders found in the sources. Theophrastus' character who makes usurious loans to market traders is (VI 3):

> vulgar in character, lacking in decency, and without principle. He is notorious for his activities as inn-keeper, brothel-keeper, and tax-farmer. . . . He does not reject any trade as beneath his dignity; rather, he acts as herald, cook, or gambles.

The orators provide a good illustration of how an advantage could be gained by presenting one's legal opponent as a professional money-lender. This is the line of attack taken by the plaintiff (again, Apollodorus) in Demosthenes' *First Speech Against Stephanus* (XLV 69):

You [Stephanus] have been far better off than you deserved, yet to whom among the mass of Athenian citizens have you ever made an *eranos* contribution? To whom have you ever given help? To whom have you done a kindness? You could not mention a single one. But while lending money at interest and regarding the misfortunes and necessities of others as your good fortune, you ejected your uncle Nicias from his ancestral home, you deprived your mother-in-law of the resources upon which she lived . . . No one has ever exacted payment from a man defaulting on the principal as you exact interest from your debtors.

As usual, there is no obligation to believe the truth of what Apollodorus says, but it might be expected to prejudice the jury against Stephanus.

Other evidence suggests that the relationship between money-lending, morality, and interest was not as clear-cut as I have so far implied. Between the extremes of interest-free loans and professional creditors, there seems to have been a grey area. It was apparently acceptable for persons who were not friends or relatives to lend to each other at interest, provided that this was done on a casual basis, and not as a means of earning a living. There are examples of these 'one-off' interest-bearing loans in the estates listed in the orators.[25]

Taken together, these arguments explain why institutional credit was so uncommon in classical Athens. Apart from usurers, who operated at the pettiest of levels, and bankers, who provided only specialized types of credit, true professional money-lenders only appear in the sources in connexion with maritime loans. For the purposes of analysis, I distinguish three types of lenders in this branch of credit operations: citizens lending casually in maritime loans; traders lending on a casual basis; and professional money-lenders. I will examine each of these categories in turn, with reference to the model of Athenian credit relations sketched in above.

The first group is the smallest. The only certain examples of citizens casually involved in maritime loans are Demosthenes and his father. Even Demosthenes' participation in maritime loans is not definite, as it forms part of an allegation in Hyperides' speech *Against Demosthenes* (frag. IV col. 17). The orator accuses Demosthenes of embezzling state funds and lending them out in maritime loans. The case of Demosthenes' father is more illuminating (Dem. XXVII 11). As a part of his estate at the time of his death he had 7,000 drachmae lent out in maritime loans 'with Xuthus'. This sum was presumably made up of a plurality of loans, and Bogaert plausibly identifies Xuthus as a middleman who looked after Demosthenes' father's maritime interests (Bogaert (1965) 141–6).

The second category of traders as casual lenders is larger, and I give only the necessary detail. In the speech *Against Phormio* ([Dem.] XXXIV 6) there are two casual lenders: Theodorus the Phoenician, and Lampis the *naukleros*, who was probably a slave. They both lent on the outward voyage only, and they both travelled with the ship. The circumstantial detail in the speech *Against Lacritus* ([Dem.] XXXV 6–9) suggests that Androcles and Nausicrates were not professional money-lenders, and Androcles is definitely a trader. The borrowers in the speech *Against Dionysodorus* ([Dem.] LVI 17) are accused by the creditors of appropriating the loan, and using it to lend in maritime loans of their own.

The largest group of identifiable maritime creditors are the professional money-lenders. The best documented example is the unnamed speaker in the speech *Against Apaturius*, who gives a brief account of himself ([Dem.] XXXIII 4): 'I have been involved in foreign trade for a long time now, and up to a certain time risked the sea in my own person. Almost seven years ago, I gave up voyaging, and having made a moderate sum of money, I try to put it to work in maritime loans.' Chrysippus in the speech *Against Phormio* ([Dem.] XXXIV 1) claims that he and his partner have frequented the *emporion* for many years, and have made many maritime loans without being involved in a court case. Similarly, Darius opens his speech *Against Dionysodorus* by talking about: 'we who are involved in trade and lend our money to other people' ([Dem.] LVI 1). From an earlier date (*c*.410 BC), I include in this group Diodotus, who appears in Lysias' speech *Against Diogeiton* (XXXII 6). Diodotus made a large fortune in trade, and when he died his estate was worth at least 15 talents, of which 7 talents and 40 minae were lent out in maritime loans. This is by far the largest single component in the estate, and easily justifies Diodotus' inclusion as a professional lender.[26]

The professional lender about whom we know the most is Nicobulus in Demosthenes' speech *Against Pantaenetus* (XXXVII 52–4). Nicobulus is an interesting case because he goes to great lengths to argue that he is *not* a professional money-lender:

When anyone asks him [my opponent], 'What valid case will you be able to make out against Nicobulus?' he says, 'The Athenians hate those who lend money . . .' For my part, I do not think that a man who lends money necessarily does wrong, although some of these people are rightly hated by you, those who make a trade of the business, with no thought of helping fellow citizens or anything else other than gain. Since I myself have often borrowed money . . . I know these people well, and I do not like them. . . . But if a man has traded as I have, making voyages and facing dangers; and having a small amount of money makes these loans, wishing not only to oblige people, but also to prevent his money being imperceptibly frittered away, why should you set him down as belonging to them?

Nicobulus tries to present himself as a man who lends only to help his friends out of their difficulties. But apart from the fact that he protests too much, the details of the case go against him. The speech arose out of an involved dispute over the purchase of an ore-crushing plant, for which Nicobulus and his partner provided the cash and charged interest at 1 per cent per month. Also, the joint loan was for 10,500 drachmae, which is larger than any loan known from the *horoi* by a factor of 30 per cent; it is almost twice the size of the biggest loan in the rest of the corpus of Demosthenes.[27]

Although it cannot be shown with absolute certainty that Nicobulus was a creditor in maritime loans, it is more than plausible. Immediately after completing the loan agreement with Pantaenetus, he set sail for Pontus. The voyage was not a success, and Nicobulus returned to Athens having lost almost everything that he had. So Nicobulus was at least involved in trade, and his allusion to having borrowed money from professional lenders in the past may refer to maritime loans. Like the speaker in the Apaturius case, Nicobulus could have used his profits to change himself from a borrower into a lender. Nicobulus sailed for Pontus before the beginning of the sailing season, and his loan to Pantaenetus could help to explain what professional money-lenders did with their money in the winter months when maritime loans were not normally possible. The exceptional size of Pantaenetus' loan, and its even more exceptional productive purpose, would have made it difficult to raise it from the conventional sources of friends and relatives; a professional money-lender was a possible answer.

In view of the almost complete absence of professional money-lenders in all other branches of Athenian credit relations, their concentration in maritime lending is significant, but not altogether surprising. If professional lenders were to find a place in the Athenian economy, maritime credit was the natural place for them. Because maritime loans did have a productive element, the charging of interest was justifiable on moral grounds. The same attitude can be detected in the Roman and medieval periods when the taking of interest on ordinary loans was restricted or banned, but exceptions were made for maritime credit.[28] In the Athenian case, there was an additional factor. Because borrowers were mainly metics or *xenoi*, professional money-lenders would not be thought of as exploiting citizens' misfortunes.

Where does all this leave Hasebroek's model? In view of the absence of evidence for citizen-rentiers as maritime lenders, some modification of the model is necessary. The only indisputable example of a citizen without trading interests lending in maritime loans is Demosthenes' father; all other citizen lenders were either actively involved in trade, or were professional money-lenders. Given the high risk of maritime loans, this is understandable. The indications are that the complexity of maritime credit made it an unsuitable field for casual lenders without practical experience in trading. This is probably the explanation of Demosthenes senior's use of a middleman to look after his maritime loans. So it appears that maritime loans had the broader function of linking poor traders with whoever happened to have spare cash, coupled with expertise in trading or money-lending. In this connexion it should be noted that the two largest lenders – Demosthenes and Diodotus – were both citizens, but neither of them were typical Athenians in that they were both comparatively wealthy without owning much land.

[5]

The 'World of the *Emporium*' in the private speeches of Demosthenes

by CLAUDE MOSSÉ

In an article published in 1938 in the *Revue des études grecques*, Louis Gernet remarked that the institution of the *dikai emporikai*, commercial actions, towards the middle of the fourth century, signified the entry of commercial law into the law of the city (186), and the existence of a clearly defined 'world of the emporium' (185, n.5). The guarantee of protection that was afforded to merchants by the possibility of bringing rapid commercial actions had as its essential goal the assurance of the city's supplies and of the advantages that it derived from having an active port, – advantages that Xenophon had already stressed in the *Poroi*. That is not to suggest that there existed in Athens 'a merchant class which played an active role in the affairs of the state or even which exerted any influence over legislation' but it nevertheless revealed the existence of a 'professional circle', a specific world of the *emporium*. On this point Gernet was in essential agreement with the views expressed by Hasebroek ((1933) 43), views according to which commerce in Athens was never an affair of the state since the majority of merchants were poor and foreigners to the city; the only part rich citizens took in commercial activities was in putting up maritime loans. Although these views found only a little support initially (Will (1954), Finley (1962)), they are now generally accepted. But since then the problem has, characteristically enough, been given a new slant; it has even been suggested that the marginality of the world of commerce was a factor in the interpretation of the 'crisis' of the democratic city of the fourth century. I have myself suggested (Mossé (1972)) the possibility of such an analysis, taking care however not to draw any conclusions of a too specific nature regarding the consequences of this marginality. Since then three articles, all produced by scholars from Eastern Europe and all influenced by Marxism, have returned to the question. With nuances that vary from one author to another, they all reaffirm the conviction that the antagonism that existed between foreigners or metics and citizens, the former being the promoters of commercial activity, the latter the beneficiaries of that activity in which they only played an indirect part, was in the last analysis the determining factor in the 'crisis' of Athenian democracy.[1] So I thought it might be interesting to return to the question, working with a limited corpus of writing, that of Demosthenes' speeches, in order to form a clearer and more specific idea of the nature of this commercial milieu, the degree of its professionalism and the closeness of its relations with the city.

What picture do Demosthenes' speeches present of the world of the *emporium* and what place do citizens hold there? From what we can learn of the social and legal status of those active in this world, it would seem possible to make a distinction between those Athenians involved in commercial affairs who do no more than provide bottomry loans, while in every other respect leading the lives of 'free men', and those for whom commerce is a profession, whether in the sense that they belong to more or less permanent commercial partnerships or whether they themselves actually go to sea. In the first category we may include Demosthenes' own father who left a fortune that included 70 *minae* of *nautika* (XXVII 11), Nausimachus and Xenopithes, whose fortunes included credits, one of them, at least, in the Bosphorus (XXXVIII 11) and probably also the Stephanus of Dem. XLV. However, the second category is much more interesting. Thus, Damon, the litigant in *Against Zenothemis* (Dem. XXXII), not only lends money to a certain Protus to go and collect a cargo of wheat from Sicily but also appears to be directly involved in the complicated deal which is the subject of the speech. The principal characters who appear in this speech meet frequently in the Piraeus. Furthermore, Damon has a number of associates (§ 21) and Protus is not simply a merchant with whom he has chance dealings. The ties that exist between him and the group formed by Damon and his associates (§§ 8 and 12) appear to be of a much closer nature. Unlike the first group we have mentioned, these men, who repeatedly stress the fact that they are Athenians (§ 23), engaged in maritime loans on a professional basis and if the full extent of their fortunes were known it seems likely that an essential part would be found to be made up of credits. That probability is even higher in the case of the litigant in the *Against Apaturius* ([Dem.] XXXIII) if, as Gernet believed, he was an Athenian. For many years he had been 'engaged in maritime business'. In later years and, no doubt, with a certain fortune amassed, he gave up actually going to sea but continued notwithstanding to live off maritime trading by means of *nautika*. He was without doubt a habitual frequenter of the trading port since, when two Byzantines arrived in the Piraeus, they came to seek him out 'in the market' (XXXIII 6). Another merchant citizen appears in the speech *Against Pantaenetus* (Dem. XXXVII). The case concerns a loan, but not a maritime one, made by a certain Nicobulus to this Pantaenetus who was running a workshop in the mining district. Nicobulus appears to be a trader who sailed to the Black Sea (cf. § 6: the typical use of *ekpleon*; cf. also § 56) whose affairs do not seem to be particularly flourishing. We may further cite the Micon who appears in the *Against Theocrines* ([Dem.] LVIII), who is described as a *naukleros* (§ 12), that is, a man who spends most of his time at sea (§ 15).

It would certainly be interesting to know who these men were and what position they held in contemporary Athenian society. We know that Demosthenes' father possessed a considerable fortune. According to his son's testimony, he ranked among the richest of the Athenians. Nausimachus and Xenopithes were members of the same social group, given that they were trierarchs, even if their family fortunes do appear subsequently to have declined.[2] Stephanus, who provides his daughter with a dowry of one hundred *minae*, is a rich man who engages in making maritime loans with the intention of becoming even richer (Dem. XLV 65ff.). He too appears on a list of trierarchs in 322 (*I.G.* II² 1632, 29). He was connected, on his mother's side, with a family which Davies describes as 'well-off but rather shadowy' (Davies (1971) 437).

What do we know of the men who appear more directly involved in commercial affairs in that they themselves go to sea or have done so in the past? Damon was related to Demosthenes. It seems reasonable to suppose that he belonged to the same social group as the men mentioned above. Maritime trade seems to be his principal activity and we know nothing of him in any other context. The name of the litigant in the *Against Apaturius* is not known. Nor do we know any more about Nicobulus, the adversary of Pantaenetus. However, a number of details suggest that his means were modest. For instance, he refers to the difficulties of his life at the time when he was obliged to go to sea and confront dangers with no way of knowing whether he would be able to repay the money he had borrowed (§ 54). As in the case of the litigant in the *Against Apaturius*, it was only once he made his fortune that he in turn began providing loans, but even then he retained certain characteristics that betrayed his origins and his adversaries drew attention to them: he walked quickly and talked loudly. We know equally little of Micon, as also of a certain Timosthenes of Aegylia who, around the sixties of the fourth century, was travelling 'on his own business'.

So it would seem that the two groups of citizens connected with commerce – on the one hand those who simply provided loans and were not professional traders and, on the other, those who had themselves gone to sea before providing loans or who still did so, corresponded to two distinct social categories. The first group, composed of men of wealth, only concerned themselves indirectly with maritime loans and those loans represented no more than a fractional part of their total fortune. Connected as they were with political circles and belonging to the group of men expected to provide liturgies, they derived material advantages from their *nautika* but their relations with the world of the *emporium* were no more than indirect.

The second group was a quite different matter: it was composed of men of modest origins much more deeply involved in maritime commerce and it had far fewer connexions with the life of the city. Commerce belonged to the private domain. This is precisely the point that Demosthenes makes to his relative Damon when the latter asks him to help him defend himself. He points out that, now that he is involved in public affairs, it is out of the question for him to intervene in the private domain (*Against Zenothemis*, Dem. XXXII 32).

However, it is important to enquire whether the distinction that I have attempted to make between these two groups is repeated at the level of their relations with their foreign partners. None of the men belonging to the first group appear to have any connexions with foreigners belonging to the world of the *emporium*. The situation is quite different where the second group is concerned. Take the case of Damon, the litigant in the *Against Zenothemis*: when he needs to bring back Zenothemis' vessel which has put into port at Cephallonia, he sends out a certain Aristophon whom he recruits in an *ergasterion* of 'disreputable men' located close to the Piraeus and it is also in the Piraeus that his meetings with the various characters involved in the affair take place. The same goes for Timosthenes of Aegylia: he is an associate of Phormion's at the time when the latter is still merely Pasion's freedman. The litigant in the *Against Apaturius* has business connexions with the two Byzantine *emporoi* who come to meet him in the Piraeus. Of course, all these are isolated examples and it could well be objected that the documentation is extremely incomplete. However, I should like now to turn my attention to three speeches that I have not mentioned hitherto: the *Against Callipus* ([Dem.] LII) which Gernet dates as 368 BC, the *Against Lacritus* ([Dem.] XXXV) of 350 to 340 and the *Against Dionysodorus* ([Dem.] LVI) which cannot be earlier than 323/322.

The *Against Callipus* speech presents us with an *emporos* from Heraclea,

Lycon by name, a client of Pasion's bank. His associate is a metic, Cephisiades, a resident of Skyros, also engaged in maritime trade. When he comes to Athens he is the guest of two Athenians, Aristonus of Decelea and Archibiades of Lamptrae and he has, in the past, had occasion to lend money to two Athenian *emporoi*, Megaclides of Eleusis and his brother Thrasyllus. Of these four Athenians, only Archebiades of Lamptrae is known in other connexions, for his son was a trierarch in 373/72 (*I.G.* II[2] 1607, 10). But in this context he is simply the host of two traders from Heraclea and he has no particular connexions with maritime commerce. On the other hand, nothing is known of the two *emporoi* to whom Lycon of Heraclea lends money. And it is characteristic that the *proxenos* of the men from Heraclea, to wit the Athenian Callipus against whom the speech is directed, makes a number of remarks about the metic Cephisiades which are, to put it mildly, of an insulting nature (§ 9).

The speech *Against Lacritus* is particularly worthy of attention given that it was made right at the beginning of the period upon which I am concentrating my analysis, namely the second half of the fourth century which, with the institution of the *dikai emporikai*, marks the entry of the world of the *emporium* into the life of the city. Foreigners and citizens appear side by side in the extensive roll-call of men involved, either directly or as witnesses, in the affair. First, the money-lenders, who are partners in a loan of three thousand drachmae are, on the one hand Androcles, a citizen, and on the other Nicostratus, a Euboean. The loan was made to merchants from Phaselis. When it comes to recovering his loan, Androcles contacts the brother of his debtors, the sophist Lacritus, through the intermediary of two other Athenians, Thrasymachus and his brother Melanopus, the sons of Diophantes of Sphettos, the deme to which he himself belongs. No other information is given about Androcles except that he declared himself to be an *emporos*. Nor do we know any more about the two sons of Diophantes of Sphettos.

Among the witnesses we also find quite a number of Athenians who in all likelihood frequented the *emporium*. Of the eight names that appear only one is identifiable: Philtiades, the son of Ctesias (or Ctesides) of Xypete, who is later mentioned as being a trierarch in 322 (*I.G.* II[2] 1632, 243). Even in his case the identification is not certain.

So the *Against Lacritus* would seem to confirm what has been suggested above, to wit that the citizens who frequented the *emporium* were men of modest means who never seem to have held important responsibilities in the service of the city. The *Against Dionysodorus* which introduces foreigners almost exclusively, indirectly confirms this conclusion. When giving an account of the bargaining which took place between himself and his adversaries, the litigant who is himself a foreigner tells the Athenian judges, without giving names, that some of their fellow citizens were present and took part in the discussion. If they had been men in the public eye he would not have failed to make the most of the point.

So although there certainly were Athenians involved in commercial affairs and although some of them were not merely money-lenders but personally took part in maritime commerce, either themselves going to sea or managing offices in the port, these Athenians in no sense belonged to the circles of leadership in the city.[3] Furthermore, although Athenians and foreigners worked side by side in the world of the *emporium*, that does not mean that they constituted a 'class of rich merchants' whose common interests, notwithstanding the legal and political differences between them, would clash with those of men with fortunes of a traditional nature. The maritime loans mentioned in the corpus range from one to seven thousand drachmae (the latter sum being the somewhat exceptional loan made by Demosthenes' father). Even if we take it that, for certain rich men not involved in the world of the *emporium*, a maritime loan could represent an investment the interest from which would be added to the revenues which they derived from the land, slave workshops or mining concessions, the 'professional' money-lender would seem, in contrast, to have made only modest profits: even with a 30 per cent interest rate, two thousand drachmae would, even at the best of times, never realize more than a six hundred drachma profit. In view of the delays and difficulties of sea voyages, such an operation did not often bear repeating. So the sums with which we are concerned are a far cry from the fortunes of those who were committed to fulfilling liturgies, and it is not surprising that we do not find among these citizens involved in commerce any names that also appear in such documents as naval inscriptions or lists of the holders of mining concessions.

But there is another aspect to the question which needs to be stressed. Not only were the Athenians who engaged in maritime commerce men of modest means; they were also the objects of, if not the scorn, at least the distrust that was meted out to those – mostly foreigners – with whom they found themselves doing business. As Nicobulus, the litigant of the *Against Pantaenetus*, reporting the words of his adversary, remarks: 'We in Athens do not like money-lenders' (§ 52). Even more significant, in my view, is the way that the interested parties themselves make similar points. Nicobulus openly admits that 'there are some money-lenders who deserve to be loathed', those whose only concern is to make an unfair profit. He declares that he himself is an honest 'worker' who has every right to make a profit on his hard-won money. And it is not surprising to find xenophobic talk on the lips of these 'little Athenians' whose affairs regularly bring them into contact with foreigners. Thus, the hostility that Androcles, the litigant in the *Against Lacritus* ([Dem.] XXXV), displays towards his adversaries is compounded by the fact that they are foreigners and, addressing the Athenian judges, he emphasises the fact that it is 'in our town' that these men have taken over 'our possessions', they who are Phaselites (§ 26). This insistence upon his own membership of the civic community and this concern to differentiate himself from the foreigners is all the more remarkable given that although Lacritus is certainly a foreigner he is not one that belongs to the world of the *emporium*, since he came to Athens to follow the lessons of Isocrates. And it is almost with bravado that Androcles declares that he, for his part, is an *emporos* and is careful to insist that the arrogance of his adversary is out of place since his – Lacritus' – own brother is an *emporos* too.

It would be easy to point to many other traces of these 'complexes' from which the Athenians involved in maritime trade suffered and against which they defended themselves both by dissociating themselves from dishonest merchants – especially foreigners – and by stressing their own integrity and their services to the city, notably through guaranteeing its grain supplies (cf. *Against Phormion* [Dem.] XXXIV 38ff.). But the most telling example, in my opinion, is that of Apollodorus, and I should like to consider it more fully.

It is not necessary to dwell upon what is already well known: the exceptional role of Pasion, a banker and the owner of a workshop of metal workers and a former slave who had been freed by his master and who received Athenian citizenship for himself and his descendants in return for his services to the city. One of his descendants was his son Apollodorus, who was to play a political role in the years preceding Chaeronea. Apollodorus was several times a trierarch and a number of speeches in our corpus are attributed to him. It is by means in particular of a 'reading' of the speeches of Apollodorus that I would like to specify what, borrowing D. Whitehead's expression, I shall call the ideology of the world of the *emporium*. They are, as is well known, [Dem.] XLIX (*Against Timotheus*), [Dem.] L (*Against Polycles*), [Dem.] LII (*Against Callipus*), [Dem.] LIII (*Against Nicostratus*) and [Dem.] LIX (*Against

Neaera). To these are sometimes added the two *Against Stephanus* ([Dem.] XLV–XLVI) which involve Apollodorus personally although Gernet believes them – the first at all events – to be by Demosthenes. The *Against Callipus* dates from 368, the *Against Neaera* from 340. We can thus follow the turns taken by the career of this figure over a period of close on thirty years. We know from the speech *For Phormion* ([Dem.] XXXVI, composed by Demosthenes on the occasion of the lawsuit between the banker and the son of his former master that Pasion had freed his slave just before he died, entrusting to him the bank and the workshop producing shields which constituted a part of his huge fortune. As well as this the banker Pasion had also given in marriage to Phormion his own wife Archippe, the mother of Apollodorus. From Apollodorus' first speeches we learn that after his father's death he had remained closely associated with his stepfather and with the world of the *emporium*. The *emporos* in *Against Callipus*, Lycon from Heraclea, was 'as were all the *emporoi*' a client of Pasion's bank (§ 3). Just before sailing for Libya he set his affairs in order, requesting the banker to hand over the money that he left deposited in the bank, a sum of 1640 drachmae, to his partner, the metic Cephisiades. Not long after, Lycon was drowned in a shipwreck. Phormion, acting on Pasion's behalf, stood by his promise and paid over the money to the metic. In a while, Callipus, the *proxenos* for the merchants of Heraclea, came forward to claim the money and filed a lawsuit against Pasion. He subsequently withdrew his suit, preferring to have recourse to private arbitration. But as Pasion died before a decision could be reached, he renewed his suit, this time against Apollodorus. In the speech that the latter composed for his own defence, he appears closely associated with Phormion, well-informed about business affairs and certainly involved in the world of the *emporium* with which his father had had connexions. However, we sense him to be already sensitive on the score of the citizenship he has acquired for he refers to Cephisiades as a metic 'without power' (§ 25). The *Against Nicostratus* reveals him still to have relations with the Piraeus and the world of the *emporium* generally (§ 17). But by now he has decided to lead the life of a 'true' citizen, even if he is only 'a citizen by decree'. He accordingly lives in the country, on the domain left to him by his father, where he grows walnut trees, vines and olive trees and even roses; and is anxious at all costs never to be accused of having treated any 'true' Athenian wrongfully (§ 18). Despite all this, he is still not completely integrated even though he is, by reason of his fortune, a man in the public eye and has been named as a prospective trierarch. The speech of 358, *Against Polycles*, is revealing in this respect.

Apollodorus is clearly particularly sensitive to the remarks of his successor in command of the ship who, learning that he has fallen into debt in order to fulfil his obligations, exclaims: 'Just see what happens when a man tries to be an Athenian!' (§ 26). Honours have clearly not rid Apollodorus of his 'complexes'. As we have already seen, in the case of the Athenian merchants whose business ties have brought them into association with foreigners and who never let slip a chance to underline the difference between them, similarly Apollodorus, in the lawsuit against Phormion twenty years after his father's death, is at pains to draw attention to Phormion's own servile origin. In the speech which he composed for the defence of the banker, around 350, Demosthenes does not fail to make that argument recoil against his adversary: 'As for nobility of birth, if you renounce Phormion as your stepfather, beware lest it make you a laughing stock . . .' Phormion's career was indeed reminiscent of that of Pasion, the former slave who had become an Athenian, and there was no need for Demosthenes to labour the point as it was lost on none of his listeners. Apollodorus' consciousness of being a citizen only by adoption betrays itself again in the words ascribed to him in the first speech *Against Stephanus*. Addressing the Athenian judges, he exclaims: 'Even if it does behove me to consider myself less than all of you, I believe I may at least set myself above him!' Ten years later, in the speech *Against Neaera*, he returns to this question of his acquired citizenship, appealing to a number of historical examples, in this instance the granting of citizenship to the Plataeans, and also to the most traditional *topoi* of the official ideology.

The reason I have lingered so long over this portrait of a *parvenu* is that I see it as exemplary. If, more than thirty years after the death of his father, the son of a rich banker, with connexions in the political world, a trierarch several times over and a member of the *boule* to boot, still feels the need to justify both his status as a citizen and himself personally, it is testimony to the distrust provoked in the city by all those who engaged in activities in the *emporium*, citizens and foreigners alike. The world of commerce in effect remained on the periphery of the city and its peripheral character was manifest in spatial terms. The Piraeus was the place where men who belonged to that world would meet. That was where partnerships of varying durability were formed and where, in the presence of witnesses, loans were negotiated. The men who frequented this *emporium* included Athenians, metics, foreigners. But, as we have seen above, these Athenians did not belong to the 'political' world despite the fact that, when involved in a lawsuit, they would be anxious to draw attention to the difference between themselves and the partners with whom they happened to be associated.

It was not possible for the city to ignore these people of the *emporium*: in the first place because it depended upon them for its grain supplies and, secondly, because, as Xenophon pointed out in the *Poroi*, their activities were a source of revenue. Hence the hastily carried through procedure of the *dikai emporikai* and the protection extended to merchants.[4]

To end this analysis of the world of the *emporium* in the second half of the fourth century, we may, I believe, formulate a few prudent conclusions. The first seems to me to be that among the men who financed commercial operations or took part in them in person, making trading voyages by sea, citizens and foreigners rubbed shoulders, entered into partnerships and shared both their risks and their profits. The second is that these men, mostly of modest means, nevertheless did not constitute a class whose common interests brought them into opposition with those whose fortunes were of a more traditional kind. As we have seen, the two groups were still deeply divided by the issue of their membership or non-membership of the civic community. Thus, even if commercial activity forged links between citizens on the one hand and metics or foreigners on the other and even if these links created common interests between them, those interests were not powerful enough to overcome the divisions made by the differences in their status.

There remains the problem of those rich Athenians of whom Demosthenes' father is the best known example, who invested a proportion – albeit a relatively small one – of their fortune in maritime loans. The problem is mentioned by P. Millett in his paper. He remarks of Demosthenes' father that he was 'wealthy without owning much land'. In the Athens of the fourth century, to be sure, land was no longer considered the only honourable form of wealth and among the twelve hundreds or so Athenians called upon to provide liturgies there were quite a number of workshop proprietors, holders of mining concessions and men who derived their income from hiring out slaves. I am not suggesting that this was necessarily a new situation or that it was peculiar to the fourth century. On this point I am in agreement with Pecirkà: it was as early as the middle of the fifth century that men whose incomes were not derived solely from landownership began to play an important role in the leadership of the city. Should we believe that it was only these '*nouveaux riches*' who invested their money in maritime loans?

I think not. But, conversely, I do not think that we can use Isocrates VII 32–3 to maintain that the practice of rich Athenians outside the world of the *emporium* making maritime loans went right back to the archaic period. Here, I am entirely in agreement with P. Millett and, by the same token, do not follow Bravo ((1974) 151–3) or Erxleben ((1974) 471–3).

Which brings me back to my original problem: can the marginality of the *emporium* be regarded as an explanation for the crisis of the Athenian city in the fourth century? I consider today that the cautious hypotheses that I formulated ten years ago may have stemmed from a concept of the nature of the crisis that depended too heavily upon *a priori* considerations. I remain convinced that the fourth century was a decisive turning point in the history of Athens and that the way had been paved for the split precipitated by the Macedonian military victory by a series of more or less visible transformations. But it seems increasingly clear to me that those transformations took place outside the sphere of commerce. In this respect, the institution of the *dikai emporikai* should be related to the collapse of the empire following the social war rather than to any developments of a commercial nature. If the world of the *emporium* remained marginal in relation to the city during this second half of the fourth century to which the speeches of the corpus of works by Demosthenes belong, it surely is because 'trade and politics' belonged to two mutually impenetrable domains.

[6]

Nile grain transport under the Ptolemies

by D. J. THOMPSON (CRAWFORD)

'Take care that the corn in the nomes, with the exception of that expended on the spot for seed and that which cannot be transported by water, be brought down . . . It will thus be easy to load the corn on the first ships presenting themselves; and devote yourself to such matters with all care and attention . . . Take care also that the prescribed supplies of corn, of which I send you a list, are brought down to Alexandria punctually, not only correct in amount but also tested and fit for use.'

(*P. Tebt.* 703. 70–87 (late third century BC))

The subordinate official who received these orders from his superior was being instructed in one of the central concerns of the Ptolemaic administration – the safe and sure provision of the grain supply. Grain, the main produce of the annually flooded Nile valley, represented the wealth of Egypt, a wealth which was ultimately the possession of the king, as owner of the land. Others cultivated the land, either as his tenants (crown peasants) or by grace and favour (owners of gift-estates, temples and cleruchs), but the king, through his administration, showed constant concern for the produce of this land.[1] Grain was important both in supporting the population of the country and in providing the surplus through which the country and the ruler might exert influence in the wider sphere of the Hellenistic world.

When Egypt was conquered by Alexander it was already well-known in the Aegean as a grain-producing country. It is no chance that in the libellous stories about the activities of Cleomenes, appointed by Alexander as tax-collector, corn is a recurrent feature (Ps.-Arist. *Oec.* II 2.33). Whilst agriculture remained the basis of the country's wealth in the Hellenistic period, the actual conquest of Egypt, together with the arrival of a new class of immigrants and the foundation of Alexandria, which was to become the new Ptolemaic capital of the country, had an important effect on traditional patterns. To meet the growing needs of the new capital and the ambitions of the country's rulers, agricultural activity was intensified under the early Ptolemies. New areas, especially in the Fayum, were brought under cultivation and new cereal strains were introduced. The most important new strain was *Triticum durum*, a tetraploid naked wheat (*puros*), which, grown on a large scale, quickly supplanted husked wheat, *Triticum dicoccum (olura)*, as the staple cereal crop of the country. Wheat was shipped in to Alexandria both as grain levied in rents and taxes (*phorikos*) and as corn purchased centrally (*sitos agorastos*) to meet foreseeable needs.

This is the background to my interest here in tracing the effects of these innovations on the internal transport of the country's grain under the Ptolemies. The old urban centres, Memphis, Thebes and the other nome capitals, remained important consumers, but under the Ptolemies the focus changed to Alexandria; the constant concern now was that there be no disruption in the downstream shipment of grain, not only for export but also to feed the city's growing population. For when Strabo, who visited the city under Augustus, noted the importance of the inland harbour on Lake Mariut he was observing the effect of important developments under the Ptolemies: 'many canals from the Nile drain into Lake Mareotis both from the south and on each side of the lake and many more goods are brought in this way than from the sea, with the result that the Lake Harbour is richer than that on the Mediterranean' (XVII 1. 7). Alexandria had become the main port in the north of the country and the boats most frequently docking on Lake Mariut were without doubt the Nile grain transports.

The organization of the production of this corn, its collection (*sunagoge*) and its transport down river to Alexandria (*katagoge*) has often been studied before.[2] Here I want to consider three aspects only: the way the shipping of grain was organized, the scale and timing of the operation and the nature of royal involvement.

The Nile naturally formed the central waterway for transport down to Alexandria. Before being loaded onto the Nile barges, grain harvested throughout the country had already been brought either by canal or by donkey from its point of production to central collecting points (*thesauroi*) on the main river.[3] The papyrus records of the transactions involved at different stages of this progress are the main source of our knowledge for the organization of the transport and shipment of grain in Ptolemaic Egypt.[4]

The organization of Nile shipping was complex. A third century BC lading receipt may serve to introduce these complexities:

'In the reign of Ptolemy son of Ptolemy Soter, Year 34; when

Neoptolemos son of Kraisis was priest of Alexander and the *Theoi Adelphoi* and Arsinoe daughter of Nikolaos was basket-bearer of Arsinoe Philadelphus, on 24 Mesore (13 October 251 BC). Dionysios, *naukleros*, acknowledges loading on the *kerkouros* of Xenodokos and Alexandros, on which Ekteuris son of Pasis of Memphis is the *kubernetes*, with the participation of Nechthembes, the representative of the royal scribes, for the destination of Alexandria for the royal treasury, together with a sample (*deigma*), 4800 artabas of barley; the grain is pure, unadulterated, sieved, and in just measure in accordance with the measure and levelling rod he himself has brought from Alexandria. And I shall make no claims.' (*P. Hib.* 98 = *W. Chrest.* 441)

In this case the *kerkouros*, the largest type of Nile transport, was owned jointly; the *naukleros* and the *kubernetes* were two separate individuals. The Memphite origin of the Egyptian captain is not surprising since Memphis had long been a centre of shipping.[5] Egyptians are often found in the role of ship's captain; they were likely to possess local knowledge of the river and its shoals. In this case, although the full capacity of the ship is not given, 4,800 or possibly 5,000 artabas was probably a full load. The cargo here was barley; in other cases loads were made up of different crops,[6] or of the same crop from different *thesauroi*.[7] The *deigmata* were sealed samples, in either pots[8] or boxes,[9] provided to travel with the cargo as a check against exchange or adulteration during the voyage.

Those involved in the management of Nile shipping, as may be seen in this receipt, were the boat-owners (here Xenodokos and Alexandros), the *naukleros* (Dionysios) and the *kubernetes* (Ekteuris son of Pasis). The *naukleros*, who in Ptolemaic Egypt was always the contractor of a ship and not its owner, might himself sometimes sail as captain (*kubernetes*) or he might employ others in this capacity. The three-tier pattern of owner, contractor and captain appears the regular pattern of management for the Nile barges of Ptolemaic Egypt. Such a structure perhaps arose from the centralized nature of grain transport in which loading orders were sent out from Alexandria, together with an officially certified measure and levelling rod. The papers were addressed for a particular loading point but might be transferred in exceptional circumstances; of these shipwreck, with consequent repairs, was probably the most common.[10] In such a regular, controlled system potential risks and profits would be well known to all concerned.

The owners of Nile barges are a shadowy group of people. Since they rarely sailed in person they are often missing from the record of transactions. Those who are known may most conveniently be consulted, recorded together with the *naukleroi* and *kubernetai*, in

Hauben's list of *naukleroi*;[11] problems of identification still remain. The use of the genitive case attached to a ship is not in itself sufficient to establish ownership, and the clear distinction between owner, *naukleros* and *kubernetes* seen in the receipt quoted above is not always so certain. When for instance in loading orders given to two *sitologoi*, as recorded in *P. Moen.* 1–3 (160 BC), the barges are listed as follows (Sijpesteijn (1978)):

'of Aratamenes, capacity 4000 artabas, on which Achilleus; (cargo) 250 artabas
of the same man, capacity 4000 artabas, on which he him[self; (cargo) 250 artabas]'

it is not clear whether Aratamenes is, as the editor assumes, the owner, with Achilles as *naukleros* and *kubernetes* on one boat and himself on the other, or whether Aratamenes is in both cases the *naukleros* who is sailing as *kubernetes* in one of the ships. I suspect the latter[12] but this loose usage can cause problems. Here, as in *P. Tebt.* 856 (*c.*171 BC) where eighteen further individuals are closely linked with grain barges for which a separate captain is often named, it would be the *naukleros* with whom the authorities would be dealing. The purpose of a particular document, loading receipts for instance or *sitologos* accounts, and those involved in the relevant transactions must always be remembered in deciding the role of a named individual.

In spite of such problems of identification some interesting observations about shipowners may be made. Amongst the owners of Nile barges the total absence of Egyptian names is striking and there is no sign of temple ownership as in earlier periods. Although a Greek name by itself does not necessarily denote immigrant nationality, the concentration of such names amongst a particular group is likely to be significant. The picture of immigrant shipowners, as in the main of immigrant *naukleroi*, is in sharp contrast both to that of the captains and to that which applied on the inland waterways of Egypt. In a third-century BC record of harbour dues on *prosagogides*, small-capacity barges, plying the Fayum canals between Crocodilopolis and Ptolemais Hormou and carrying a variety of freight, the taxpayers, who were (except in the case of royal boats) probably also the owners, all have Egyptian names.[13] On the Nile in contrast all the large barge-owners have Greek names and some are those of good Alexandrian families. It may well be that wealthy Alexandrians, recognizing the constant demand for grain, invested in Nile shipping. The shipping itself they then let out to contractors.

Shipowning was not confined to men. Some of the women shipowners were queens (Kleopatra II certainly, Berenike possibly) and Archeboula, Agathokleia (sister of Agathokles) and Philotera would seem to be from prominent Alexandrian families.[14] There was other royal interest in shipowning, but on the whole it seems to have been slight (Hauben (1979)). A royal barge, *kontoton*, with one Horos serving as both *naukleros* and *kubernetes*, is recorded carrying corn from the Koite district (*P. Hib.* 39 (265 BC)), and in the mid second century BC various small boats (*kerkouroskaphai*) of the queen, probably Kleopatra II, are listed carrying small quantities of *phorikos* wheat;[15] in two of these cases (*P. Lille* 22–3 (155 BC)) the *naukleros* is also described as *misthotes*. In addition she had at least two large *kerkouroi* which could carry 1,000+ artabas (*P. Tebt.* 1034 (*c.* 151–150 BC)). The shipping interests of Kleopatra were probably managed indirectly.[16] With regard to taxes royal boats were treated differently, as may be illustrated from the harbour dues of the Fayum *prosagogides* already mentioned.[17] Harbour dues, according to this record, normally stood at 50 per cent of the freight charge, but in the case of these royal boats 75 per cent went to the crown and 25 per cent to the *kubernetes*; the rate suggests a profitable business for the crown. Royal shipowning under the Ptolemies seems however to have been in the nature of private investment rather than for the purposes of control. In the main ownership was in private hands.

It was the *naukleroi*, the contractors, who carried the main responsibility in the Nile transport of grain. The identification of this class is even more difficult than that of the owners. Conveniently listed by Hauben (1978) they regularly bear Greek names though Egyptians and Levantines (see page 70 below) also occur in this role. Otherwise it is not possible to place them in society. Also unrecorded are the details of the relationship between *naukleros* and owner on the large Nile ships. Two letters from the Zenon papers do however give some idea of possible forms of contract. *P. Cairo Zen.* 59649 is a memorandum to Zenon from an unnamed individual putting forward a range of alternative proposals for running a boat. The royal tax on the boat for the year is 292½ drachmae and the annual wages bill (3 sailors at 7½ dr. a month and the *kubernetes* at 10 dr.) is 390 drachmae. A variety of ways of spreading this cost between Zenon and the *naukleros* are suggested. In another letter, *P. Mich. Zen.* 60 (received 11 May 248 or 247 BC), Pais, a *kubernetes*, records the discontent of sailors who are sailing at a third share (*triton meros*), whereas when monopoly goods are being shipped the rate is a half. The boat, he reports, also needs repairs since it is old. If the boat is registered for monopoly use (and it is interesting to see how the state protected its interests) Pais, who seems here to be acting also as *naukleros*, is willing to pay an annual rent of 800 dr. for the boat in question. *P.S.I.* 328 records the repairs as carried out, but what exact arrangement they agreed on is unknown. Various payment arrangements are clearly possible in ship-renting and I assume from disclaimer clauses in their receipts (*W. Chrest.* 441.21, qu. p. 66) that the contractor carried the risks as well as putting up the capital for the voyage. Transport costs might also vary and accounts survive providing some information on how these might work out,[18] but since in most cases a vital piece of information (the distance covered, the size of the cargo or the sums involved) seems to be missing it is not possible to calculate regular transport rates. It is noteworthy that no evidence survives suggesting any sort of preferential treatment, either in taxes or customs dues, given to those transporting grain, however important this activity might be to the government.

In the first century BC a new development in ship management is first recorded in documents from the Herakleopolite nome. This is the existence of organized groups of *naukleroi*, such as the *Naukleroi Hippodromitai* from Memphis whose activities are recorded in *B.G.U.* 1741–3 (63 BC). This group had a *prostates* who seems to have been a short-term functionary (Apollophanes in early July, Malichos in July–August) and a recorder, *grammateus* (Eudemos), who held office for a longer period. Two *naukleroi* are named (Zabdion son of Artemidoros and Apollonios) who may also have served as *kubernetai*. A similar arrangement is probably recorded in *S.B.* 8754. 7–8 (5 February 77 BC)[19] where Dionysios and Heroides, *hoi pros tei naulosei*, act together in a similar capacity, designating the ships which are to be loaded with grain. It has been suggested that this was a Memphite group of smaller *naukleroi* who joined together to compete with the larger operators from Alexandria (Boerner (1939) 43). Perhaps. It is also possible that this first-century development arises from contact with similar groups elsewhere in the Aegean, particularly in Delos. Others earlier, perhaps in a less formal way, are known to have joined in sharing (one assumes) both risks and profits. *B.G.U.* 1933 (third century BC)[20] records four men with different boats (two *kerkouroi*, a *skenagogos* and a *paktotos*) who join to fulfil an order together; the first-century partnerships may have developed from such joint enterprises.

One of the bills of the Memphite Hippodromitai, *B.G.U.* 1742 (18 July 63 BC), reads as follows:

'To Ammonios. Year 18, 14 Epeiph (18 July 63 BC). To . . . *antigrapheus* of the *thesauros* near Tilothis. Load for (transport to) Alexandria for the royal account, according to the instructions of Diogenes, *sungenes*, *strategos* and in charge of the revenues, aboard the ship of 1,200 artabas capacity of [Zabdion] son of Artemidoros which has been designated as under orders by [Apollophanes], *prostates*, and Eudemos, *grammateus* of the Hippodromitai from Memphis, [corn, which is fresh,] unadulterated and sieved; it is to be measured with a measure checked against the (official) bronze measure, using a valid levelling rod; five guards, *phulakitai*, are to travel on board, from the class of cleruchs, men who have provided good guarantees, and the sample, sealed in unbaked earthen-ware jars, will be [given over to their care] and, with the consent of the sailors on board, they shall escort the load, (as instructed) by the official who controls the grain supply on the quay:[21] 1,200 artabas of wheat. Supply receipts and counter-receipts [for them as is fitting].'

Two features may be noted. Firstly Zabdion, like Malichos in *B.G.U.* 1743. 5, provides evidence for the continued involvement of the Syro-Phoenician community of the city in Memphite shipping. The need to import ships' timbers into Egypt had led to early contact with the Levant, and by the reign of Amenophis IV in the fourteenth century BC the Phoenician goddess Astarte had been assimilated into the Memphite pantheon as consort of Ptah, the patron god of the city.[22] Herodotus (II 112) saw her temple in the city, that of the foreign Aphrodite, close to the Phoenician quarter, the Tyrian Camp. The Phoenico-Egyptians of Memphis remained a recognizable group in the Ptolemaic period[23] and the Hippodromitai Zabdion and Malichos suggest that they continued to play an active role in shipping, an area of economic activity where they had long been important.[24]

Secondly of interest is the need for check and counter-check, for sealed sample and armed guards, which highlights the problems of escorting the grain safely to Alexandria. In the Roman period legionaries often sailed on board[25] and throughout the Ptolemaic period armed guards, either on board[26] or on escort ships[27] protected the grain against adulteration, theft or attack. Five guards for 1,200 artabas suggests the need for a high level of security, a security which must often have been breached.[28]

Most of the surviving evidence, including that for the three-tier structure of management of owner, contractor and captain, comes in the context of traffic downstream to the capital. Instructions were issued in Alexandria, probably by the official in charge of grain on the quayside,[29] and these were relayed to the officials involved with its release in the nomes. At least in the first century BC the *naukleros* could only fill his ship after he had taken a royal oath to transport the grain to the city unadulterated and without delay.[30] When the ship was filled he issued receipts for the grain to the officials involved, to the representative of the royal scribe(s), the *oikonomos* who checked off the cargo and to the *sitologos(oi)* who released the grain from the *thesauros*.[31] From the point of view of the administration the use of private contractors seems to have worked free from problems; it also shifted the responsibility for filling the barges on their upstream voyages. From the point of view of the contractors there was always a guaranteed downstream cargo, and it is unlikely that their large grain-barges went empty up the Nile. The cargoes which filled them on their upstream journeys are, however, rarely recorded. It was only in passing through the customs posts that they attracted royal interest. Such barges might carry food and other goods from their homeland for the new settlers of the Egyptian countryside. *P. Cairo Zen.* 59110 and 59548 record Patron's *keles* in the autumn of 257 BC carrying south to Memphis goods for Zenon sent on the instruction of Amyntas: 2 *keramia* of salted tunny, 6 (or 5) of Rhodian dried figs, 5 *keramia* of Caunian (figs), 2 large Cynthian cheeses and 20 Rhenaian, a winter sheepskin cloak and 2 *keramia* of sweet old Chian wine.[32] Other commodities from Alexandria might find a market upstream and there was a new demand for imported metals; its carriers might attempt to evade customs dues.[33] The initiative therefore of individual shipowners and contractors had full scope on the voyage up the Nile with a guaranteed cargo of grain to fill the hulls on the way back downstream.

Alexandria was the normal destination of grain ships but shipments were also made to other centres.[34] Traders might sail both up and downstream in the search of good markets or better deals:

'Sosos to Zenon. I received your letter in which you asked me to put aside 100 artabas of wheat which we have on board and to sell the rest at the highest price we could get. Now as for reserving the corn, know that it is no longer possible. For not being aware that you would be wanting it, we sold the whole cargo of wheat at the harbour over against Aphroditopolis . . . (*P. Mich. Zen.* 28. 1–10 (29 March 256 BC))

Other commodities too might vary in price according to season and availability,[35] and the new immigrants, like Zenon and his circle, with access to information might commission shippers to take advantage of these changing prices. Yet in terms of the overall bulk of Nile traffic this individually directed, small-scale, commercial activity was probably insignificant.

There was an enormous range of Nile boats with variety in both size[36] and name; the variety of the latter is a measure of the importance of river-transport within the country. The *skaphai* of the Memphite *naukleroi* (in *B.G.U.* 1742–3) held 1,200 and 1,800 artabas of wheat, and that in the similar record (*S.B.* 8754. 10 (77 BC)) 2,500 artabas. The smaller *kerkouroskaphai* of Kleopatra II mentioned earlier held 250 and 300 artabas (*P. Lille* 22–3). The most common however of the Nile grain boats was the *kerkouros*, with a capacity range from 1,000 to 18,000 artabas.[37] 1,000 artabas represents 4,500 Roman modii or, on the basis of Pliny's figures,[38] 30.65 metric tons. The most commonly recorded size of *kerkouros*, that of 10,000 artabas, held 45,000 modii or 306.5 tons, and the largest, of 18,000 artabas, held 81,000 modii or 551.7 tons. These were the barges which regularly brought the grain downstream to Alexandria.

The minimum quantity of grain regularly shipped to Alexandria was that needed to feed its population. In normal years a substantial quantity will also have been exported. More exact quantification is difficult. The figure Diodorus Siculus gives for the free population of the city in the mid-first century BC is 300,000 (XVII 52. 6). On the basis of the more general statement of Diodorus (I 31. 6–8) that in his day Alexandria was the largest city in the world, Fraser argues that this figure is too low for the entire free population and that a figure of one million for the total population of the capital, free and otherwise, is more likely.[39] All calculations have a large margin of error; only parameters are possible. One modern reckoning for subsistence minimum is 250–300 kg of unmilled wheat per person a year,[40] whereas the F.A.O. daily average figure for consumption in a hot country with high birth and death rates is 1,194 calories a head[41] which, on the equivalence of 3,150 calories to a kilogram of unmilled wheat,[42] gives an annual figure of 139 kg. The daily grain allowance of 1–2 *choenikes* paid to employees of the *dioiketes* Apollonios in the third century BC works out at 9–18 artabas or 233–466 kg a year;[43] many must have eaten less than this. At 150 kg (4.9 artabas) per person a year, a population of 500,000 would require 2,450,000 artabas a year, and a population of one million, 4,900,000 artabas. At 200 kg (7.2 artabas) a year the requirement would be 3,600,000 artabas for half a million, 7,200,000 artabas for a million. In boats carrying 10,000 artabas the lowest requirement (half a million at 150 kg a head, or approximately 75,000 tons) would be 245 loads a year; at the highest (one million at 200 kg a head, or approximately 220,000 tons) 720 loads, or about two boats a day, would be required to bring the necessary grain to Alexandria. In addition of course was any surplus for export. In practice the grain came in boats both large and small and the unloading quays of the Lake Harbour of Alexandria will have been constantly alive with activity.

Grain was moved downstream throughout the year. Minor fluctuations in this operation may be illustrated from a granary account from Ptolemais Hormou (*P. Tebt.* 856 (*c.*171 BC)) which, at the end of the Fayum canal network, was an important Nile port serving the Arsinoite nome.[44] The period covered by this somewhat fragmentary account is the half year from Mesore to Tybi (September to February). Besides recording other granary payments it lists grain-ships loaded at the port. These were as follows:

grain-ship/artabas	Mesore September	Thoth October	Phaophi November	Hathyr December	Choiak January	Tybi February
prosagogis/1,900				2		
kerkouros/5,000						1
kerkouros/9,000				1		
kerkouros/10,000		1	1	4	2	4
kerkouros/11,000				4		
kerkouros/12,000	1		1	1	1	
kerkouros/16,000				1		
kerkouros/18,000				1		
TOTAL artabas	12,000	10,000	22,000	142,800	32,000	45,000

The distribution of sailings is interesting. Mesore, with only one ship, is the high point of the Nile flood, and the period runs through until the month before the new harvest, which took place in late March–April. By far the largest shipment, 142,800 artabas (642,600 modii or 8,086.5 tons) went in Hathyr, once the flood had subsided, and assuming that the ships left Ptolemais Hormou loaded, a total of 263,800 artabas (1,187,100 modii or 4,377 tons) was shipped out in this period. The annual total shipped from this one Nile port will probably have been more than double this amount since the missing period includes the months immediately following the harvest. Indeed a document from the first century AD, *B.G.U.* 802 (AD 42), records 270,808 artabas (8,300 tons) shipped out from the Fayum in the period from the harvest until 17 July. Possibly over 600,000 artabas (*c.*18,000 tons) a year left Ptolemais Hormou for Alexandria, the equivalent of 60 loads of a 10,000 artaba *kerkouros* and the same figure as the income from the Herakleopolite nome in 51–50 BC.[45] This would represent over a boat load a week, on the assumption that shipping proceeded throughout the year.

This pattern is supported by other dated evidence for Ptolemaic grain transport. With the exception of September, at the height of the flood, documents spread throughout the year. The number of such documents is not great – 6 each for June, August, December; 5 each for January, March, April; 4 each February, May, July; 3 for November and 2 for October – but their chance survival supports the record from Ptolemais Hormou showing constant activity in grain transport. The Nile flood is the only limiting factor.

The great barges laden with wheat, barley, olyra and lentils which sailed down to Alexandria represented the income of the king, the wealth through which Ptolemy competed with other Hellenistic monarchs. Equally, if not perhaps more importantly, they carried food to meet the needs of the population of Alexandria. These needs were great. Alexandria was subject to disturbances at the best of times and the Ptolemies could not afford to let the citizens go hungry. Ptolemy III Euergetes recognized this when, in a time of shortage (*sitodeia*), he imported grain, at considerable expense, from Phoenicia, Syria, Cyprus and elsewhere.[46]

In normal circumstances rent and taxes from the countryside could meet the requirements of Alexandria. Sometimes however there was a need to supplement these and additional grain was bought by the central authorities. The existence of this *sitos agorastos*, bought in bulk and shipped from source together with the *phorikos* grain,[47] shows the king, or his administration, as well aware of the need to secure supplies sufficient to meet the needs of his capital.

The first century BC was the most troubled of the three centuries of Ptolemaic rule. With continual struggles in the ruling house, the country was split, Alexandria in turmoil. The regular corn-supply will frequently have been endangered and this is the period when (as in *B.G.U.* 1742 above) cleruchs appear as armed guards escorting the cargoes. As military men settled by the crown on land which they held under favourable conditions, cleruchs were able to provide guarantees for the safe arrival of this grain. They might also be expected to have some personal interest in the successful fulfilment of their task. In this use of cleruchs central concern for the smooth flow of the corn-supply seems to play a part.

On 27 October 50 BC a royal decree was promulgated which forbade, on pain of death, the shipment of corn to elsewhere than Alexandria (*C. Ord. Ptol.* 73). Such a decree goes beyond the normal extent of royal control and would seem to belong to a year when the authorities were worried about the availability of corn. A loan contract from the same year (*P.S.I.* 1098. 28–9) foresees the possibility of corn reaching a price of over 3,000 copper drachmae which is well above the normal price, and the instructions preserved as *B.G.U.* 1760. 23 (51–50 BC) for the collection of grain from the Herakleopolite nome have a tone of urgency about them over and above the norm. Whether these measures are to be connected with Auletes' overseas commitments or, as I think more likely, with a poor Nile and bad harvest that year, remains uncertain.

It is however clear that from time to time exceptional measures were taken to secure a free flow of grain to Alexandria. In 108 BC for instance the *dioiketes* sent orders for the payment in Upper Egypt of sailors on two grain-ships under Pamphilos who is described as *ho par' hemon prokecheirismenos epi ton epispoudasmon tou purou* (*P. Grenf.* II 23 = *W. Chrest.* 159). The date of the *dioiketes'* letter is 10 January but, as so often with bureaucratic delays, it takes until 1 June before the wages were actually paid. There are three points of interest here: state involvement in the payment of the sailors, the description of Pamphilos as responsible for expediting the grain, and the date of the order. State officials were regularly involved in the collection of grain, as rents and taxes, and in its storage in the *thesauroi* but, as we have seen, transport and shipping were normally in private hands. Here however state involvement extends to the shipment of grain which suggests some form of requisitioning. Pamphilos' appointment was perhaps equivalent of that over one hundred years earlier of Theogenes who is described as *epispoudastes*, and appears in the context of requisitioning donkeys for grain transport; the document is dated 10 February 214 BC.[48] In a further case the order for requisitioning came from the *dioiketes* on 15 January 207 BC (*P. Tebt.* 704. 20–24). Evidence for this practice is not common in Ptolemaic Egypt[49] and it is perhaps significant that the only detailed documents to provide evidence for requisitioning in connexion with grain, and, more particularly, for the appointment of an *epispoudastes* (not, it appears, a regular appointment) all come from the winter months preceding the harvest when, in bad years, supplies in Alexandria might be running low. The Ptolemies, concerned to avoid grain shortage in their capital, would seem, in certain years, to have taken exceptional measures to bring the grain down to Alexandria. Content in normal circumstances to rely on the services of independent shippers, ultimately the Ptolemies seem to have been very conscious of the needs of the inhabitants of their capital city.

[7]

Marseilles, Rome and Gaul from the third to the first century BC

by CHRISTIAN GOUDINEAU

'The problem for us is less to elaborate new and complicated methods . . . than to pose the appropriate question.'

(M. I. Finley, *The Ancient Economy*, 25)

Let us try, without illusions.

A number of monographs and many articles have been devoted to Marseilles,[1] and inevitably commerce has featured prominently: was not Marseilles founded by merchants?[2] One point emerges clearly from a detailed study of this literature: no recent analysis has provided major new insights on the accounts given in the ancient sources.[3] Various publications may have added the results of recent excavations to the existing body of data, while others have clothed well-known ideas in up-to-date language, but in both cases without the slightest change of substance.

Yet I think there are, if not new questions to pose, at least some surprises to manifest, or some uncertainties to express, in relation to the 'classic' schema which Sir Moses has summarized very clearly, in saying of Marseilles that it 'served as an entrepot for products exported to the barbarians of the interior or imported from them' (Finley (1973) 131). Why? First, perhaps, because the textual tradition is less categorical and less clear than is usually suggested. Secondly, because the development of archaeology in our region for – say – twenty years (a development which has been little exploited for historical synthesis) has tended to establish anomalies. I am aware of the risks – which have often been pointed out[4] – that one runs in trying to utilize pieces of fieldwork that are still limited in number and often dictated by urgency, in order to revise or reinterpret a well-built framework of scholarship. But I hope you will allow an archaeologist to reflect on discoveries which seem to him to conflict with received ideas, and to dare to venture into that alarming territory where the counting of sherds and drawing of structures yields to the burning (or chill) winds of theoretical reflexion.

According to the usual scenario, Marseilles exchanged certain Celtic goods with others from the Mediterranean world or from its own producers. Among the former (it is usually said) are: tin (attested),[5] skins (not attested), cereals (not attested, or virtually not),[6] slaves (poorly attested),[7] salt (not attested).[8] I leave on one side the matter of mercenaries. None of these 'products', of course, leaves the slightest archaeological trace except, strictly, tin, but then there is no prospect of analyzing all ancient Hellenistic bronzes (later ones also, since re-smelting is possible). We therefore have, from concrete evidence, *no idea* of the importance of these imports. If we believe it to have been considerable, we cannot justify this with reference to precise texts (there are none), but by arguing from the reputation Marseilles enjoyed in antiquity, and from what is known in general of the activity of Phocaean foundations. Let us note, nevertheless, that Strabo – to whom we shall return – does not once use the word 'commerce' in speaking of Marseilles.[9]

If Marseilles exchanged (and we cannot suppose otherwise if we take into account the limited circulation of coinage in Gaul before the middle of the second century BC), with what did she supply these barbarians – or their chieftains? There is a clear answer. The literary sources – sparse as they are – say wine, and that alone.[10] Theoretically this is broadly sufficient: the reputation of wine-lovers (not to say drunkards) that the Gauls shared with other barbarians (cf. Diod.V 26. 2–3) surely corresponds to reality: even at a very high price (as is usual in this type of situation in all periods), wine found takers, the more so since its consumption met certain needs of Gallic 'sociability'. To which we must add a detail: that at this period, as at Athens, the sale of wine was accompanied by that of the 'drinking service', that is to say the various receptacles which, theoretically at least, enable its preparation and tasting to become ceremonial.[11]

If Marseilles's imports could not have left any traces, the same is not true for its exports. Massaliote wine was transported in amphorae which can be identified easily, even when they are fragmentary, thanks to their very characteristic shape and to their fabric recognizable by the presence of particles of mica. More generally, the whole assemblage of 'Massaliote pottery' is distinctive and easily characterized.

So, if we cannot follow the traces of the Gallic products which Marseilles either used or re-exported, we should be able to find those which she exchanged for them – if the theoretical scenario works. What do we find? The answer is clear: in the interior of Gaul, for the Hellenistic period, virtually nothing, anywhere.[12] No amphorae, no pottery – except for a negligible amount – which could hardly be the result of chance: yet of the hundreds of archaeological excavations in France, more than a quarter concern the period which interests us.

Should we then modify the model and suppose after Villard ((1960) 159–61) that following the 'upheavals' which would have marked the transition from the first to the second iron age (Halstatt-la Tène), the Celts would themselves have taken in hand commercial movements, with a chain of indigenous middlemen carrying out transactions from the suburbs of Marseilles up to the north, even as far as Cornwall? Implausible as it might seem, let us retain this possibility of multiple and diversified exchanges, with Massaliote products being 'diluted' in proportion as one goes further north. In this case, the most abundant traces should be found in the south. Is this the case? Let us distinguish amphorae from other pottery.

Pottery

Massaliote pottery is found in abundance at Marseilles itself (obviously) and in those establishments which were institutionally bound to it, for example Agde or Olbia[13] which Strabo (and others) call Massaliote comptoirs. On the other hand, in all the other excavated sites, local hand-made pottery persists at least to the time of Augustus (and even beyond) for all wares used for cooking or storage of foods.

If Marseilles had launched its own wares from the sixth century BC, for example, the so called 'céramique grise' (grey ware) inspired by the 'Aeolian bucchero' of Asia Minor, or again the 'pseudo-ionienne', these productions were, *almost immediately*, the object of local imitations, with a repertory of forms and decorations with little relation to the Marseilles pottery.[14]

On any *non-Massaliote* site in the third and second centuries BC, Massaliote pottery forms a very small part of the assemblage, at most 5 per cent (some mortars and table wares), generally much less, around 1 per cent. It is a derisory amount, especially if we note that, unlike the Etruscans, Marseilles did not export metallic vessels.

Ceramic imports from elsewhere are certainly attested. Leaving aside the products of Greece or of Asia Minor which are sparsely represented (Megarian bowls[15]) and those of Iberia ('céramique grise ampuritaine', 'sombrero de copa' – which are relatively late and scarce), the most important point is the abundance of Campanian wares, from the vessels of the workshops of 'petites estampilles'[16] ('small stamps') to the great series of Campanian A originating in Magna Graecia.[17] Were these products distributed by Marseilles (as she had previously distributed Attic products)?[18] One cannot say: shipwrecks only in exceptional cases give the name of their shipper. Nevertheless two points arise: imitations are produced quite quickly in Gaul as in Iberia,[19] and, above all, the highest distribution of Campanian ware corresponds to the years of the Roman conquest.[20]

Amphorae

It is very difficult to assemble satisfactory statistical data on the diffusion of Massaliote amphorae: quantitative methods of recording are not very far advanced in France and, more importantly, useful stratigraphical associations are often lacking – not through the fault of excavators. Nevertheless, in the last few years, some points are being established: first, that in absolute terms, *on any site*, the total number of amphorae dating from the sixth/fifth century is much greater than that of Hellenistic amphorae. Secondly, from subdivisions of the period covering the third-first centuries, a number of phenomena emerge which had hitherto not been appreciated. The table below, which is derived from the results of excavations in the Vaunage (nr. Nîmes) gives a detailed illustration of data which are generally repeated on other sites. It gives (for *thousands* of sherds) the percentage of amphorae in relation to local wares, and, secondly, the percentage of Massaliote amphorae in relation to Italic amphorae.[21]

Date (BC)	% of amphorae (vs. local wares)	Amphorae (%) Massaliote	Italic
250–225	0.89	100	0
225	3.19	100	0
225–200	3.30	93.8	6.1
200–175	1.96	97.2	2.7
175	2.79	75	25
175–150	4.41	42.2	57.7
150	4.46	33	66
150–125	4.12	33	66
125	3.46	22.7	77.2
100	30.10	0.65	99.3
100– 75	44.86	0.58	99.4

The table calls for various comments. Let us make three observations:

1. From 100 BC, the archaeological evidence shows a prodigious increase of imported wine. It is tempting to compare this with the statistics on shipwrecks summarized in the following table:[22]

Shipwrecks on the Mediterranean coast of France:

Before 2nd cent. BC	9		
2nd & 1st cent. BC	54	comprising:	
		second century	14
		late second/early first century	13
		first century (not more closely datable)	11
		first half of first century	10
		second half of first century	6
Empire (after Augustus)	33		
Uncertain date	7		

In fact, this table is only of interest as a comparison of data on Italian commerce at the end of the Republic and under the Empire. For us, it has no value, since Marseilles did not need boats to distribute her wine in Gaul. Nevertheless, it gives some sort of support to the statistics set out earlier, or rather it illustrates them. Let us therefore note, first, that the consumption of wine on south Gaulish sites is increased by a factor of about 10 after the conquest of 125. It is already known that in the interior the increase from this same date seems even more marked,[23] and that from the mid-second century Italian wine replaced that of Marseilles. It totally replaced it (even in the area *very close to Marseilles*) from around 100 BC.

2. Statistics can be interpreted in a variety of ways: why this increase in the consumption of wine? What was the exchange product? What new conditions were there, not only on the political but socio-economic fronts? And so on. A. Tchernia (ch. 8) has suggested some avenues of enquiry. That is not my present concern. I conclude, first of all, that all explanations so far offered of the replacement of Massaliote by Italian wine are valueless. They include:

A disease affecting Massaliote vines – which Plutarch, for example contradicts (*Marius* XXXVII).

A change of containers – amphorae replaced by goatskins. This has now been disproved, since we have recently learnt that the so-called 'Gallic' amphorae (those which would be used under the Empire) are the direct descendants of Massaliote amphorae, and their kilns and wasters have been found at Marseilles itself.[24]

An imitation by Marseilles of Italian Dressel I amphorae – no chemical analysis has been able to confirm this.

All that is false.

3. In fact all these data prove the rarity of Massaliote wine and of its distribution. We may also observe that no text has ever suggested the opposite. Strabo does not say one word on its export, and Athenaeus (I 48.27c), later, described Massaliote wine in this way: 'It is of good quality, *it is scarce*, it is thick, it has body' – to say nothing of other authors (cf. Martial X 36).

From the time of the Roman conquest of Transalpine Gaul, therefore, there was a *quantitative leap* of great importance, which proves, by contrast, the weakness of Massaliote exports. We need not concern ourselves today with the reasons for this change (presence of the legions, Romanization of the elites, lower price etc. . . . one can think of several, without forgetting that these statistics relate to non-urbanized sites, where there is no indication of any military presence). What I would like to stress is that, *judging by archaeological finds*, Massaliote products are very rare on all the excavated sites, at a time when similar products were imposed by Roman domination, with a gigantic rate of increase in the space of a few years. Nevertheless, Marseilles is regarded as a great power. How are these contradictions to be reconciled? Yet again by the non-objective nature of archaeological data?

There is an easy and simple solution. This is to affirm that, after having been founded to practise commerce, Marseilles became a city of 'classical' type, living from its *chora*. Strabo (IV 1.5) argues for this. Having indicated that, 'to begin with, the Massaliotes trusted in the sea' (an expression which he normally uses to designate piracy rather than commerce,[25] which Justin (XLIII 3) seems to confirm in speaking of the Phocaeans in general) he stresses the 'energy' which allowed them to establish strongholds and also to conquer territory.[26] Several authors refer to Roman assistance: apart from Strabo, Polybius, then Cicero and Caesar.[27] Posidonius' host, Charmolaus, possessed estates in Liguria (i.e. probably in the Alpes-Maritimes) which he was using indigenous labour to cultivate (Strabo III 4.17). Both the extent and the chronology of this *chora* have been much discussed.[28] But that does not matter: it existed in the Hellenistic period and it must have reached its greatest extent in 49.[29]

Having been founded to play a commercial role, then, did Marseilles in the course of time become a colony of classic type, living from its territory?[30] This suggestion is not only defensible; it explains both the anomalies which we have just noted (exchanged goods became rare) and the difficulties which Marseilles encountered with the barbarians (who laid siege to its comptoirs, Nice and Antibes, in 154, and then to Marseilles itself in 125)[31] in an attempt perhaps to liberate or recover territories.

This solution is eminently reasonable, and it is not without reservations – or a spirit of adventure – that I intend, *at least partially*, to question it. Why? Because, again, all that we have just learnt from the last twenty or ten years of archaeological research inclines us to caution. The problem is not that no trace of 'colonization' can be found: we would not know how to define it, except by pre-Roman cadastration (non-existent, except near Agde), which might be the trace of a 'Massaliote colonization'. But it is at this period (third-second and even first century) that traces of a typically indigenous civilization are found – even in proximity to Marseilles – in all the material remains of daily life: objects of local provenance or from Celtica, characteristic rites ('têtes coupées' – decapitated heads) and so on. I am not underestimating the discrepancies (well known even today in Africa or South America) between economic domination and ways of life. All the same, every colonization, even one of agrarian type, imports not only the structures but also the objects of domination (from Coca-Cola to table-knives). Also, the literary tradition has preserved, for the peoples of southern Gaul in the second century BC, an image of power and of savagery which is hardly compatible with an extended Massaliote *chora* – and these were the justifications *a posteriori* for Roman imperialism.[32] It remains to see if, in the face of these difficulties, it is possible to propose another approach.

Let us reread a passage of Strabo (IV 1,5), in the translation of H. L. Jones (Loeb edition). To restore the argument I have removed a digression:

> In earlier times they had a good supply of ships, as well as of arms and instruments that are useful for the purposes of navigation and for sieges; and thanks to these they not only held out against the barbarians, but also acquired the Romans as friends, and many times not only themselves rendered useful service to the Romans, but also were aided by the Romans in their own aggrandizement (. . . . . .)
>
> But at the time of Pompey's sedition against Caesar they joined the conquered party and thus threw away the greater part of their prosperity. Nevertheless traces of their ancient zeal are still left among the people, especially in regard to the making of instruments and to the equipment of ships. But since, on account of the overmastery of the Romans, the barbarians who are situated beyond the Massaliotes

became more and more subdued as time went on, and instead of carrying on war have already turned to civic life and farming, it may also be the case that the Massaliotes themselves no longer occupy themselves so earnestly with the pursuits aforementioned. Their present state of life makes this clear; for all the men of culture turn to the art of speaking and the study of philosophy; so that the city, although a short time ago it was given over as merely a training-school for the barbarians and was schooling the Galatae to be fond enough of the Greeks to write even their contracts in Greek, at the present time has attracted also the most notable of the Romans, if eager for knowledge, to go to school there instead of making their foreign sojourn at Athens.

There are some difficulties in this text,[33] but as their interpretation affects the general meaning little I will ignore them.

In general we need only take account of the concluding sentence to draw attention to Marseilles's civilizing role in teaching the Gauls to speak Greek and educate themselves (even though Strabo is speaking here of the writing of contracts)[34] and we can set beside this text the 'Gallo-Greek' inscriptions[35] or the passage of Caesar concerning the famous tablets of the Helvetii (*B.G.* I 29, cf. VI 14). Marseilles 'instructress of the Gauls', 'educator', 'mother of progress': the tears of emotion this idea invokes are still shed in public life as in scholarly publications.

It is nevertheless useful to relate this text to Justin's of the second century on the 'teaching' of Marseilles (XLIII 4): *Ab his igitur mansuefacta barbaria, et agrorum cultus et urbes moenibus cingere didicerunt. Tunc et legibus non armis vivere, tunc et vitem putare, tunc olivam serere consuerunt.* Although it was taken literally at the start of the century, it has since then been regarded as a vague or as an emphatic statement. However, we should remember that Justin was summarizing the writings of an Augustan author, Trogus-Pompeius, a southerner from close to Marseilles,[36] and that he may have illustrated this thesis with specific examples. And we can illustrate each phrase in the sentence by recently discovered archaeological material.

– *vitem putare*: attempts at viticulture are attested in Languedoc at an early date.[37] Some of the *dolia* from Ensérune have representations of bunches of grapes.[38] Cicero's text (*Rep.* III, 9.16), whose context is 129 BC, could be referring to Languedoc (cf. Nicolet (1978) 687).

– *olivam serere*: oil presses are now known on protohistoric sites of the second century at Entremont (near Aix) and also at la Courtine (near Toulon). There is palaebotanical evidence for the cultivation of the olive near Fos. (Note that in these cases we are speaking of establishments which were certainly not under Massaliote domination: Entremont most strikingly, but also la Courtine, carry traces of violent destructions dating to the campaigns of 124–123).

– *urbes moenibus cingere*: it has long been thought that this expression meant that a 'model' (a city surrounded by defences) had been imitated (e.g. Baratier (1973) 24). Recent discoveries go further. We now know, firstly, that the Massaliote 'model' was preceded by other defensive works, and secondly, that, beside indigenous ramparts following their own tradition, we find fortifications which are not only inspired by Massaliote models, but imitate them so faithfully that they can only be the work of the same engineers: namely the rampart of Saint-Blaise, the fortified gate of Glanum. Also, certain monuments or works reproduced Greek plans and Greek techniques, for example central towers (Mauressip near Nîmes, le Baou des Noirs near Vence in the Alpes-Maritimes), the *bouleuterion* of Saint-Rémy. Firstly, these sites are not Massaliote: this is obvious for Mauressip and le Baou des Noirs; and it is highly probable that Saint-Blaise, for long considered a station of Marseilles, was besieged in 124–123; as for Saint-Rémy, the traces of indigenous culture (rite of decapitated heads, 'crouching' figures) prove that we are at least dealing with a 'mixed' establishment. Secondly, for how many fortifications and important establishments is evidence lacking? The majority, all those which urbanization (Roman or modern) has destroyed, notably all those of the Rhone valley. We are beginning therefore to grasp that Justin's remark (*didicerunt*) goes well beyond the meaning usually given to it: it is possible, perhaps probable, that Marseilles (in the Hellenistic period) offered the *services* of engineers and architects working in native country from the Alpes-Maritimes to the frontier of the Pyrenees. Let us leave out the plan of certain *oppida*: we have too few and the hypotheses advanced remain weak.[39] Nevertheless, *mutatis mutandis*, we link up with the ceramic data: developments took place which suggest not just imitation (which is impossible spontaneously), but real instruction, with all that that implies.

I shall risk going still further, by returning to the first part of Strabo's text. The Massaliotes possessed 'a good supply of ships as well as of arms and instruments that are useful for the purposes of navigation and of sieges'. The phrase which follows this is particularly interesting. Following Strabo, let us distinguish two things:

1. Thanks to that, 'they acquired the Romans as friends'. To my knowledge, little attention has been paid to that phrase. The indestructible friendship between Marseilles and Rome remains largely myster-

ious. What were the 'useful services' that Marseilles rendered to Rome?[40] Marseilles's role at the time of the Second Punic War seems to have been a minor one, and after that it is always Marseilles that has recourse to Rome. For earlier periods there is no clear reference. But if we consider that Marseilles, a town of engineers and mistress of the crafts of navigation and (artillery) sieges, was able to aid Rome in this area, in expertise and in technical projects carried out, one side of this 'friendship' seems to become clearer. Rome's weakness in this field until the third century is well known. That no text makes direct reference to it is no cause for surprise: a discreet silence has always surrounded this type of 'service' and only rare allusions can be gleaned from ancient texts. There is nothing impossible, therefore, about the idea that the *beneficia* recognized by Rome were of this nature.

2. The same phrase of Strabo contains a well-worn *topos*: 'arms and instruments . . . thanks to these they held out against the barbarians'. Let us not press this passage, which has been discussed a thousand times. The most curious part is its ending: 'on account of the overmastery of the Romans, . . . the Massaliotes themselves no longer occupy themselves so earnestly with the pursuits aforementioned'. Perhaps there is a mistake here in the translation: not the Massaliotes but the Gauls who, in becoming civilized, no longer had the same taste for warfare. But it does not matter much, because the meaning of the passage can only be: 'while the Gauls had a taste for warfare, Marseilles was a great power in the manufacture of military devices; now that they are civilized, the city has turned to rhetoric'. Are we to imagine that an important part of the activity of Marseilles was devoted to swelling a stock of armaments exclusively to defend herself? The texts show, on the contrary, that she was not capable of this (hence her appeals to Rome).[41] Is it impossible, on the other hand, to suppose that in the same way as she 'sold fortifications' she could sell the technology of aggression, not only to the Romans but also to the barbarians? If one disregards the topos, why not? This in any case would explain certain facts. First, the presence of catapult bullets on sites in the south whose destruction does not correspond to any historical date.[42] Secondly, the upsets which Nice and Antibes experienced (in 154) and then Marseilles herself (in 125). Finally and above all, her own decadence. One could imagine, following Strabo, that a town of military engineers could change its pattern of life. The leadership (assuming that the *charientes* are Massaliotes and not Gauls – but it makes little difference) could become orators the more easily since ancient civilization did not distinguish, like our own,

between specialized fields. The sole difference would be that the engineer employed technicians and workmen while the orator needed nobody.

Marseilles, in the Roman period, is a city of minor importance: the epigraphic evidence alone shows this. In the Hellenistic period she enjoyed great renown, and yet she seems to have had little commercial importance (contrary to the state of affairs at her origin). How is this contradiction to be explained? Undoubtedly by the existence of a *chora* which Rome confiscated after the siege of Caesar. Yet various factors lead us to wonder if, in exchange for Gallic products, Marseilles did not export 'invisibles' or 'near-invisibles', notably military technology, both defensive and offensive, from which Rome equally benefited.

I have intentionally limited myself to this example, although there are other pointers – in Strabo especially – towards further research. I have been conducting the (risky) experiment of confronting texts with archaeology and proposing an explanation when there is a clash. If, at least in part, I am not too greatly mistaken, let us observe that from antiquity onwards this type of service has been hidden under very generalized labels, just as now the concepts of cultural exchange and technical aid conceal notions and realities that are very disparate: from the teacher to the mercenary, from the film to the machine gun, it is difficult from state documents to find out precisely where we are. It also happens that certain services rebound against those who offered them – and that a call is made for others. Nevertheless it is a 'civilizing role' that is often the subject of competition between great powers, in the same way as, for the south of Gaul, one could say, if one was called Trogus-Pompeius, *'Gallia in Graeciam translata videretur'*, but if one was Pliny the Elder, *'Italia verius quam provincia'*. Business and ideology . . .

[8]

Italian wine in Gaul at the end of the Republic*

by ANDRÉ TCHERNIA

The diffusion of Dressel 1 amphorae (the main carriers of Italian wine) in the second and first centuries BC constitutes the most spectacular evidence of the export of agricultural produce from Italy in the ancient world. The amphorae were produced as containers for the wines of the Tyrrhenian coast, and typologically they represent the final stage in the evolution from the Graeco-Italic amphorae which in many cases had been produced for many years on the same sites. One can date to approximately 130 the evolution in the form of these objects which corresponds to the change in the archaeologists' nomenclature for them. A number of the principal chronological reference points are particularly connected with the trade with Gaul: the Dr. 1 of Entremont cannot be later than 123, if the traditional chronology can be accepted for this *oppidum*; consular dates painted on the amphorae have been found at Ampurias (119) and in addition at Vieille-Toulouse (103).[1] In the stratigraphies of Nages these amphorae begin to appear in large numbers between 125 and 100, in those of Tournus between 120 and 80.[2] They disappear completely about one hundred years later, during the last but one decade of the first century, at which point they are replaced by a new model, the Dr. 2–4.

1. *An exceptional trade*

It is many years since Bohn (1923) indicated the frequent incidence of Dr. 1 in the *oppida* of independent Gaul. More recently distribution maps have been drawn up.[3] The dots representing findspots of Dr. 1 are clearly numerous. C. Panella ((1981) 58) writes: 'The data that we have collected should be interpreted with caution. Nevertheless, they clearly indicate a commercial expansion.' Now, conclusions relating to the economy should be drawn only with the utmost prudence from a study of maps indicating diffusion, for such maps inevitably incorporate two defects. In the first place, if they refer to an extended territory, they can take only published material into account, and there is a danger that they will reflect not so much the state of the remains as that of archaeological studies. Furthermore, they represent each site of discovery by one dot, regardless of whether a single or a thousand amphorae were discovered there. The quantitative evidence thus entirely, or almost entirely, eludes us. All the same, we should not regard such maps as totally useless nor should we believe that until we have at our disposal exhaustive archaeological inventories no conclusions can be drawn. That would be both foolish and utopian. Faced with objects produced by the million and (as we shall see) in some instances in more than a hundred localities within a single department and sometimes more than a thousandfold on a single site, such exhaustiveness would be valueless. It is, on the other hand, very important to have at least a rough idea of the relationship between the published selection and the actual extent of what has been found, since – unfortunately – the relationship between what has been found and what actually exists inevitably remains, with very few exceptions, a matter of pure speculation.

Only local research workers are in a position to list the total known remains from any particular region, whether these be published or not. In this respect, recent enquiries have made three interesting tests possible with regard to the distribution of the Dr. 1 in Gaul. The current published distribution maps indicate, in respect of the four departments of Brittany, seven sites where Dr. 1 amphorae have been discovered. A recent inventory (Galliou (1982)), conducted by the *Direction des antiquités de Bretagne* has indicated fifty-five sites. The authors of the distribution maps knew of seven sites in the department of Saône-et-Loire. Thanks to research undertaken by an archaeologist from Burgundy, it is now possible to locate thirty-three (Vaussanvin (1979)). Finally, in the Aude, where all the maps indicate a greater density of sites – thirteen according to Daphne Nash ((1978) 321–2) – Guy Rancoule and Jean Guilaine ((1979) n.32) know of close on a hundred. In the three regions under consideration, the sites known to regional archaeological specialists are roughly five to eight times more numerous than those indicated on the general maps, and that proportion is a relatively constant one.

Now let us consider the quantity of objects in the various cases. In Brittany, there are only 123 amphorae scattered over the fifty-five sites where discoveries were made. The figures are very different for the Saône-et-Loire. At Châlon, a nineteenth-century archaeologist, studying the dredging operations conducted in the Saône, calculated that more than 24,000 amphorae had been extracted from the bed of the river

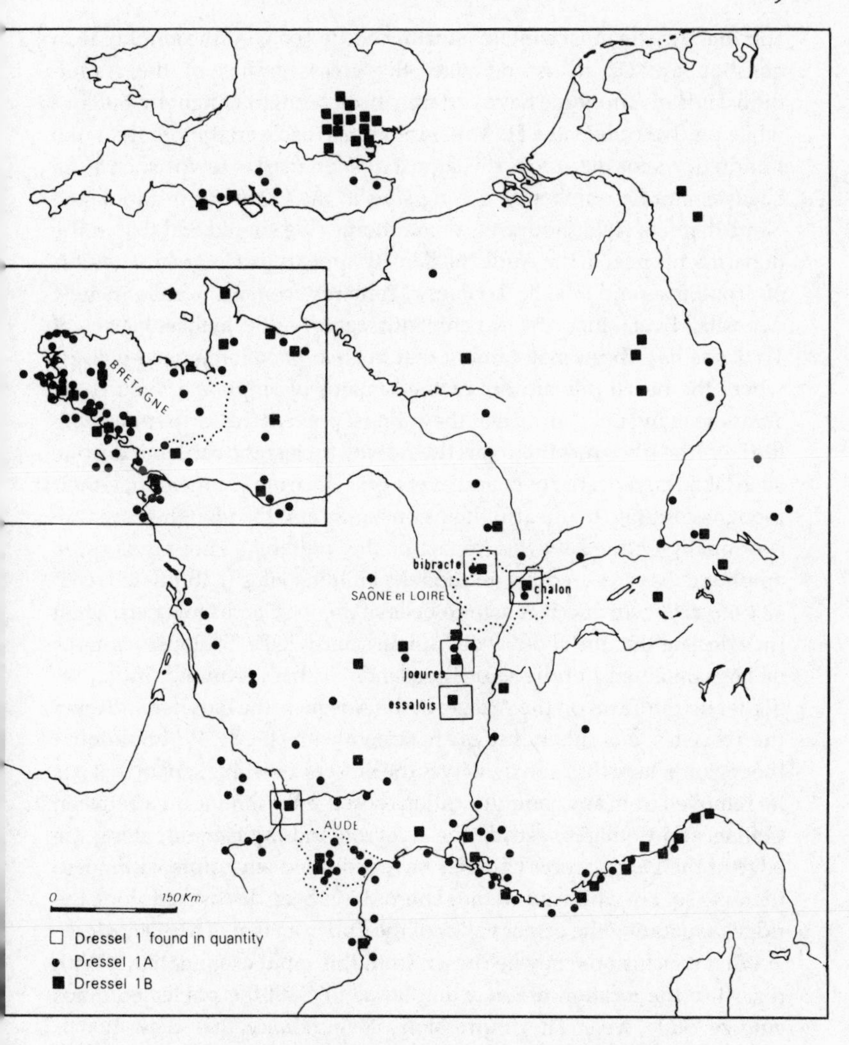

Distribution of Dressel 1 amphorae in Gaul and Britain
(after Peacock (1971) and Galliou (1982))

The enclosed area is that dealt with in the work of P. Galliou. Dr. 1 amphorae are thus very much over-represented there by comparison with those from other regions, and it would be absurd to conclude that Italian wine was exported to Brittany in particular.

and that the site must contain a further 200 to 500,000:[4] the amphorae in question are Dr. 1. At Bibracte, the great *oppidum* of the Aedui, thousands of amphorae have certainly been brought to light by Bulliot,[5] while on five other sites H. Vaussanvin has discovered more than one hundred. As for the Aude, the largest *oppida* – market towns such as La Lagaste – and a number of mining sites in the Corbières or Montagne Noire districts yield thousands of amphorae. We should add that in the departments next to the Aude the density appears just as great. The sites of Toulouse and Vieille-Toulouse certainly contain Gaul's richest deposits. Ever since the seventeenth century the archaeologists of Toulouse have been maintaining that in areas containing necropolises, where the burial pits are full of the remains of amphorae, 'you come across so many intact urns that they almost prevent the earth from being fertile';[6] 'the labourers there cart them away to clear the earth but despite such labours, repeated over and over again since time immemorial, their ploughs continue to unearth them constantly and the plough-shares are continually blunted by the impact of this pottery'.[7] Thousands more amphorae have turned up on modern building sites (Labrousse (1968) 143–60, 207, 230) and it is safe to believe the local archaeologists when they declare that the sub-soil of Toulouse and Vieille-Toulouse contains or has contained hundreds of thousands of them. Around Toulouse, higher up the Tarn, on the Ariège, in the Ausques, the Elusates and even the Tarbelles, a number of sites are strewn with sherds. Without doubt the region where the high density is the most astonishing, given that it is far removed from any communication routes, is the mining area between Ceilhes and Camarès, astride the Aveyron and the Hérault, along the edge of the Larzac: recent articles have indicated ten points within less than 150 sq. km where numerous sherds have been discovered along the ridges separating the upper valley of the Orb from that of the Dourdon.[8]

What conclusions may be drawn from this rapid examination?[9] With regard to the location of Dr. 1 amphorae in Gaul the published maps emerge quite well. The impression of abundance that they give is confirmed and the unevennesses of distribution are accentuated rather than modified. Over the maps' blank zones many points could certainly be added, but in most cases each one would represent no more than a few amphorae. Meanwhile, the zones where we have found the greatest concentrations to lie are those where the density of the known sites was already the greatest: the Aude, the Aveyron, the Tarn, the Hérault and the Haute-Garonne, in that order, are the departments where Daphne Nash mentions the greatest number.

The quantitative evidence provides newer information if we examine the situation of the wine trade in Gaul under the Republic in relation to (a) exports to other provinces and (b) the evidence provided by other amphorae at other periods.

a) On the maps of C. Panella or M. Beltran[10] for Spain, and on that of D. P. S. Peacock for Britain, the density of points seems to be almost as great as in Gaul. However, Peacock has provided detailed information on the quantities found there: on the sites in Britain only a few fragments of amphorae or a few intact ones were discovered, in many cases no more than a single one and in only two cases as many as a few dozen, namely at Camulodunum and Hengistbury Head. In Spain, investigation of the publications indicates that on the Iberian sites, similarly, no more than a few dozen amphorae at most have been discovered. Several thousand sherds have been found at Ampurias; the only sites where quantities appear to have been large enough to cause the excavators any surprise were the mines of the Sierra Morena.[11] It would appear that, overall, imports of Italian wine contained in Dr. 1 amphorae were higher than anywhere else in those areas of Gaul situated to the south of a line drawn between the mouths of the Garonne and the Rhône.

b) On the sites in Gaul occupied long enough to have received several different types of amphorae, Marseilles, Ibero-Punic and Graeco-Italic amphorae are much less numerous than the Dr. 1 type. C. Panella's remark about the expansion of trade, quoted above, is thus entirely confirmed.

Let us consider another type of amphora well known for its abundance in Gaul and along the Rhine, namely the Dr. 20 which was used from the time of Augustus to that of Gallienus for transporting oil from the valley of the Guadalquivir. It would be possible to produce a map showing their distribution just as spectacular as that for the Dr. 1 amphorae.[12] But, apart from Rome, there is not a single site where Dr. 20s have been discovered in their thousands. In the case of Gaul, a quantitative study leads one to reverse Emile Thevenot's statement of fifteen years ago: 'Spanish exports are much higher, in terms of absolute volume, than the exports of wines from Italy'.[13] The truth is, in fact, precisely the reverse.

Among all the trade movements that the presence of amphorae reveals in the west, the export of Italian wine to Gaul during the second and first centuries BC appears to be a unique phenomenon. This is so because, in the first place, quantitatively speaking, there is more evidence here than anywhere else, except for Monte Testaccio; and secondly – and above all – because it is the only important trade movement exporting food products over large distances where the principal destination was not Rome or the armies stationed along the *limes*. The difference in the distribution patterns for the Dr. 1s and the Dr. 20s, concentrated mostly in Gaul and Germania along the Rhône-Rhine axis, provides telling evidence. As for the quantitative predominance of the Dr. 1s, this is also confirmed along the French Mediterranean coastline by the number of sunken wrecks: a survey of 1975 counted 29 wrecks containing Dr. 1 out of a total of 103.[14]

On the basis of this figure, I have made an attempt to calculate (or rather to guess) the dimensions of the import trade. My tentative estimate, of which I will offer a detailed explanation, even if not justification, elsewhere, is in the range 50,000–100,000 hl per annum (but I consider the higher figure more probable). With a trade of 100,000 hl per year, some forty million amphorae would have been unloaded in Gaul in the course of the century or so during which the Dr. 1 amphorae lasted. This does not appear implausible in the light of the observations that we have made regarding the number of discoveries made on land. Nor is a total of 100,000 hl per year incompatible with the production of the vineyards on the Tyrrhenian coast under the Republic. A. Carandini has recently suggested a figure close to 50,000 hl for the Cosa territory alone.[15] 100,000 hl would certainly amount to only a small proportion of the wine consumption of Rome at its peak.

Finally, to see these exports in better perspective, we may compare them with what represents a historical record in the wine trade of pre-industrial times, namely the exports of wines from Gascony to England and Flanders at the beginning of the fourteenth century, before deliveries were interrupted by the Hundred Years War. The average for the seven years for which records exist between 1305 and 1336 is about 750,000 hl.[16] 'This was the largest international trade in the medieval western world.'[17]

2. *The consumers*

Who drank all this wine? There appear, *a priori*, to be only two clients possible: the Gallic elite and the Roman armies. Plenty of legions passed by way of Gaul from 125 to the time of Augustus and there can be no doubt that the officers, and possibly the men too, drank wine. The question that needs to be resolved is whether, as some distinguished scholars maintain, these were indeed the chief clients, and whether the Roman military presence did, in effect, represent the motive force for the trade. For that to be so, wine would have had to be part of the ordinary rations for the troops and the *annona* would have been responsible for arranging regular deliveries. But that was not the case: the usual beverage was *posca*, a mixture of vinegar and water.[18] Distributions of wine are not reliably attested until the beginning of the third century AD.[19]

The archaeological evidence points clearly to a Gallic and civilian consumption. It was the *oppida* of Gaul, in the Transalpine region as well as in barbarian Gaul, that, together with the mining regions, received the overwhelming majority of amphorae. The exceptionally plentiful and precise texts from Posidonius to Caesar which mention deliveries of Italian wine in Gaul also all indicate that the buyers were Gallic.[20] The famous *Pro Fonteio* taxes (XIX and XX) have been understood by M. Labrousse ((1968) 143) and, in particular, G. Clemente ((1974) 132), as having operated solely against the Gauls. There can, in fact, be no other possible interpretation, if one poses the question of how to integrate into Cicero's text Ammianus Marcellinus' quotation (XV 12.4) of a lost passage that runs as follows: '*Gallos post haec dilutius esse poturos, quod illi venenum esse arbitrabantur*'. The phrase *Video, iudices, esse crimen et genere ipso magnum; vectigal enim impositum fructibus nostris dicitur* . . . can only be a purely rhetorical play, as G. Clemente has correctly pointed out: Cicero is making a defence at this point, not an accusation. The only possibility of understanding the lost passage in which Cicero was refuting the *crimen vinarium* is the following: granted, the tax affects our products. But in reality it only operates against the Gauls. So those drunkards have to pay more for their wine, do they? There is a perfectly simple way for them to make up for the increase caused by the Fonteius taxes: instead of drinking their wine neat, they should mix it with water, as do all civilized people.

The conclusion to be drawn from the passage at the beginning of the *Gallic Wars* (I 1.3), where Caesar suggests that the Belgae imported less wine than the Celtae and Aquitani, corresponds roughly to the one that can be drawn from an examination of the maps of distribution. In an exactly comparable fashion the amphorae found in abundance among the independent peoples living around Toulouse and in the *oppida* or mining districts of the Aude provide a perfect illustration of the interpretation I have offered of the *Pro Fonteio*.

We can go even further if, to account for the hundreds of thousands of amphorae in Toulouse, we adopt a hypothesis drawn from a comparison with Aquileia, another frontier town under the Republic. Strabo (V 1.8), unquestionably basing his remarks upon an earlier source, describes Aquileia as an *emporium* where the Illyrians used to come to collect their wine which had arrived by sea. They transported it home after having transferred it into their own barrels. A text taken from the *Gallic Wars* (VIII 42.1) tells us that to the north of Toulouse, on the frontier with independent Gaul, barrels were used by the inhabitants of Cahors. If other peoples in the region did the same,[21] Toulouse would seem to have been the place where the independent Gauls came with their barrels in order to collect wine brought there by the Romans in amphorae, and the exceptional concentration of discarded amphorae used for the purpose of filling in burial pits is easily explained. The at first sight surprisingly high level of consumption on the part of Toulouse is thus reduced in the light of the consumption on the part of other sites all around; there, as we have seen, amphorae have also been discovered in large numbers: so only some of the wine was transferred into barrels.

We can grant that there are no grounds for doubting that consumption on the part of the Roman legions contributed towards increasing the deliveries of Italian wine (and the more so whenever these legions were stationed in areas where such deliveries were habitual whether they were present or not). All the evidence, however, invites one to see the key to the trade as consumption by Gauls. Extravagant predilection for wine on the part of the Gauls was proverbial in the ancient world.[22] For the elite, wine was a prestige commodity, 'a sign of wealth and for that reason an instrument of power'.[23] Wine was used in the agonistic giving of gifts between tribal chiefs – the potlatch analyzed by Marcel Mauss, a practice which he describes as 'overdeveloped among the Celts of Gaul and Ireland'. When the practice was at its peak a gift of wine was considered as prestigious as one of gold or silver; in some circumstances it was worth sacrificing one's life for.[24] Wine was redistributed as largesse to dependent peoples, for example during festivals such as those held by Luerius, the father of Bituitus.[25] During the period with which we are concerned it was also used in exchanges between one people and another, sometimes even within the framework of a monetary economy: in the area controlled by the Aedui, one of the sites richest in amphorae is Essalois, an *oppidum* of the Segusiavis on the left bank of the Loire, where the number and diversity of Gallic coins are also quite exceptional.[26]

The abundance of amphorae in centres such as Bibracte, in river ports where cargoes were handed over, in all *oppida* that may have served as markets or depots, can therefore be easily understood. It is quite another matter when it comes to accounting for the considerable quantities found on mining sites in isolated areas, in the Corbières, the Montagne Noire or the upper valley of the Orb[27] and also for the extremely extensive diffusion of amphorae in the Aude, in particular, where fragments have been found in caves which otherwise show no signs of human habitation except during the barbarian invasions and the Religious Wars (Rancoule and Guilaine (1979) 440). There are no obvious technical reasons to explain the presence of amphorae in mines or to account for their having been transported there when empty. All in all, the archaeological data tends to suggest that in the mining sites and regions of the South-West, redistribution took place on a sufficiently large scale to create – at least to some extent – a popular consumption of imported wine, a most unusual phenomenon in the history of wine-drinking.

3. *The goods exchanged*

The problem of what goods the Gauls exchanged for their wine is one that has several times been posed and, in most cases, resolved by a heterogeneous list of the products usually used in exchanges between the Roman and barbarian worlds. Admittedly, anything and everything *may* have been exchanged for amphorae of wine and, at some point or other, probably was. But the imports of wine in Gaul are out of the usual run and we need to describe the conditions that made them possible more precisely. The texts mention three categories of goods arriving in Italy from Gaul: metals, products from herd-raising (wool and hams) and slaves.[28] Let us examine each in turn.

a) The huge iron works whose slag covers dozens of hectares and whose production can be measured in thousands of tons a year in the Montagne Noire, the Cher and the Yonne, would seem to suggest that iron was the most important exchange commodity, were it not for the fact that they were not flourishing until somewhat later: none of them have so far been dated to before 60 BC. They are on the whole post-Caesar, those in the Yonne later still. As in other mines, there are quantities of amphorae in the earliest trenches excavated in the slag heaps of the Montagne Noire, but that is only relevant to the end of the period with which we are concerned.

On the other hand, the silver, copper and lead mines of the Montagne Noire, the Corbières, and the Rutènes were started or considerably extended at the end of the second or beginning of the first century.[29] Observations made of the particular concentration of amphorae sherds in many of these mines are confirmed by a relationship which is just as clear at a regional level. The region that extends from the Rutènes district to that of the Tarbelles in the Basses-Pyrénées contains the zones richest in amphorae. The abundance of metal – gold (probably obtained from gold-washing), silver and copper – is furthermore better attested in this area than in any other part of Gaul by the texts and by archaeology.[30] Why is it that the Aveyron is one of the richest departments in Dr. 1 in the whole of France if not because of the silver from the Ruteni?

The picture that I am suggesting assumes that the exploitation of the mines of Transalpine Gaul was left to the natives. We have, unfortunately, no direct information regarding their regime under the Republic, but in a province where the administration was particularly lax, such a situation is altogether plausible. It is the solution that has been adopted for the iron and copper of Macedonia after Pydna (Livy XLV 29.11). The connexion between mining sites and amphorae is confirmed on both sides of the frontier of Transalpine Gaul. A lingot of lead stamped with the name of the Segusiavi[31] and a passage in Suetonius (*Tib.* XLIX) both prove that cities in the area might well have exploited their own mines – at least up until the time of Tiberius.[32] There is therefore nothing to prevent us relying on the very clear congruity of the maps showing on the one hand the distribution of mines and, on the other, the concentrations of amphorae and concluding that, in the south west, wine was exchanged first and foremost for metals.

Then there are the other regions to consider. In Bâle and the *oppida* of the upper Rhine and the upper Danube (Uenze (1958)), we may similarly refer to the gold-washing that took place. But among the Arverni and in the territory belonging to the Aeduan confederation, mines exploited during the republican period became few and far between. As for Châlon and the river valleys to the north, here we may refer to the famous trade in British tin (Diodorus V.22 and 38). But Peacock ((1971) 173) has already pointed out that the rarity of amphorae along the French coasts of the English channel indicates that continental tribes did not act as intermediaries in exchanges. The same applies to the lower Loire. In contrast, the few amphorae recovered from the sea off the coasts of Vendée and southern Brittany[33] suffice to attest the existence of an Atlantic route. R. Dion, basing his remarks upon geographical arguments, has for his part interpreted Diodorus' overland route as passing by way of the Garonne and the Gallic isthmus.[34] British tin, therefore (in addition to the products of local Gallic mines), is a better explanation for the abundance of Dr. 1 amphorae in the Gallic isthmus than it is for their presence in central Gaul.

b) Despite Flaubert, who in 1881 had his Bouvard and Pecuchet maintain that the Gauls had taught the Romans to trade in hams just as they had taught the Greeks metaphysics and the Etruscans divination, the idea of sizeable exports of Gallic hams and articles of clothing to Italy has enjoyed considerable success. Admittedly Strabo wrote some arresting lines on the subject of Gallic exports to Rome and Italy (IV 4.8). However, elsewhere he makes similar claims for exports to Rome of hams from Cisalpine Gaul (V 1.12) and articles of clothing from Padua (V 1.7). It is clearly not reasonable to believe that a country where the raising of sheep and pigs was already well developed[35] should have imported both from Gaul and from Cisalpine Gaul salt pork and wool in quantities sufficient to have played a role of any importance in its commercial exchanges. The reputation enjoyed in Rome by the hams of the Sequani (Strabo IV 3.2), the Cavari and the Comacini (Varro *R.R.* II 4.10) rested upon their quality rather than their quantity. A few amphorae of wine were from time to time exchanged for salt pork or wool but this cannot account for the hundreds of thousands of objects found on the bed of the Saône.

c) Now we come to the slaves. Diodorus, in a well-known text, actually describes how they were bartered for wine. It is the only text that specifically mentions any particular article being exchanged for wine (V 26.3): 'Being inordinately fond of wine, they gulp down what the merchants bring them quite undiluted. They have a furious passion for drinking and get altogether beyond themselves, becoming so drunk that they fall asleep or lose their wits. Many Italian merchants, prompted by their usual cupidity, consequently regard the Gauls' taste for wine as a godsend. They take the wine to them by ship up the navigable rivers or by chariot travelling overland and it fetches incredible prices: for one amphora of wine they receive one slave, thus exchanging the drink for the cupbearer.'

Two other texts also mention exports of Gallic slaves to Italy. The first is to be found in Cicero's *Pro Quinctio* (VI. 2): there, we learn by chance, from his meeting in Volterra a convoy of *pueri venales* from Gaul, that the company formed by Quinctius and Naevius to trade with Gaul was, among other things, engaged in the slave traffic. The second text, which is less well known, comes from Afranius, the prolific author of *Comoediae togatae: 'Liber natus est; ita mater eius dixit in Gallia ambos cum emerem'* (*Gram. lat.* I 119). Diodorus draws upon Posidonius; the *Pro Quinctio* describes facts relating to 83; Afranius was born around 150. Here, contemporaneous with our amphorae, within a period of forty years at the most and possibly as few as twenty, are three texts alluding to sales of slaves in Gaul. Given the rarity of ancient sources that mention the slave trade at all, this concentration is significant, as is confirmed most tellingly by the number of Gallic slaves present in Italy in the period that immediately followed: that of Spartacus' rebellion.

Spartacus' two Celtic lieutenants, Crixus and Oenomaus had under their command an autonomous band of Gallic and Germanic slaves: 30,000 men according to Appian, of whom 20,000 were killed in 72 by Gellius' troops.[36] When the final defeat came, a further 35,000 Celts according to Livy (*Per.* XCVII), or 12,300 according to Plutarch (*Crassus* XI 3), were killed along with Castus and Gannicius, who had replaced Crixus and Oenomaus as leaders. Of course, these figures are only as valuable as we care to make them; ancient estimates of the total number of slaves who followed Spartacus vary from 70,000 (Orosius V 24) to 120,000 (Appian BC I 117). Nevertheless, the Gauls accounted for a large proportion of Spartacus' band and, that being so, there must have been at least some hundred thousand Gallic slaves in Italy at the time. I certainly do not believe that, as has sometimes been suggested, Spartacus' Celts were the survivors or descendants of the prisoners captured by Marius from the Cimbri and the Teutones. A full thirty years later, not very many of them can have remained alive and it is very unlikely that, in those times, they can often have been in a position to produce children. There were no doubt a number of campaigns in Gaul between 102 and 73 (Goudineau (1978) 690–1), but, as Finley has demonstrated (1962), Graeco-Roman slavery cannot have depended solely upon war and piracy, but implied an organized slave trade on a large scale; and the same is manifestly true where the Gallic slaves in Italy are concerned. According to Varro (*R.R.* II 10.4) they were regularly employed as shepherds. It is not credible that the work force for Italian agriculture was dislocated in the way implied by Westermann when he maintains[37] that Thracians and Gauls were almost completely eliminated from the slave population between Spartacus' revolt and the Gallic War. So we are left with the texts referring to the slave trade that we have cited above.

Assuming there to have been 300,000 Gallic slaves in Italy – between 10 and 15 per cent of the slave population – and allowing for a 7 per cent rate of replacement,[38] only one quarter of which could, in those times, have been assured by natural reproduction, a total of 15,000 slaves must have been brought from Gaul during each warless year.

Diodorus, or Posidonius, was shocked by the inequality of the 'terms of trade' in the exchange of one amphora for one slave. But the background for his account is clearly one of potlatch rather than commercial exchange (Daubigney (1981)). In potlatch, the gift made in return is necessarily greater than the original one given and the Roman merchants exploited the development of this practice in Celtic societies. At the time of Posidonius, the traffic was just beginning to expand and it is conceivable that his account is indeed correct. As the exchanges multiplied they in all probability came gradually and increasingly to resemble truly commercial exchanges and the inequality of terms was reduced. However, it is possible to set a limit to this evolution. In Herculaneum, an ordinary adult slave was worth between 900 and 1,000 sesterces,[39] that is to say 60 amphorae of wine at the lowest possible price for production (Columella III 3.10). In central Gaul, in the first century BC, a Roman merchant would no doubt consider that when he paid ten amphorae in exchange for a slave, he had been overcharged. To remain within reasonable bounds let us suggest that, if we abide by our original working hypothesis – 100,000 hl of wine exported and 15,000 slaves imported – the slave trade may have accounted for between one tenth and one third of the goods exchanged for Italian wine.

4. *Features of the trade*

There were markets where the barbarians exchanged slaves for wine at Tanais, Byzantium and Aquileia.[40] But Diodorus' text makes another point: Italian merchants were penetrating barbarian regions in order to effect exchanges. The only exact parallel is to be found in the lexicographers, where they explain the meaning of the expression *haloneton andrapodon*: this was the expression used to describe a worthless barbarian slave because merchants were travelling to the interior of the land, taking with them salt in exchange for which the Thracians would provide them with servants.[41]

This comparison may help us to understand the wine trade in Gaul. The salt merchants were in search of slaves and nobody would claim that their aim was to extend the market for salt or to increase the value of the salt marshes. Diodorus' text makes the same point: the merchants in question did not set off for Gaul for the purpose of selling an amphora of wine but in order to bring back a slave. Seen from this point of view, the presence of millions of amphorae for Italian wine in Gaul does not result from an effort to step up the market for wine. Rather, the amphorae of wine were an advantageous exchange currency for the metals and slaves of which Italy was in need.

Twenty years ago, François Villard was, reasonably enough, posing similar questions on the subject of Marseilles wine: 'We come back to this question: what were the people of Marseilles receiving in exchange? Can we really believe that the desire to sell their crops for a good profit can have impelled them to travel so far afield? . . . For the people of Marseilles, wine was no more than a commodity that could be exchanged for a product that was, in their eyes, much more valuable'.[42]

The same interpretation seems feasible where Italian wine is concerned. The text of the *De Republica* (III 9.16) relating to the prohibition against the peoples of the Transalpine planting vines and olive trees 'so as to increase the value of our own olive groves and vineyards', as Cicero puts it, is extremely perplexing as there is no other measure in Roman legislation with which it can be compared. Cicero's testimony makes it clear enough that this was an imperialistic measure in the sense that, if applied, it operated in favour of the ruling Romans for reasons relating to the interests – or, to be more precise, *prudentia* – of the victors. But should we go further and see it as 'commercial imperialism', as a means of acquiring new commercial outlets? It is now agreed that Cicero's text is not anachronistic and that the measure referred to dates from before 129 (Goudineau (1978) 687). It is contemporary with the beginnings of the trade with which we are here concerned. The Romans were beginning to realize the unique role that wine could play in enabling them to acquire metals and slaves. They were trying to protect a way of providing themselves with provisions that Italy could not do without, guaranteeing these imports for themselves, rather than being protectionist. There are plenty of parallels for such motivations, starting with Domitian's edict on the uprooting of vines to guarantee an abundance of wheat. One consequent effect would have been to set a higher value upon the vineyards best situated to export wine to Gaul. Sixty years later Cicero was sufficiently aware of the situation to see this as the motivation for the measure.[43]

Let us recapitulate the various conditions which made it possible for the Romans to use wine as an exchange currency. First the Gallic passion for wine and the practice of potlatch which, quite apart from their propensity for drunkenness, made them consider the gift of wine as an honour, the possession of wine as an instrument of power and the giving of gifts in exchange for it as a duty. In this sense, the ground had already been prepared, on a smaller scale but in a long-standing tradition, by the people of Marseilles. But Marseilles had neither the needs nor the level of production to induce them to seek to organize traffic on the scale that Rome initiated as soon as it had acquired better situated bases within barbarian territories than its predecessors. Toulouse was one of the key points in the trade: it is no doubt not merely by chance that, after the Ahenobarbus milliary, the most ancient Latin inscription in Gaul comes from the town where the most amphorae have been found (*C.I.L.* XII 5388). The particularly close alliance with the Aedui, 'the brothers of the Roman people', made it easy for the Romans to penetrate further into independent Gaul. This was particularly important when it came to moving slaves from one point to another: the setting up of depots, ensuring supplies for them and the organization and surveillance of caravans demanded an infrastructure of quite a different nature from that of, for instance, the tin trade. These are all reasons why Marseilles amphorae (or, in the south-west, Ibero-Punic ones) disappear during the second half of the second century, to be replaced by Graeco-Italic and Dr. 1 amphorae.

By multiplying the occasions for the giving of gifts and counter-gifts between the Gallic peoples and the Romans, the Italian merchants conferred an exchange value upon commodities which had until then above all had a use value.[44] That goes without saying when the effect of the exchange is to turn a dependent servant into a marketable slave, but the same applies where metals, even precious ones, are concerned. According to Posidonius (Strabo IV 1.13) the Tectosages had no conception of luxury, which may account for the large quantity of sacred treasures found in their district. Bartering gold for consumer goods clearly gave gold a more profane use. Exchanges took on a more commercial character. The sphere of social and geographical wine redistribution was considerably extended, the prestige involved in the wine being maintained notwithstanding, and the need for exchangeable commodities increased. Gaul met this need not only by drawing upon its dependent peoples but also, in some regions, by exploiting its subterranean wealth. One of the most noticeable effects of the increase in exchanges is the opening of markedly intensified exploitation of mines in the south-west at the very end of the second century or at the beginning of the first.

In short, so long as it was in exchange for wine, the Gauls were prepared to relinquish goods they possessed and for which the Italians had more use. We should also remember how short the sea journey involved was and the well known advantages of the river network.

These conditions, which are peculiar to Gaul, explain the abundance of Dr. 1 amphorae found there. Archaeologists have discovered treasures in the form of coins that date from the same period in the lower Danube region where the Romans paid for their slaves with denarii,[45] just as during the third century BC, before the Roman vineyards had been developed on a commercial scale, they paid the Cisalpine Gauls in gold and silver in exchange for their captives (Zonaras VIII 19).

The social transformations that resulted in Gaul from the increase in the consumption of wine have been studied in depth by A. Daubigney ((1979) (1981)). There is therefore no call for me to dwell upon the aggravation of the relations of dependence that the trade under consideration both presupposed and provoked. That point is clearly made by the exchange of a dependent person in return for an amphora of wine. But it is also relevant where metals are involved. There can be no doubt that the development of the mines occasioned considerable population movements and the abundance of amphorae in mining areas could be explained by the fact that wine was instrumental in facilitating and determining such movements. The text in which Posidonius (Athenaeus VI 25.233D) notes that the Helvetii and other Celts had their goldwashing performed by women and men lacking in physical strength can be similarly understood: it calls to mind certain aspects of the conquest of the New World, where the Indian chiefs, left free to choose which workers to send the Spanish *encomenderos* would provide women to do the goldwashing in the muddy rivers.[46]

For want of more detailed information, I have been obliged to study the traffic under consideration in very general terms. The reality was, no doubt, very different: the distribution of Dr. 1 amphorae varied not only from place to place but also in time, in the course of the century when they were current. A better understanding of the chronology of their sub-categories and a study of the distribution of these will one day make it possible to produce a more diversified and detailed picture. At all events, the situation changed some time during the first ten or fifteen years of Augustus' reign. Dr. 1 amphorae stopped being produced in Italy between 20 and 10 BC. They were replaced by a different shaped vessel, the Dr. 2–4, imitations of the amphorae from the island of Cos, and these became increasingly pervasive from the beginning of the second half of the century onwards. Now, compared with Dr. 1 amphorae, Dr. 2–4 are extremely rare in Gaul. Nowhere have they been discovered in large numbers. Wherever they have been found – and their sites, similarly, are not clearly so numerous as those where Dr. 1 have been discovered – the individual items could be counted on the fingers of both hands.

A more normal pattern for a wine-producing economy now becomes detectable. Gaul now, especially in the west, depends for its consumption of wine, which appears to be much lower than hitherto, upon the closest wine-growing district, namely Hither Spain. Amphorae from that region often take the place of Dr. 1 on the same sites, although in much smaller quantities. A few years later, towards the end of Augustus' reign, the first wine amphorae manufactured in Gaul appear, and vine cultivation begins to expand rapidly, spreading – as usual – northwards.

It is tempting to see this as an effect of Augustus' reorganization of Gaul which began with a census in 27 and with his stay at Narbonne. Under the Empire, a number of slaves continued to be bought in the provinces although in contravention of legal prohibitions;[47] unrestricted trade, of the dimensions we have envisaged, was no longer possible. Was the same true where metals were concerned? There is one Gallic copper ore that is called Livianum because the mine where it was extracted belonged to Livia (Pliny *N.H.* XXXIV 2.3–4). This is the only hint we are given (and it is a slight one) of the changes that occurred in the organization of the mines under Augustus. We can take it that in barbarian Gaul the mines must have passed into Roman hands. In the new province of Narbonensis there is no reason why certain cities should not have retained the right to exploit their own mines, at least until the time of Tiberius (Suet. *Tib.* XLIX).

One point emerges however. In western Languedoc, where the amphorae, although plentiful, are ten or twenty times less so than around the Narbonne-Toulouse axis, most of the *oppida* remained occupied until the end of the first century A D.[48] Vieille-Toulouse, on the other hand, was abandoned between the beginning of the Empire and the end of the millenium (Labrousse (1968) 83 and 105) and in the Aude, for all the *oppida* 'the curve of a graph plotting the intensity of activity would seem to be the same: rapid progression during the first half of the century; decline in gradual stages after the Gallic War; abandonment of or almost total disaffection from the *emporium* by the beginning of the first century A D' (Rancoule (1980) 129). During this same period, the copper and silver-bearing lead mines of the Corbières or Lastour-Fournes in the Montagne Noire fell into decline.[49] The whole exchange system was collapsing and with it the economic activity and native urbanization for which it had, in this region, been the principal impulse.

Were the causes of this collapse internal or external? If we assume that most of the wine passed beyond the frontiers of Transalpine Gaul, it may be that the supply dried up when the peoples of Aquitaine lost their means of exchange and the valley of the Aude ceased to be a transport route. Other hypotheses may also come to mind.

Whatever the case may be, the trade that we have been examining presents all the characteristics of one that operated beyond the frontiers of the empire. It depended upon the different use two different civilizations made of particular commodities and, if it also took place to a certain extent in Transalpine Gaul, that was on account of the very low level of integration of that province.[50] The trading stopped at a moment when Gaul was undergoing significant historical transformations. In my opinion, the end of the trading is connected more with the history of Romanization than with that of the internal fluctuations affecting the Italian vineyards. We should not forget that, although the 100,000 hl that we have proposed represent a trade of very considerable proportions for any pre-industrial period, and although they played an important role in the history of Gaul, the fact remains that they are relatively insignificant in comparison with the consumption of Roman Italy – representing less than one tenth of the quantity of wine that the inhabitants of Rome alone consumed under the Empire.[51]

[9]
Pottery and trade in the Roman period*

by GIUSEPPE PUCCI

I

In 1754 Horace Walpole added to the English language a new word: serendipity. If the term was new, what it signified had been known all over Europe for a couple of centuries, since the first Italian translation of the Persian tale concerning the three sons of the King of Serendip who, observing a series of traces on the ground, were able to describe with precision something (a camel) which they had never seen. In Voltaire's pamphlet *Zadig ou la destinée*, a dog takes the place of the camel, and Zadig, deciphering the tracks, guesses that it is a bitch, that she has recently had puppies, that she limps with the left foreleg and has very long ears. But when he states that he has never seen her, the Queen's soldiers do not believe him and arrest him.

Often the archaeologist is in the very same situation in which Zadig found himself (including the danger of condemnation, this time by incredulous historians): he must guess the nature of something that he is largely ignorant of – for example, trade in the Roman world – by means of traces which are on the ground, or – more frequently – underground: first of all by means of pottery.

In comparing the archaeologist to Zadig I have been preceded by an eminent British scholar. A century ago Thomas Huxley entitled one of the lectures he gave on Darwin's theories *On the method of Zadig*. The sub-title, *Retrospective prophecy as a function of science*, might seem a contradiction in terms: 'but', Huxley observes, 'prophecy as much applies to outspeaking as to foretelling, and (. . .) it is obvious that the essence of the prophetic operation does not lie in its backward or forward relation to the course of time, but in the fact that it is the apprehension of that which lies out of the sphere of immediate knowledge (. . .) The retrospective prophet (would that there were such a word as 'back-teller'!) affirms that so many hours or years ago, such and such things were to be seen'.

The method of Zadig, according to Huxley, is shared by astronomy, geology, palaeontology, archaeology, history. In short, all diachronic sciences resort to traces, signs, clues, to the empirical knowledge inferred from observation or experience.

I am far from declaring myself a follower of Huxley. I am simply claiming the right of the archaeologist to use the archaeological finds in order to build up a coherent system of scientific knowledge valid not only for the study of the materials themselves, but also for a more general understanding of that which lies behind them and which today we cannot perhaps know otherwise.

So far I have intentionally avoided the word 'evidence'. This term has a probatory force in itself. Pottery cannot strictly be evidence to indicate what trade was in the Roman world, to define its essence, its structure, its articulation. But pottery can be regarded as a sort of spy, or a symptom of a much more complex reality. It is the context which supports the single pieces of circumstantial evidence. In the same way, ceramology is not self-sufficient, is not a surrogate for the history of trade and traders.

Pottery is just one of the sources we can use to reconstruct that history, a source with a standing not lower than that of other sources. Many historians are reluctant to put sherds and literary sources on the same level. Finley ((1980) 50) complains of economic histories of the ancient world which do not mention slavery. One could cite a long list of books in which authors deal with commerce in antiquity virtually without mentioning archaeological evidence. Ancient literary texts need to be interpreted with the aid of philology. Manufactured goods, including pottery, need a proper philology. Many historians do not master that kind of philology, and are either indifferent to or suspicious of those sources.

Nevertheless I prefer the historian who totally ignores archaeology to the historian who merely 'shops' in the supermarket of archaeology, choosing those items which fit his theories more readily.[1] Each form of knowledge has its own epistemological system which can suffer neither violent manipulations nor extrapolations. Some historians pretend to utilize the results of archaeological research without understanding its methods. Some others baulk at the material difficulties: whereas the historian can find his sources collected in a single good library, the archaeologist must seek his sources elsewhere by means of excavations which are lengthy and require money and a complex organization. However dull the meticulous descriptions of sherds in archaeological reports may appear to ancient historians, they are indispensable for further study.

Zadig's science, that is the knowledge of the archaeologist who picks up pottery in a trench or in a field survey, is in a way the ultimate example and perhaps most sophisticated display of the knowledge of the primitive hunter who watches the tracks of his prey. Some historians, who are used to working on texts and documents, still regard this as a lower form of knowledge, and have contempt for the 'science of illiterates'. They could be reminded of an ancient Chinese legend which ascribes the invention of writing to an official who had observed the tracks of a bird on the shore. In other words, the knowledge of the historian who relies upon written sources has a close relationship in a remote past with the knowledge of the hunter who, during thousands of years, learnt how to guess from tracks the shapes and movements of invisible prey. At the origins of western culture the two forms of knowledge were not separated. The historian and the physician, the politician and the potter, the seaman and the hunter operated within the conceptual sphere of *metis*, that is of conjectural knowledge.[2] Even in modern times the historian is in no position to repudiate the empirical knowledge of the researcher who ranges in a series many individual micro-observations, since he employs the same technique himself.[3] That is indeed the reason why both literary and archaeological sources can be analyzed by means of the same instrument: philology.

We can define the philological method in a variety of ways. In a general sense it means the process by which particular facts are verified and established in their unmistakable individuality. This is as true for the text of an ancient author as for an ancient amphora. In both cases we are dealing with individuals.

One could object that a literary source, although created by an individual, testifies to the culture of a social or intellectual group at a given epoch, whereas a pot offers a more restricted range of information. Yet artefacts, usually unintentional witnesses in contrast with texts, can tell us much about the culture of both producers and purchasers. Artefacts are the preeminent original sources for the history of illiterate and subordinate social strata. And it may happen also that artefacts disprove by the force of facts, by the force that facts are given when linked to each other in a significant chain, the statements of an author – ancient or modern – which, issuing from a human being, may be tendentious or wrong (cf. Carandini (1979a) 60ff.).

The philological approach is appropriate for individuals. And in fact a philological method is necessary in finding individuals by excavation, in indentifying and analyzing them, in defining the chronological context. But – to return to pottery – much Roman pottery was mass-produced in standard patterns and distributed on a large scale. This means that an enormous quantity of individuals which are virtually identical to one another can be ordered in a typology. This is very important from an epistemological point of view. Setting up a typology does not mean putting 'one damn thing after another'.[4] We can pass – without renouncing philology – from the micro-observation of individuals to another sphere of knowledge in which the segmentary information that the single unit can provide is related to and integrated with the whole represented by an entire class or group.

And that produces remarkable results. In the first place, quantification is employed in the study of a precapitalistic and prestatistic society in a sector in which the written sources generally provide unreliable figures, if they do not omit them altogether. If not today, in the future we will be able to grasp in some degree the dimensions of some productions and trades. I am not enough of an optimist to imagine that we will ever be able to determine the total quantity of commodities produced by a workshop or to reconstruct the book-keeping operations. But, to borrow an epigram: 'There is a limit to what we can do with numbers, as there is to what we can do *without* them.'[5] Villard tried to reconstruct the economic history of Marseilles between the sixth and fourth centuries BC on the basis of 598 sherds of Greek pottery, 447 of which date from the second half of the sixth century.[6] This was too hazardous (Goudineau (1974) 105). But if you excavate a villa completely, and keep a systematic record of every kind of pottery; if you restore the vases and employ in their classification some current quantitative methods, you will be able in the end to determine the ratio of, for instance, local to imported manufactures. If you – or rather future generations – multiply the numbers of such full investigations of single units of production and cover an entire area, if you dig the whole of Monte Testaccio or explore thoroughly some centres of production that have survived in some degree, in the end you will have produced a rather less impressionistic picture of ancient reality.

Antonio Gramsci wrote some fine pages in his *Quaderni dal carcere* (cf. Carandini (1979a) 230ff.) on what he called the *societas rerum*, the world of objects and commodities, the extra-linguistic field *par excellence*. In the case of these objects – he says – it is necessary to discover statistics and trends. On them we can found an experimental science of history. But –

and this is the point – these objects interest us for their human and social content. The objects which man produces have their own morphology, but they reveal a more complex morphology of attitudes, social rules and behaviour, values and symbols. The anonymous productions of commodities are the cultural patrimony of the masses, and we can understand it only in the quantitative dimension; only if we can range the individual phenomena in long series can we understand the point of repetitions and variations. In the same way, only through long geological periods can we appreciate and explain the variation of species.

For these objects quantity means something that cannot be confused with an arithmetic sum. The opposition of quality and quantity is actually an opposition between two different kinds of quality. Quality and quantity are in a sense two sides of the same coin. Quantity means a higher or a lower degree of homogeneity, consistency, standardization – all qualitative concepts.

In this sense quantitative and typological studies of pottery can provide circumstantial evidence relating to manufacturers and the conditions under which they worked.

But the main question, which we started from, remains: what can pottery tell us about the Roman economy? How can we use pottery for 'retrospective outspeaking' of Roman production and trade?

In *Capital* Book I, ch. V, Marx is dealing with tools and mechanical instruments, which he calls 'the articulated bones and muscles of production'. On the other hand he describes the means of transport and containers as the vascular system of production. Among the latter he mentions barrels and jars. So, if we refer to the ancient world, amphorae, dolia and the like, from an economic point of view, fall directly within the sphere of production, and in this sense they can be useful in sketching out the features of an organism that we cannot analyse as a living body (Carandini (1979a) 78ff.). They are spies who can help us to outline the dynamic picture – I stress dynamic – of some basic products exported in large part as exchange values.

But the real battles between historians and archaeologists are fought over the economic significance of tableware, not containers; and the level of the argument is exemplified in questions like the following: how reliable would an economic history of France be which was based on the export of Limoges porcelain? (Goudineau (1974) 109). But – even if we were to admit, as we cannot, the validity of such comparisons between the ancient and the modern world – it is clear that pottery was never a pivotal sector of the economy in antiquity.

The ancient pottery industry did not need an exorbitant outlay, and – in general – pottery was not a luxury article. Price poses a difficult problem. Relevant literary sources are scanty and elusive. We must always pay due regard to the context, often satirical or facetious. When Martial says *asse duo calices emit* (IX 5.22), that is nothing but a proverbial phrase like the English 'two-a-penny' or the Italian 'a quattro un soldo'. But Martial, on the other hand, warns: *arretina nimis ne sperne vasa monemus* (XIV 98). We must also distinguish between different kinds of pottery. A Pompeian graffito (*C.I.L.* IV 5380) informs us that the price of a *pultarium* or a *patella* was one *as*. But that is coarse kitchen ware. Terra sigillata was not the cheapest pottery available. Certainly pottery was never very expensive, not even Attic red-figure.[7] But a commodity which in a production centre is cheap may be more expensive elsewhere, and not only because of the cost of transporting it over a long distance. There is a psychological dimension that is easily missed. Was the Attic ceramic of a tomb at Tarquinia worth the same in its findspot as in Athens? Long distance trade does not automatically imply the existence of a world market and an equivalence of prices. There are certain vases made in Gaul which imitate Arretine vases and bear the stamp *arretinum verum* (*C.V.Arr* 132). They will not deceive a good archaeologist, but surely they might have deceived some Gallic customer, a brave peasant, for instance, who did not know the true Arretine pottery but knew the reputation of Arretine ware and was therefore ready to pay a bit more for it. A grapefruit is not a luxury good. Sicily and Israel have similar climates, and Sicilian grapefruit are of good quality. Nevertheless, Sicilians buy the Jaffa-stamped grapefruit, and pay more for them.

Pottery was not a luxury. But what are the parameters of luxury? Is Trimalchio a valid parameter, Trimalchio who himself used only *calices fictiles inauratos* (Petr. *Sat.* LXXIII)? One can object that by this epoch some eccentric kinds of pottery fetched very high prices: *eo pervenit luxuria ut etiam fictilia pluris constent quam murrhina* (Plin *Nat. hist.* XXXV 163). Are the acquaintances of poets a valid parameter, such as those of Juvenal, who were ashamed to dine with pottery tableware: *fictilibus cenare pudet* (III 168)? This dish satisfied Roman soldiers. How was it regarded by a Gallic peasant? Anyway, can we judge the economic importance of any commodity by its price alone? Is it correct to compare the output of a small workshop with a restricted local market with that of a workshop of Arretium, or Puteoli, or Pisa? From La Graufesenque graffiti we learn that the average batch of vases from a South Gallic oven was 30,000. One text lists 166,000 items of the same shape.

What matters is not only how much the producer gains from a single piece, but also how many of them he sells (one single trained potter can easily make over two hundred vases per day). Ancient historians must begin to reckon with pottery produced in great quantities. Many commodities have a low price: in a modern storehouse many items (often imports) cost less than 50p. A German producer of pencils and erasers may be not as famous as Mr Ford, but his products may have an even larger market, and his enterprise may be sound enough. Josiah Wedgewood made his fortune on the basis of not the reproduction of the Portland Vase, but the enormous quantity of pottery for everyday use distributed through an excellent commercial network.[8] Indeed, one might ask the superficially naive question: if the economic value of Roman pottery was so insignificant, why was it traded on so large a scale? Freight-rates were low, but hardly non-existent. So, what use was there in sending such goods into faraway regions, if the profit was negligible?

Moreover, in the shipwreck of Riou 1, pottery seems to have been not the secondary but the main cargo.[9] It is usually assumed that only decorated or fine pottery was exported; but in some shipwrecks the main cargo, apart from amphorae, was common ware (i.e. neither sigillata nor glazed ware).[10] And if thin-walled pottery can actually be regarded as a particular kind of common pottery, how do we explain the export of Cuman[11] or African kitchenware in the period preceding the export of the finer red slip ware?[12] The more humble the commodity, the more important the symptom. One can argue about the interpretation of such a phenomenon, but the statement that ancient long distance trade concerned only luxury goods is quite simply untrue.

Of course, if there is a trade that is geographically extensive, it does not follow that markets are intimately linked. The ancient world did not know formation of a market price through a mechanism of equivalent exchanges, nor did any other precapitalist society.[13] But it should be possible to set up a typology of economic contexts, articulated by periods and by regions, and to try to define each context by analyzing the connexion between local and interregional markets. Obviously, some connexions are less significant than others for this purpose. It is more interesting to find a Spanish oil amphora in Africa than in Rome, the focal point of the imperial *annona*; or a potsherd from central Tunisia in Algeria or in Tripolitania, where a virtually identical pottery was produced.

Pottery did not ordinarily travel alone. It was shipped together with necessities, first and foremost foodstuffs, that is, the products of agriculture. It was stowed in the interstices of the primary cargo, in piles between amphorae, as we observe in the shipwrecks, or alongside more perishable goods.

We will always be badly informed concerning the trade of these perishable goods, but given the nature of our sources, we have no better instrument to enable us to determine the variations in intensity and quality of exchanges, in a given period of time within a given area, than pottery – I mean of course sufficient pottery to enable us to establish typologies and stratigraphical seriations, from which alone we can derive chronological and quantitative data suitable for making comparisons. By turning sporadic observations into a close and systematic analysis of single contexts, we will produce something not definitive, but nevertheless different from economic history in the style of Heichelheim or Tenney Frank.

But it must be clear that the real economic importance of the phenomena which pottery points to can be judged only by relating them to all available sources: literary, epigraphical, numismatic, archaeological.

To a certain extent, ceramology can help us to understand not only the trade, but also the sphere of production. I do not say that we can move automatically from objects to relations of production, but the exhaustive study of a ware can shed light on the history of a manufacture, on the rise and decay of a certain productive unit based on a particular organisation of labour, and this can constitute a chapter of the history of a given social formation.

Therefore, I cannot agree with the affirmation that it might be worthwhile writing the history of pottery but not history through pottery (Goudineau (1980) 109). This is not a genuine alternative. The real issue is to determine the conditions and the limits within which it is possible to write both.

II

There is not space to give a comprehensive description of developments in the production of pottery in Italy in the Republic and Principate.[14] I simply state the fact that *grosso modo* in the period between approximately the second century BC and the second century AD Italian commodities achieved a hegemony in the provinces which they did not have before – when production was basically for self-consumption or for a local market – or after. How should these phenomena be interpreted? I confine myself to asking what are the implications of the growth of a substantial export industry for the economy of cities, and how is the decline of the industry to be explained.

Did there exist in the ancient world any 'industrial' towns? Scholars under the influence of Weber and his ideal-type of the consumer city reply in the negative. They do not deny that there were some urban manufactures geared to export, but argue that well-documented cases are few and can be regarded as exceptions and economically irrelevant.

As Finley acutely observed ((1973) 21–2), David Hume did not know a single passage in any ancient author where the growth of a city was ascribed to the establishment of a manufacture. But should we look to ancient authors for a statement of an economic kind? The most we can expect from our literary sources is a comment such as the elder Pliny's (*Nat. hist.* XXXV 160) about towns famous for their potteries (*in esculentis): et sic gentes nobilitantur et haec quoque per maria terrasque ultro citroque portantur, insignibus rotae officinis*. Of course, this is different from the assertion of a causal relationship between the establishment of a manufacture and the growth of a town, but Pliny's passage nevertheless deserves attention. The key-word is *nobilitantur*, and *nobilitas* is a moral, not an economic concept. Yet the term which Pliny opposes to it has a clear meaning. *Esculenta* are ordinary tableware. What Pliny wants to underline is that *nobilitas* comes to these towns not from aesthetically pleasing products, but, on the contrary, from those which are prosaic and utilitarian.

I do not intend to force the evidence and multiply the number of supposed industrial towns. But I wonder if the Weberian definition of the town as a consumption centre is universally applicable in antiquity.[15] Does it apply to the period under consideration, in which some Italian urban manufacturers employing slave labour exported on a large scale over land and sea to the same widely separated markets which received Italian agricultural goods?

Hopkins has remarked on the growth of trade between 200 BC and 200 AD as well as on the growth of towns.[16] But the development in his view was confined to the provinces. He pays little attention to the expansion of Italian production and exports. But before exporting *coloni*, Italy exported commodities, in the phase of imperialistic expansion.

Hopkins affirms that towns exchanged urban-produced commodities with the country: urban artisans in provincial towns absorbed a part of the total value of taxes *in loco*, as payment for their work of providing provincials with those commodities which they had to sell to pay taxes. This was undoubtedly a service rendered by town to country, and it does not easily fit Weber's typology. But Italian urban centres were also exporting to provincial markets, at least until the crisis of the second century AD. How easily does this fit Hopkins' model?

The villa, a seat of rural manufacture, was connected with the town in many ways. The men who created it came from the town. They lived partly in the town and partly in the country. There were of course absentee *domini*, but they were a degenerate phenomenon, in the view of the *scriptores rerum rusticarum*. The initial capital came from the town, either in a literal sense or in the sense that it derived from political activity, wars of conquest or civil wars. The means of production were an intrusion; the exceptionally large quantity of cheap slave labour was an alien imposition on 'natural' conditions of production in the countryside. The villa itself, the Varronian type at least, its architectonic structure, its building technique and its luxury decor had an urban model and origin (the *dominus*' residence is named by ancient authors the *pars urbana*).

The ancient town was not always, everywhere, merely a centre of consumption. In the period I am speaking of, there was a limited but significant rise in exchange value,[17] and one might wonder whether conspicuous citizens were always merely landowners or whether they did not play the role (more or less disguised or delegated) of the merchant, at least in respect of their own crops.

In a merely arithmetic calculation all these phenomena will appear as exceptions, since they are all limited to specific periods and regions. The region of the villa system is virtually restricted to the major valleys of central Italy, and the region of the Italian manufactures extends from Etruria to Campania. But what in Weber's schema can be an irrelevant exception, in another conceptual framework can appear a dominant exception (Carandini (1979b) 221). The productive capacity of this restricted epicentre is deduced from its area of influence, which the archaeologist can detect, with all due reserve, from pottery.

I do not mean that amphorae and tableware are strictly comparable or that the villa system and urban manufactures are the same thing. But it is evident that the growth of an intensive agriculture and a development in the production of commodities ran parallel.

There is another coincidence. By the second half of the second century AD all the villas we know from Etruria to Campania were either abandoned or had converted from intensive and specialized cultivation to extensive cultivation and pasturage; the farms were incorporated into imperial estates or allotted to tenants.[18]

Some scholars do not hesitate to call this a crisis. Crisis does not mean that Italian agriculture has come to an abrupt end, nor that all Italian landowners were in distress, nor that agriculture no longer created wealth. But the rural landscape changed in central Italy and undoubtedly the system of production changed too.

At the same time the containers which had carried agricultural products from central Italy faded out. The suggestion that amphorae might have been replaced by barrels is unconvincing. Amphorae were used all over the Roman world until late antiquity, whereas barrels, like water-mills, were known, but never employed on a large scale, except perhaps in continental Europe (cf. Panella (1981) 275 n.19). And contemporaneously Italian manufactures from central Italy disappeared from provincial markets. As regards pottery, the traditional explanation for the crisis is competition from the provinces: Italy lost her provincial markets because provincial potters had the advantage of proximity to the market and a cheaper product. There is something in this, but the factor of distance cannot be decisive. The Arretine branch-factories in Lyon, for instance, were closer to the *limes* centres than the Rutenian workshops in Montans or La Graufesenque. Recently another theory has been advanced: provincial potters conquered continental markets because Italian potters abandoned those markets following a collapse of the demand for their product in the internal market. The standard of living of Italians had risen so far that more luxurious tableware was preferred to the product of the kiln (Goudineau (1974) 109).

This explanation is hardly persuasive. Sigillata was still in demand in Italy, as archaeology proves, and it was imported into Italy from Gaul and the East, although the standard of the imported ware was no higher than that of Italian pottery. Meanwhile the workshops of the Po Valley produced and exported sigillata into the second century.

In my view, the crisis originated in the structure of the industry. In the golden age of Italian pottery, a large number of medium-sized and small workshops carried out the process of production with the use of a labour force of skilled slaves working together with a high degree of cooperation. The situation changed in the period of the late Italian potters. The moving of the workshops from Arezzo to a site near the port of Pisa coincided with a concentration of enterprises. But the poorer quality of the product betrays a much lower level of cooperation within the labour force, which is probably related to problems of supervision.

A comparison with the situation pertaining in agriculture is instructive. The slave system was successful in the medium-sized villas, in which the work of the slaves could be controlled and coordinated; but Columella, although a supporter of the use of slave labour in agriculture, issued warnings concerning the difficulty of overseeing slave workers on large estates.

Provincial systems of production, on the other hand, were more flexible and well-coordinated. Slaves were employed, but for secondary tasks. In fact, the slave mode of production, in its definitive form, was never exported from Italy to the provinces. An attempt was probably made, in connexion with the establishment of provincial branch-factories. That development, which implied that the producer was becoming merchant in respect of his own products in order to sell in distant markets, was the furthest that the ancients advanced on the path which leads to the birth of industrial capital. But the setting was alien to such a revolutionary development. Small peasants and free artisans were too closely integrated, and slaves were never the prevailing labour force. The Gallic system was a mixed one, marked by a close connexion between town and country, and a different development of forces of production.[19]

Dogmatic marxism was in error when it read the world of antiquity, without discrimination, as a slave society. Slavery was not ubiquitous nor uniform. In its economically most developed form, the slave system was surprisingly limited in space as well as in time. But many of us hold that in central Italy in the late Republic and early Empire the introduction of slave labour led to the most important case of pre-capitalistic development in history.

Development is not to be confused with take-off, and there was an eventual return to pre-existing economic forms. Yet an embryo is a living body whatever its prospect of birth. And to choose to overlook this fact is to make a moral or a political, not a scientific judgement.

APPENDIX: *A note on the status of potters*

We are too badly informed about Roman potters to know whether or not they were little Wedgwoods. Some of them wrote their names on their products and thus live on in the archaeological handbooks or in the 'Gutemberg galaxy' of the *Corpora inscriptionum*. We do not have significant monuments, funerary or other, that certainly concern potters. No potter is known to have held a public office or to have been a public benefactor. But the survival rate of inscriptions is notoriously low. Similarly, we can deduce little from the fact that no excavation has turned up a rich house belonging to a potter. Not a single house has been excavated in Arezzo, Pozzuoli, Pisa or Lezoux. And there is little chance of unearthing a well-preserved house in any of these sites in the future.

There is the possibility that behind potters bearing names which sound 'vieille noblesse' there are aristocrats either directly involved in the production or acting as patrons. There is a tantalizing letter in which Augustus calls his friend Maecenas *iaspis figulorum* (fg. 47 Malcovati). The text is suspect, and it would be rash to base an argument on it. We have no epigraphical record of a *collegium* of potters in Arezzo.

Potters' *collegia* are rarely attested even in Gaul; a single text (*CIL* XIII 8729) mentions a *mag* (*ister*) *fig* (*ulorum*). Sometimes potters belonged to *collegia* of *fabri*.

In the Gauls and in Germany we know some *negotiatores artis cretariae*, who traded other goods, like wine and clothes, at the same time. The only pottery merchant we know from Pozzuoli is a freedman, M. Modius Pamphilus, *figulus propolus* (Pucci (1977) 13). *Propolus* is rare. We would expect *propola*, which undoubtedly means a small retailer. I cannot say if *propolus* has a different meaning, nearer to the Greek *propoles*, a warrantor in commercial transactions (cf. Finley (1973) 203 n.63).

But in general the traders recorded above do not seem important enough personages to control production, transport the products and sell them in the provinces. They are more probably small local shopkeepers. On the other hand, the massive export to the military camps on the *limes* – which led to a high degree of standardization – has suggested to some scholars a coordinating traders company supplying the army.

[10]

Grain for Rome

by PETER GARNSEY

1. The needs of Rome

Grain was the basic food in classical antiquity, providing perhaps two-thirds to three-quarters of the calorific requirements of the average consumer. It was less important in the countryside than in the city, at any rate where the rural population was well placed to supplement cultivated cereals with meat, vegetables and the fruits of the forest, river and marsh. But in this paper we are interested in the grain consumption of residents of a city, Rome, roughly from the first century B C to the early third century A D. In this period Rome was inhabited by three-quarters of a million to a million people. Of the grains known to antiquity, wheat was preferred by the urban consumer, and it was wheat that was imported in quantity to Rome.[1]

Let us say that Rome had one million inhabitants, who required a minimum of 30 modii (200 kg) of grain or grain equivalent per head per annum (providing *c.*1745 calories per day), of which requirement 75 per cent was furnished by grain. Rome thus needed to import at least 150,000 tonnes of grain per annum.[2]

For the actual consumption rate of grain I opt for a figure in the region of 30 million modii or 200,000 tonnes.[3] This would reflect the higher standard of living enjoyed by at least the more prosperous section of the population: court, administration, soldiers, senators, equestrians and better-off members of the plebs. Some commentators would double this figure.[4] It is not inconceivable that import levels did occasionally reach 60 million modii. The quantity of grain dispatched from the major surplus-producing regions must have varied greatly in response to widely fluctuating harvest levels, and governments were no doubt alive to the advantages of putting in store the surplus from good years. (It does not follow that specific import targets were set on the basis of estimated grain consumption rates, available storage facilities and existing grain stocks.) But as a *consumption figure* 60 million modii,

400,000 tonnes, is wildly improbable, representing not much less than three times Rome's basic needs in grain. It does not help the case that each of those entitled to state grain apparently received it at the rate of 60 modii or 400 kg per annum (Sall. *Hist.* III. 48). No Roman government could have expected the million residents of Rome, or even the recipients themselves, to have consumed grain at the rate that is implied. The truth is that the figure of 60 million modii is the result of a misguided attempt to exploit or 'save' two ancient *testimonia*. The author of a fourth century Epitome (*de Caes.* I.6) gives a figure of 20 million modii of Egyptian wheat exported annually to Rome under Augustus, while Josephus (*B.J.* II 383, 386) has Agrippa II state that North African grain exports ran currently (in the mid-first century AD) at twice the level of those of Egypt and fed Rome for eight months in every year. Neither passage can bear much weight, and to combine the two is a quite unacceptable procedure.[5] I place no more credence in two other texts which fit my own results better. A scholiast on Lucan (I 319) would have us believe that in Pompey's day Romans consumed 80,000 modii of wheat a day (a little over 29 million modii, a little less than 200,000 tonnes a year). Again, the figure of 75,000 modii per day in the *Vita Severi* (XXIII; cf. VIII), if it stands for a total consumption rate, which is not how the author presents it,[6] gives a similar result for the reign of Septimus Severus, towards 27½ million modii, or somewhat over 189,000 tonnes. But the ancient evidence is too thin and of too poor quality to provide a test of the acceptability of my assumptions.

2. *Sources and status of imported grain*

From early in its history, whenever the return from its own territory was deficient, Rome tried to secure grain by river and sea from Etruria and Umbria on the one hand, and from Campania on the other. These areas (and doubtless also Latium) continued throughout Roman history to make a small but useful contribution to Rome's total grain requirement. Less accessible areas of Italy were not called upon to supply Rome except in emergencies. As the population of the city grew, additional sources of grain were found abroad, and in the first instance relatively close at hand. Grain from Sicily, Sardinia and North Africa reached Rome intermittently from the second half of the third century BC through sale or diplomatic gift, and later, as these areas came under Roman sway, regularly as tribute and rents from public land (cf. Cic. *imp. Cn. Pomp.* XXXIV). Contributions from other areas of the West, particularly Gaul, cannot be ruled out. But there is no reason to suppose that grain was *regularly* imported from the East before the annexation of Egypt in 31 BC.[7]

North Africa probably sent more grain to Rome than any other region under the republic, perhaps ca. 8 million *modii*, and increased, perhaps doubled, its contribution under Augustus and his immediate successors.[8] This is reconcilable with our conjectured total consumption rate in Rome. Other areas of the empire are known to have sent grain to Rome, including Gaul, the Chersonese, Spain and Cyprus (cf. Pliny *n.h.* XVIII 66–8). But ordinarily Rome was able to sustain itself largely on African, Sicilian, Sardinian and Italian grain from the West, and Egyptian grain from the East. From AD 330, when Egyptian grain was diverted to the newly founded Constantinople,[9] the city, now considerably smaller, leant on the traditional Western sources of supply.

The grain that found its way to Rome was, in the first place, state grain, coming in the form of taxes in kind from tribute-paying provinces, or of rents in kind from tenants of *ager publicus* or of imperial estates. The state also bought from merchants or landowners at source. Such purchases could be substantial. In the first century BC, in years when Sicily was producing around 30 million modii of wheat, it paid a tithe of 3 million modii, and at least in some periods, for example, for three years after the passage of the lex Terentia Cassia in 73 BC, sold a second tithe annually to the state. Verres was instructed to pay three sesterces per modius for this second 3 million modii, and, in addition, to buy up a further 800,000 modii at 3½ sesterces per modius (Cic. II *Verr.* III 136). Other grain undoubtedly came onto the market through the regular activity of private merchants, whether from Sicily or other grain-exporting provinces, Egypt included. In the early Empire private grain merchants at Puteoli were able to acquire and market grain from Alexandria in considerable quantities (*A.E.* 1972, 86).[10]

The amount of imported grain produced on land owned directly by the state increased measurably under the Principate, as emperors built up their holdings of grain-bearing land in the surplus-producing regions of the empire. On an imperial estate in N. Africa, an exaction of one-third of the crop is attested, representing presumably rent plus tax (though the texts also allude to rates of one-eighth and one-fifth; *C.I.L.* VIII 25902 I 25ff., *cf.* II 8; 20210). Private estates in Africa continued to contribute tax grain, though whether at the rate of a tithe or a quarter or something in between is unclear. I hold, against a commonly accepted view,[11] that the Roman state continued to draw tax grain, as well as a slowly growing volume of rent grain, from Sicily in the post-Caesarian and early imperial period. State purchases of grain, for the city of Rome as distinct from for local or military use, continued under the Empire also. If as some scholars think the state increasingly took upon itself direct control of the food supply of Rome, leaving less and less scope for private enterprise, then buying and requisitioning may have been extensively resorted to.

3. *Middlemen*[12]

Under the Republic the state sold contracts for collection of tax grain and rent grain and for its transport to Rome or to the army.[13] To the extent that contracts for collection and transport were sold to the same people, or more accurately to the same companies or *societates*, tax-collectors doubled up as shipowners. There is nothing surprising about this. The contractors who supplied the armies overseas – who are among the first *publicani* to appear in the historical record – are the likely owners of the transporting vessels. This is easily believed, for example, in the case of the two men, who having with seventeen others taken a contract for supplying the Spanish armies, demanded insurance money from the state for some dilapidated ships carrying cargo without value, which had been scuttled en route (Livy XXIII 48.5ff., 215 BC). The culprits were apparently of equestrian status and therefore not affected by the recently passed lex Claudia barring senators from the ownership of merchant ships of any size.[14]

Again, tax-collectors were also 'wholesale traders', insofar as they disposed of such stocks of grain as they were able to collect over and above the amount they had contracted to deliver to the state authorities for civilian or military consumption. The Asian *publicani* and those of the provinces organized by Pompey had substantial stocks to sell, if as seems likely the state did not as a rule draw on the grain of the East except for the provisioning of such armies as were stationed there.

The *publicani* made substantial profits. The original bid might occasionally have been over-optimistic in respect of the amount of grain that would come in as tithe. But the *publicani* are unlikely to have found themselves short very often. The attempted renegotiation of the Asian contract in 61 BC which was backed by Crassus is almost unique in the historical record (Cic. *Att.* I 17.9; cf. Livy XXXIX 44.7ff.). Moreover, the connivance of the governor, who was often under obligation to the *publicani* if not actually in league with them, must have enabled them frequently to take more of the harvest than was permitted them by the law.

The scale of the profits made in the province of Asia and in other provinces in the region may be inferred from Caesar's substitution of a fixed payment for the tithe, and his reduction of the total tax liability of the Asian province by *one-third*, presumably without loss to the state (App. *B.C.* V 4; Dio XLII 6.3).

The Asian *publicani* were rich Romans and Italians of equestrian rank, inevitably, as the contract for the Asian tithe was sold at Rome, for five years, and involved the pledging as security of land worth millions of sesterces by the successful bidders. In contrast, the Sicilian tithe was sold by the governor in Sicily, city by city. This provided an opening for local men of relatively limited resources. Romans were not excluded. We know of an equestrian based in Syracuse, Minucius Rufus, whose bid for the *decumae* of *Leontini*, situated in the richest grain-producing area of Sicily, was foiled by the intrigues of the governor Verres (Cic. *II Verr.* II 75). Rufus was one of a sizeable group of Romans, a number of them of equestrian status, and Italians, active in Sicily. Some were, *inter alia*, owners or renters of land. *Publicani*, collectors for example of the *portoria*, customs, or of the *scriptura*, pasture tax, are sometimes referred to by Cicero. We also meet a grain exporter in the person of C. Avianius Flaccus, a friend of Cicero from Puteoli (Cic. *ad Fam.* XIII 75).[15] Cicero in the letter asks a governor of Sicily to grant Flaccus favours in respect of both the port of export and the time. He does not omit to mention that Pompey as *curator annonae* had made similar concessions to Flaccus over a three year period, again at his request. The grain trade is not specifically mentioned elsewhere in Cicero. This is not necessarily significant, just as Cicero's silence on the subject of the banking activities of Italians in Sicily is not significant.[16] Be that as it may, the exceptional profits available to Italians in Asia were clearly not matched by those that could be derived from tax-collection in Sicily and the trade in Sicilian grain.

To sum up: although the class of businessmen of which we are talking does not come into sharp focus, their place in Roman, Italian and to some extent provincial society, and the range of their economic activities, can be plausibly reconstructed. Some were equestrians and municipal aristocrats, and they had close links with members of the senatorial aristocracy. They included, on the one hand, tax-collectors and cultivators (notably in North Africa, Sicily and Campania) who secured grain in large quantity, and on the other hand, investors, shippers and traders who were involved in disposing of it profitably. (But these two broad categories were not mutually exclusive.)

The destiny under the Principate of this group, and in particular the *publicani*, is a matter of considerable interest. The imperial *publicani* are a shadowy group. The patchiness of the sources is in some degree responsible for this. But an administrative development is also relevant. It seems clear that the services of *publicani* as collectors of the revenues were gradually dispensed with. By the second century AD tax-grain was normally paid over by producers and proprietors to city-magistrates or liturgists acting under the general supervision of imperial officials. Some would date this development considerably earlier. Anyway, this system was already established in its essentials in late Republican times, not only in provinces like Gaul and Spain where *publicani* were apparently never employed, but also in the Asian provinces, from the time (also in the late Republic) that *publicani* began to make *pactiones* with the cities for the payment of agreed amounts (e.g. Cic. *Att.* V 13.1). Caesar abandoned the use of *publicani* in Asia, and Augustus followed suit in Egypt. Aside from a Tiberian reference in Tacitus (*Ann.* IV 6), there is evidence for the survival of *publicani* as collectors of tribute (with the cooperation of the cities) only in North Africa (*I.L.S.* 901) in the first century AD, although they appear to have collected rent in kind on imperial estates in Sicily (*I.L.S.* 7193 = *C.I.L.* III 14195,[4] AD 103–4).

The change in the tax system from Republic to Empire had very serious implications for the *publicani*, since the tax contracts played a key role in the creation of their wealth. It must be very doubtful whether there was a group of comparable means and influence among the middlemen involved in supplying Rome with grain under the Principate.

One possibility to be explored is that the *navicularii* and *negotiatiores* known from sources for the imperial period were in some way successors of the *publicani* of the late Republic. Certainly, to the extent that the *publicani* of the Principate continued to collect grain stocks, they may be supposed to have sustained an interest in the subsidiary enterprises of wholesale trading and shipping.

However, to pin down the *navicularii* and *negotiatores* is itself a major undertaking, even if we confine our attention to those in whom emperors were particularly interested, namely, those engaged in the service of the *annona*.[17] Claudius' reign was marked by food shortages, and he is the first emperor known to have offered inducements to shipbuilders and shipowners. Anyone who had a ship capable of holding 10,000 modii, a little under 70 tons of wheat, and was prepared to involve it in provisioning the city with grain for 6 years, could gain exemption from the lex Papia Poppaea (in the case of Roman citizens),

Roman citizenship (in the case of Latins) or the *Ius III liberorum* (in the case of women).[18] About a century later the Antonine jurist Scaevola, pointing apparently to a similar measure of later date, stated that to qualify for exemptions, one had to own a ship with a capacity of 50,000 modii of wheat, or several (five?) ships of 10,000 modii each. What is more, the privilege he mentioned was the substantial one of exemption from public liturgies (*Dig.* L 5.3). Immunity from public liturgies (and we might as well say from *other* public liturgies) was available to *navicularii* at least from Hadrian's time (*Dig.* L. 6.6.5). The first attested attempts to limit the privilege, evidently greatly valued, are also Hadrianic. For Hadrian, immunity was available to those who invested 'the greater part' of their resources in the enterprise, and did not respond to financial success by reducing the proportion of their goods invested (*Dig.* L 6.6.8). His successor Pius warned against 'phantom' *navicularii* merely interested in escaping liturgies (*Dig.* L 6.6.9), and Marcus and Verus against those who claimed immunity without either launching their ships or investing most ('to pleon meros') of their wealth in the enterprise (*Dig.* L 6.6.6). Scaevola, a near contemporary, insists that the newly constructed ships must actually sail or others be put in their place (*Dig.* L 5.3).

This is the moment to bring up a terminological problem raised by the exemption texts, reflected in the other primary sources, and relevant ultimately to the identity of these middlemen and the precise nature of their activities.[19] Callistratus, the Severan jurist who has preserved most of the relevant material, indicates that immunity was available to *negotiatores* as well as *navicularii*. One wonders how firm a distinction existed in his mind between the two groups, who, respectively, 'annonam urbis adiuvant' and 'annonae urbis serviunt' (*Dig.* L 6.6.3) When the Divi Fratres (Marcus and Verus) write in a rescript, quoted in Greek, of *naukleriai* and *emporia* (which is expanded as 'ton siton kai elaion emporeuomenon eis ten agoran tou demou tou Rhomaikou), there is no implication that they contemplated alternative channels of investment (*Dig.* L 6.6.6). Hadrian, moreover, appears to conflate the two in a letter of which Callistratus gives us the substance (rather than, I think, the *ipsissima verba*) (*Dig.* L 6.6.8). No doubt *negotiatores* who were not *navicularii* did enter into contracts with the state, and if their services were valued sufficiently highly, they were rewarded with special privileges. But the legal texts spell out only the extent of the services by which *navicularii* may earn *immunitas*. The implication is that in official circles shipping and trade were considered to be interconnected, and in such a way that the latter could be virtually subsumed under the former for all intents and purposes.

Who, then, were the *navicularii* – and the *negotiatores*? The corn traders (those involved in the provisioning of Rome) who come into the light of day in the period of the Principate are drawn from the freedman class and the municipal aristocracy of Ostia, itself permeated by descendants of successful freedmen.[20] In addition, individual inscriptions show groups of unnamed grain *negotiatores* or *mercatores* participating in corporate activities, raising a temple in Rome (*C.I.L.* VI 814) or commemorating a prefect of the corn supply (*C.I.L.* IV 1620 = *I.L.S.* 1342). The organization of *mercatores frumentarii* and of others concerned with the grain supply of Rome into *corpora*, companies, registered by the state, is a second century development, at least in Ostia, and beneficial to both sides.

The *navicularii* of the inscriptions are drawn, it would seem, from this same 'middle-class' of freedmen and their descendants, foreigners, and the arriviste sector of the leadership of port cities. M. Frontonius Euporus and L. Secundus Eleuther, two *navicularii* of Arles (the only two whose names are known) have been classified predictably as freedmen serving *operae* for local aristocrats whose landed investments provided the financial basis of their enterprises.[21] No doubt there were *navicularii* who belong to this category. But we note that we are dealing here with two men who were, among other things, Augustales, one of Arles, the other of Aix, that is to say, members of a wealthy and influential freedman elite whose benefactions and other services to a city might (in due course) be expected to win for any sons membership of the local aristocracy. There is no need to see them as front men for established landowning gentry.[22] It can indeed be assumed that they were landowners themselves. In short, I see no reason why these self-styled *navicularii* should not be taken at face-value as shipowners rather than, for example, dependent shipcaptains. Whether Euporus and Eleuther were involved in supplying either Rome or the Rhine armies (the presence of so many corporations of shipowners, sailors and traders on the North-South river route in Gaul can hardly be fortuitous) is unknown. The chances are that they were, presumably as members of the five *corpora naviculariorum* of Arles known from the inscriptions of Arles and Beirut (*C.I.L.* XII 672; III 14165^8). But there were clearly many shipowners to whom the legal texts do not relate, since they did not meet the requirements laid down for *immunitas*.

Even so, those texts do not exclude people of their social background.

The *navicularii* whom they consider for *immunitas* are recruited from the whole class of *possessores* below senatorial rank. Senators could not claim public *vacatio*, Scaevola reminds us, because technically by the lex Iulia they were not permitted to own ships. The *navicularii* were men (and women) of means who chose to invest some of their resources in shipping, rather than be drawn into the performance of other more onerous, inconvenient or expensive liturgies. They were avoiding among other things, according to the Severan jurist Paulus (*Dig.* L 3.9), incorporation in the city councils, whose members provided the core of the liturgical class. They were, furthermore, landowners. This is not directly attested before the fourth century, but should be self-evident.[23]

4. The state and private enterprise[24]

Under the Republic, the interest of the state authorities in grain imports to the capital appears to have been normally limited to the selling of contracts for the collection and transport to Rome (and to the armies) of tax-grain and rent-grain. The grain imported in this way may be supposed to have been sufficient for the government's own needs, and for the distribution to qualified Romans of subsidized and later free grain, but insufficient for the population of the capital as a whole. Only in emergencies was the government prompted to further action, and such action, most obviously the purchasing of additional supplies of grain, was usually ad hoc and not designed to ward off future crises. Even the lex Terentia Cassia of 73 BC may have been merely a temporary measure requiring Verres, but not as far as we know other governors of Sicily, to purchase a second tithe annually. Even Pompey, who in 57 BC was given special authority as *curator annonae* to buy up grain, does not appear to have made lasting changes in the system of supplying the capital. Moreover, we hear virtually nothing in the sources of attempts to supervise or regiment shippers and merchants or to protect the consumer against unfair profiteering. The incident of 189 BC involving the fining of traders by aediles for speculating in grain is unique in the historical record (Livy XXXVIII 35.5). The lex Iulia de annona (*Dig.* XLVIII 12), which among other things made it a criminal offence punishable by a fine to hold up the flow of grain to Rome or through any other ruse to force up the price of grain, might in principle go back to Caesar and indeed to his consulship in 59 BC. It is more likely to be Augustan; at any rate, if it was enacted in 59, there is every sign that it was not enforced in the years immediately following, when grain prices fluctuated wildly, bringing not only material profits (to traders) but also political rewards (to Pompey).[25] There is the possibility that the state periodically intervened in the market to dispose of surplus stocks of grain, at market or below market prices, but we hear nothing of this practice.

There was a change of direction under the Principate. Emperors, whatever they themselves thought of the *frumentatio* (cf. Suet. *Aug.* XLII 3), could not afford to neglect the corn-supply. The *praefectus annonae*, an imperial appointee, was a symbol of their public commitment to it. Egypt was now sending substantial amounts of grain, and in general, because of the efforts of emperors, grain was coming in through taxes in kind, rents in kind, requisition and purchase, in sufficient quantity to restrict severely the scope of private profit. The lex Iulia de annona could be invoked against speculators.

There is, however, much room for disagreement about the extent of state intervention and the scope left for private enterprise. First, our vision of the size of the city and the total volume of grain imports will colour our interpretation. It is, I believe, no coincidence that the severest critic of the interventionist position believes that Rome consumed annually about 60 million modii of grain, that is, more than double the highest estimate of the amount of state-owned and -purchased grain entering the city (Casson (1980)). Second, the evidence for the dealings of the state authorities with traders and the market is very fragmentary and bound to give rise to widely contrasting views.[26] For some, the few examples of government intervention evoke a regular pattern of behaviour, for others they are completely exceptional and indeed establish the case for free commerce. Third, individual texts are ambiguous and incomplete. Under Trajan, says Pliny, the fiscus did not requisition, it purchased (*Pan.* XXIX). But at market or below market rates? Were state purchases advantageous to traders or not? Does a whole pattern of supplementary acquisition of grain (by requisition or purchase) underly this text? Again, a sentence in Tacitus suggests that the *praefectus annonae* was 'expected' to make a profit: Faenius Rufus won popularity with the people because he neglected to do so (Tac. *Ann.* XIV 50.5). Are we to infer from this that such profits were an offshoot of the prefect's function (for which there is no other evidence) of interfering in the market in the cause of price-stability, typically by releasing surplus state grain?[27]

I reconstruct, speculatively, as follows. Firstly, the shipowners on whom the government had always relied to bring in the grain remained free agents. They did not become public employees performing compulsory services as members of self-perpetuating corporations with closed funds until the late third and early fourth centuries. The five *corpora* of *navicularii* of Arles, known from the inscription of AD 201 who were in dispute with the *mensores* were fully aware that they were bound only by the terms of their contracts to serve the *annona*, and that their interests were not sunk in the interests of the Roman state (*C.I.L.* III 14165^{8}).

Secondly, the steady growth of *imperial* grain production reduced the amount of grain available to private merchants and so gradually eroded their position. What is in doubt is the rate of change. I do not accept the argument of Rickman that the decline was slower than has been thought because of a change from taxes in kind to money taxes, because I believe such a change in the tax system of Sicily and N. Africa to be illusory. In addition I set Rome's total grain consumption lower than he does, at around 30 million modii; my estimate of the amount of grain needed for the city over and above that originating on imperial estates is correspondingly lower. Nevertheless Rickman is right to assert that there was considerable room for activity by private merchants at least in the first century of the Empire.

Thirdly, those *negotiatores* with whom the government made contracts to supply grain to the state, and to whom it offered immunity from public liturgies (as the juristic writings of the Principate attest), were no more state functionaries than were the *navicularii*, with whom they overlapped. They were bound to the performance of their contract, but that is all. There is no need to suggest that such contracts were weighted against the traders, that for example the state regularly imposed a below-market price for grain sold to the *annona*.[28] The top echelon of *negotiatores*, those who are prominent in the inscriptions, were prosperous, and presumably this owes something to their dealings with government officials, to whom they frequently express gratitude. The impression derived from the legal and historical sources is consistent with this picture: the Roman authorities, obsessed with problems of supply, strove to increase the number of shippers performing state service by contract by offering inducements in the form of privileges and favourable terms, rather than by exacting compulsory services. That Rome was fed as a result of the operation of something less than *libero commercio* or *laisser faire, laisser passer*,[29] is neither here nor there. But talk of *dirigisme*, though not in the same way anachronistic, is also inappropriate.

APPENDIX: *The upper classes, agents, and trade*

No one will seriously entertain the proposition that men of status in Roman and provincial society travelled with the produce of their estates as ship-captains or merchants and sold it on the docks or in the market place. Yet many scholars accept that the freedmen, slaves and foreigners who appear to dominate these relatively specialized and low status occupations were necessarily front-men or agents for a class of investors in trade consisting of wealthy landowners from not only the municipal aristocracy and equestrian order, but also from the senatorial class.[30]

The thesis is difficult to establish for several reasons. In the first place, the legal texts which attest the use of slaves by masters, sons by fathers, and freedmen owing services (*operae*) by ex-masters in a wide variety of commercial undertakings, leave the social status of the principals in complete obscurity. The epigraphical evidence poses a similar problem, in that it frequently presents us with a businessman of freedman status without any reference to a patron. In such cases it seems to me pure speculation to insist, first, that behind him must have lurked a patron controlling his operation and pocketing the lion's share of the profits, and second, that that putative patron was necessarily of high social standing.

I find it more plausible to suppose that, for example, M. Frontonius Euporus, *navicularius* and Augustalis of Arles (*C.I.L.* XII 982), or C. Novius Eunus, dealer in grain and other foodstuffs at Puteoli (*A.E.* 1972, 86), were exercising at least de facto independence. The juristic evidence points not simply to an 'agentization' of commerce and trade, but also to the high degree of independence that freedmen and even slaves in business could secure (Garnsey (1981)). And if we must look for patrons and masters behind freedmen and slaves in business, there is no better place to start than with a 'middle-class' of investors and commerçants consisting of relatively successful and well-off freedmen and their freeborn descendants, and aliens, and (an overlapping group) arriviste politicians and civic leaders from port cities where trade played a significant role in economic life.

In any case, neither juristic nor any other kind of evidence compels us to believe that upper-class Romans regularly invested in trade through their dependents, and the evidence that they did so is insubstantial. This is one area, it may be suggested, where the prosopographical approach is never likely to bring tangible results (in contrast perhaps with late

Republican politics). How often, we may ask, can a link between any particular freedman (or slave) and a putative aristocratic patron be firmly established, not to mention the nature of their economic relationship, and indeed the precise nature of the 'dependant's' activities? My conjecture is that at least in the case of grain, trade touched a limited number of upper-class Romans, and it was anyway ancillary to the production of grain on their estates and, in the case of equestrians, the collection and transport of grain owned by or owing to the state by contract.

[11]

Urban elites and business in the Greek part of the Roman Empire

by H. W. PLEKET

In the lively debate provoked by Moses Finley's *The Ancient Economy* no consensus has been reached on the nature of economic life in antiquity. In particular, while none deny the primacy of agriculture, the place of manufacture and commerce – or 'business' – is vigorously disputed.

One characteristic of the debate has been the regular recourse to historical comparison. Finley's polemic is directed in the first place at Rostovtzeff's assumption that the difference between ancient and modern economies was quantitative rather than qualitative.[1] In addition, his assertion of 'the low status of the professional traders and manufacturers throughout Roman history'[2] is built at least in part on a contrast between the imperial and urban elites of antiquity and the commercial bourgeoisie of the Italian and Flemish city-Republics of the late middle ages and early modern period – who 'nestled into town government'.[3]

John d'Arms' critique (1977) (1981) of Finley leans on a comparison of the mentalities of the Roman imperial nobility and the French nobility of the eighteenth century. His observation that in the French case a contempt for 'business' coexisted with a commercial bourgeoisie encouraged him to believe that in the Roman Empire similar negative views were compatible with the existence of a commercial bourgeoisie in the localities and at least indirect involvement in trade at the highest level of Roman society.

Paul Veyne, for whom the great break lies in the nineteenth century, which experienced 'a phenomenon of growth of quite unprecedented dimensions',[4] attacks the assumption that the absence of a commercial bourgeoisie is necessarily a sign that business was of marginal significance in Rome in comparison with other pre-industrial societies. In his view – and I accept his argument – it points to a difference in the organization of society, to a lack of correspondence between social classes and economic activities, more precisely to the permanent availability of slaves and free dependents (freedmen in particular) for the execution of commercial enterprises (Veyne (1979) espec. 277–8), rather than to a fundamental difference in the dimensions of the non-agrarian sector. Both Veyne and d'Arms seem to imply that the reductionists/ 'primitivists' may have made pre-modern Western Europe too modern and antiquity too primitive.

The attempt to make a meaningful comparison of the size of the 'non-agricultural sector' in ancient and later pre-industrial societies is vitiated by the lack of quantitative data for (at least) the former. It is true that Jones considered that late imperial data are adequate to establish a precise ratio (95 per cent: 5 per cent) between the contribution of agricultural and non-agricultural enterprise to the state revenues and the wealth of the Empire. But the argument is weak, resting as it does on extremely scanty evidence, returns for the 'trade tax' (*collatio lustralis*, chrysargyron) from Edessa and for the land tax from two Egyptian cities (Jones (1964) 465). One of the many objections that could be raised is that the tax was bypassed by small men through the operation of *patrocinium*,[5] and by the landed elite through what I think was the common practice of investing in business through the intermediary of slaves, freedmen and perhaps other free dependents. Urban aristocrats did not themselves act as *negotiatores* (cf. *C. Th.* XIII 1.4 A D 362), but if they did business through dependents, and moreover presented this as trade in the products of their own estates, they could easily escape the chrysargyron.[6]

Meanwhile the impropriety of arguing back from Late Empire to Principate on the basis of such evidence needs no stress. One consideration that must be borne in mind is that the chrysargyron operated precisely in a period in which the number and prosperity of urban craftsmen and traders was seriously reduced.

Finally, even if we were attracted by Jones' argument, we would still need comparable material from other societies to produce a case for the relatively small size of the business sector in the Roman Empire.

The most interesting method currently used to assess the level of trade and commerce in the Roman Empire is that of the model, as employed by Keith Hopkins. Particularly noteworthy is his argument that, in order to be able to continue paying taxes in money, the tax-exporting provinces (especially Asia Minor and Greece) must have exported goods and products to the tax-receiving areas (Italy and frontier provinces).[7] In this way he establishes a link between taxation and the growth of long-distance trade.

Though Hopkins perhaps underestimated the amount of tax levied in kind under the Principate, I agree that some coinage must have been earned back, for example, by the sale of requisitioned grain to the army and the export of textiles, marble[8] and similar luxuries. Hopkins also posits an important interregional trade in staple foods like corn (to which may be added wine and oil) in addition to the transport of tax-corn, a huge redistributive operation. In the end, however, he sticks to the overall picture painted by Sombart, Weber and Finley:[9] the monetary commercial economy is merely a thin veneer spread over a large subsistence economy; the ancient city was not a Hanse-city, a city which produced wealth by exporting its articles, but remained a consumer city, one which served its own elite who paid for whatever goods they required with the surplus taken from the peasants in the form of rents. Hopkins apparently does not believe that we can even begin to close the gap between Roman cities and medieval and post-medieval European cities. On that matter I have three points:

1. It is perhaps not correct that the (post-) medieval cities in general were characterized by the regular opposition of 'commercial burghers' and 'rural aristocracy';[10] this may be valid for the period of the *rise* of the medieval cities but not necessarily for the period of full-grown urbanism; and it is that which should be compared with the situation in the Roman Empire.

2. It is not correct to assume that all medieval and post-medieval cities were invariably 'producer-cities' on the Hanseatic model.

3. There may be room for a fruitful comparison between (a-typical) Hanse-cities and (a-typical) large harbour-cities in the Roman Empire.

Useful as the comparative approach may be, in the end the relative unimportance of trade is supposed to be shown by the absence of a prestigious class of urban merchants, a bourgeoisie. In this respect Hopkins joins Finley and the Weberian ranks are closed again. As I said above, the absence of an urban bourgeoisie does not necessarily reflect the backwardness of trade and manufacture, but rather a different organization of society, a different social structure. In other words, with Paul Veyne I believe it to be not improbable that the level of business did not differ decisively as between Roman and later societies, and that the contribution to this branch of the economy by the Roman urban aristocracy, largely indirectly through the intermediary of middlemen (slaves, freedmen and other dependent figures), was equivalent to that of the bourgeoisie of later periods.[11]

I believe that one cannot emphasize enough the fundamental *social* (rather than economic) difference between, on the one hand, a bourgeoisie directly engaged in business, and on the other, an urban and agricultural elite investing in business and entrusting their interests to agents.[12] In the Greek East it is by no means easy to find examples of *direct* involvement of members of the urban elite in business; by 'direct' I mean that they are referred to as businessmen by themselves or by others. Veyne was not the first to misread the Erastus inscription (*Syll.*[3] 838) as attesting 'a self-confessed professional trader turned local notable'.[13] Lucius Erastus often sailed the seas, was useful to his city and specialized in transporting Roman dignitaries – Hadrian included. As a result of all this 'he wants to become a member of the council'. Hadrian intervenes for him and writes that he is willing to pay the entry fee. The correct interpretation is exactly the opposite of Veyne's. The Ephesian council members were not prepared to accept a *naukleros* (shipper) in the council, not even among the *inferiores* (as opposed to *primores*) who presumably existed in the council of that city as in the council of nearby Clazomenae in Hadrian's day.[14]

I know of only one example from Asia Minor in which a person calls himself a *naukleros* and *bouleutes*: a shipper and councillor. It is a certain Telesphorus, son of Telesphorus, whose sarcophagus was found in Nicomedia.[15] Since he mentions no offices he presumably belonged to the *inferiores* (or *pedarii*); L. Robert has recently collected and discussed the impressive epigraphic evidence concerning Nicomedian shippers, which shows that they transported their goods all over the oikoumene.[16] But Robert largely ignores the question of their social status or the broader problem of the importance of trade in the Roman Empire. There is no parallel in these texts to Telesphorus' council membership. One Nicomedian trader (*emporos*), Asklepiades, was also honorary citizen of the Phrygian city of Aezani, and did business in Tomis where he buried his brother and business partner. This was, as Robert says, a big businessman, whose interests extended from S. Phrygia to the Euxine. Yet he did not belong to the urban bouleutic class, not even to the lower echelon within that class. Nicomedia is known to have had a junior and senior association of *naukleroi* which, like all ancient professional organizations, was in the habit of electing top local politicians as patron. But since such patrons do not seem to have been active in the trade in question, and not to have been office-holders within the association, they do not help us to determine the social status of members.[17]

In the same article, Robert has also drawn attention to a passage in the 38th speech of Dio of Prusa (§ 32). Dio emphasizes the vital importance of Nicomedian sea-trade for neighbouring Nicaea; Nicomedia lets Nicaea share in the goods transported by sea. The passage unfortunately is corrupt. The argument seems to be that Nicaea owes its share in imported goods partly to Nicomedian favour. Dio adds in parenthesis that 'it is the city of Nicomedia which should grant favours officially and not certain people privately'. Robert seems to mistranslate; 'one should be grateful to the city for all this, and not to some private individuals', and suggests that the latter were a pressure-group of Nicomedian shippers who claimed the gratitude of the Nicaeans. Whatever the truth of the matter is, Dio obviously defends the views of the city, or, more realistically, those of the elite to which he himself belongs, according to whom the criticisms of a number of shippers were not to be tolerated. The latter apparently claimed a voice of some importance in urban life but were rebuffed. In other words, Telesphorus was no match for the urban elite.

Ruggini[18] recently suggested that a Chian inscription offered an example of an important politician, a *nauarchos* ('admiral'), who was simultaneously president of the association of 'merchants in the agora' (*archonta ton kata ten agoran*) and consequently himself involved in their business. The man was honoured by the '*naukleroi* and *ergastai* (shopkeepers, petty-traders) in the harbour-area'. But L. Robert saw that this man was president not of the agora-merchants but of the urban magistrates in charge of the agora.[19] No big businessman, then, but another top politician, admiral and chief of the market-officials, honoured as patron precisely because of his politico-military functions; as *nauarchos* he was the man to protect the *naukleroi* against pirates.

On Nicomedia, we may echo the judgment of Liebeschuetz ((1972) 73–83) in connection with fourth century Antioch, that it lacked a politically and socially important merchant class. But we should elaborate the comparison. In Antioch it was not unusual for *councillors* to own ships (Liebeschuetz (1972) 46, 75, 165). They were among the landed and shipowning elite on whom the transport of tribute-corn to Constantinople was imposed. If imperial pressure for the fulfilment of this liturgy was continuous, this does not reflect any shortage of ships but rather a reluctance to contribute ships. Investment in ships by the elite was common all over the Greek world. Dio of Prusa writes that the urban rich supported themselves by investment in usury, leasing of tenements, slaves and ships (cf. Brunt (1972), 10). The astrologist Ptolemaius lists among profit-making activities building, agriculture and shipowning plus trading (*naukleria*).[20] Lucian describes the situation of a man owning five ships, and Rougé, who admittedly too easily turns *pragmateutai/oikonomoi* into *commercial* agents, this time correctly writes that the passage would have been incomprehensible 'if in the period in which he was writing the East had not known enterprises of maritime transport where individuals had several ships'.[21] In all these passages there is no special pleading; on the contrary, owning ships is represented as normal for the rich. I do not understand why Liebeschuetz ((1972), 83), after pointing out that shipowning among councillors was not unusual, goes on to write that 'it is an indication of the low development of trade under the later Empire that the provisioning of the capital cities could not be imposed on a professional merchant class'. In my view the absence of such a class is significant for the *organization* of trade, not its dimensions. For the economic historian it is unimportant whether, let us say, 500 Antiochean ships were the property of a landowning aristocracy of between 100 and 500 men, or of a small professional merchant bourgeoisie. For the social historian, on the other hand, it is highly relevant. Investing in trade was normal for an aristocrat; to be a trader, humiliating. In this connexion Veyne's 'Gelegenheitshandel' (cf. above note 12) perhaps does not convey the right message. The term is acceptable in so far as it suggests that landowning was the economic basis which guaranteed stability, whereas trade was derivative; it is unacceptable to the extent that it implies that landowners dabbled in trade only occasionally, as a sideline. A sideline it was, but one with structural significance, as it were – and there were other sidelines too.

Lucian's little dialogue *The Ship* provides another interesting detail. Adeimantus, who dreams about possessing a large freighter, believes he would gain a handsome profit from investing in a merchant-vessel. There is no reason to take his 'twelve Attic talents' literally, but the basic assumption is that a large freighter is a wealth-generating possession: 'what a happy life I should have had if of a sudden some god had made the ship mine: I would have helped my friends, and sailed in her myself sometimes, and sometimes sent my slaves' (*Navigium* 13). He proceeds, not unexpectedly, to describe the conspicuous consumption he dreams of: a house near the Stoa Poikile, slaves, clothes, carriages and horses.

Adeimantus has 'Peiraeus-fever' and loves the idea of sailing his own ship. There is something of a parallel from the world of agriculture in the attitude of Antoninus Pius, who took a hand in the work of the farm for recreation (Fronto, *ad M. Caes.* IV 6.1).[22] Neither would have appreciated the label of *naukleros* or *georgos* respectively. Adeimantus prayed to Hermes 'Kerdôos' (*Navigium* 18), but there is a vast social distance between him and the *naukleros* who in a Thasian text is called *archikerdemporos* the chief profit-making merchant, worshipping Hermes

'Kerdemporos'.[23] The shipowning urban elite surely did business, but equally surely was not 'in business'. Adeimantus had slaves 'in business'; and he was not alone.

In Antioch Libanius' friend Lollianus used slave agents to operate his ship (Liebeschuetz (1972) 46 n.3). Plutarch (*de liberis educandis* VII) in an important but neglected passage unmarked by special pleading states in a 'matter-of-fact' way that people turn their first-rate slaves into farmers, *naukleroi, emporoi,* estate-managers and bankers.[24] Of course not all recorded *naukleroi* in fact were slaves. The Nicomedian *naukleroi* were free. However, we should not ignore the possibility of links with the landowning aristocracy. Veyne[25] drew attention to a passage in the *Philogelos,* a book full of jokes about the 'ideal-type' of the pedantic scholar, the professor. In § 50 the joke lies in the professor's having a *naukleros* as a debtor.[26] It was presumably common for landowning intellectuals (and scholars were generally members of the landowning upper-class) and landowners in general to have *naukleroi* among their debtors. In the Pergamene magnate L. Cuspius Pactumeius Rufinus, consul in AD 142, who is said to have asked the oracle in Didyma how to exact an oath 'from his own *naukleros*', we have a wealthy landowner using either a slave or a debtor as *naukleros.* L. Robert was right to conclude that he had 'an enterprise of maritime commerce'.[27] One professor who was also an extremely wealthy estate-owner was the sophist Damianus, said by Philostratus to have had a private harbour built near his coastal estate for the use of merchant-vessels.[28] If there is an implication that in Asia Minor the private harbour was exceptional, the situation may have been different elsewhere. In Tripolitania archaeology has shown that large coastal villages seem to have had their own harbours.[29] At any rate Philostratus does not imply that it was unusual for a landowner to have been involved in the shipping of the products of his own estates. He records that the wealthy father of a sophist from Byzantium owned *thalattourgoi oiketai,* ('slaves earning their livelihood from the sea') (*V.S.* p. 103 (Loeb)). Did they function as agents of their well-to-do owner, or were they involved in fishing? My conclusion is that behind the many *naukleroi* who are on record in inscriptions may have lain wealthy members of the urban elite who leased ships to *naukleroi,*[30] put slaves (or freedmen) in charge of ships, or provided capital to small independent *naukleroi.*[31]

In the Roman world an influential shipowning and trading urban bourgeoisie is unlikely. Though we did come across one shipper councillor, the shippers as a group turned out to be of lower status, not involved in local politics. However, in my view the estate-owning urban elite in harbour cities of some size and importance were involved indirectly in trade as shipowners. In as much as they availed themselves of the services of agents, free or unfree, and lent money to small, independent shippers, they in fact functioned as bourgeois shipowners such as those who in later European history in cities like Amsterdam came to belong to the urban elite. The latter did not sail themselves, but either used other people as ship captains (in Dutch: 'zetschippers') on their own ships or chartered tonnage on other people's ships.

A recent study by W. Brulez[32] on the profitability of shipowning in early modern European history shows clearly that both in the Mediterranean area and in N.W. Europe shipowning gave 'trivial or nonexistent net returns'. Though we cannot do the sums for antiquity, I have no doubt that the same is true for Graeco-Roman society. It is striking that, both in the Roman Empire and in 15th–16th century AD Genoa and Venice, the government had to support private shipbuilding by attractive subsidies, which never proved to be attractive enough. From Brulez' survey one is entitled to infer that in this period in general the social status of the shippers, whether independent or agents, was not high. This is perfectly in line with what we know about our Greek shippers. As to Hanseatic cities where some shippers did possess 'high social rank', Brulez suggests that it is not always clear whether shipping was in fact their main profession. They may well have combined shipping with commercial activities. Shippers consistently tried to become merchants; the reverse did not occur. In other words, cases like that of our Nicomedian shipper Telesphorus who managed to penetrate into the bouleutic class (probably the lower echelon) may have been as exceptional for Nicomedia as for later European harbour-cities. Telesphorus, as so many shippers, probably combined shipowning with commerce. In this respect he is again a perfect parallel for those rare later shippers who managed to acquire high social status. It is a comparison of this kind which inclines me to the view that pre-industrial European history has been modernized and Roman imperial history 'primitivized' too much.

Brulez's article emphasizes the importance of the merchant as against the shipper. The merchants of pre-industrial Europe were on the whole little interested in shipowning, and the profits derived from the latter were marginal when compared with those from commercial operations. This brings us to the problem of the merchant in the Greek part of the Roman Empire.

Plutarch (*de liberis educandis* VII) wrote of slaves functioning as merchants (*emporoi*) for their masters. Two centuries later Basilius mentioned five sources of wealth: corn, wine, wool, trade (*emporia*) and, of course, banking.[33] The role of shipper (*naukleros*) and merchant (*emporos*) might be and often was filled by one man, but there are examples of merchants who booked space on somebody else's ship for their cargoes.[34] A third category of merchant traded overland and had little or nothing to do with ships. Except for traders in luxury-items which could bear the heavy costs of land-transport, these will have been engaged in local trade (in wool, wine, grain and oil). They are to be distinguished from the local retail dealers (*kapeloi*) who often, though not always, were identical with the small craftsmen who produced the articles concerned.

Our sources present basically the same picture with respect to *emporoi* and *naukleroi*. The number of self-styled *emporoi* who also enjoy high social status in their cities, that is, hold magistracies and are members of the town-council, is exceedingly small. Most epigraphically attested *emporoi* are undistinguished. An interesting exception is offered by an honorary inscription from Thyatira (Asia Minor).[35] The slave-trader (*somatemporos*) Alexandrus has been market official (*agoranomos*) of the city and thus belonged to at least the lower echelon of the urban elite.[36] Characteristically he did not himself buy and sell in his city. That was the business of the dealers on the slavemarket (*hoi tou statariou ergastai*) and of the slavebrokers (*proxenetai somaton*), who both honoured the big merchant publicly. Artemidorus from nearby Daldis, the author of a dream-book, held it to be perfectly conceivable that slave-traders could make large profits from their trade (*Oneirocritica* III 17 (T p. 211)). He was right: Alexandrus is praised for having paid lavishly for entertainment during a feast in honour of the imperial family. The only other Greek slave-trader known to me is a freedman Aulus Caprilius Timotheus whose relief was found in Amphipolis. He was presumably an agent working for a patron who invested money in the trade, without being a trader himself (*S.E.G.* XXVIII 537 (ca. 100 AD)). Timotheus explicitly mentions his patron, thereby, as it were, expressing his dependence. In the recent catalogue of slave-traders of W. V. Harris ((1980), 129–32), the predominance of freedmen is striking. Non-freedmen in the list do not seem to have had much social prestige. Harris pointed out that those who enjoyed high social status did not shrink from advertising their interest in and connexion with the slave trade, but this does not alter the fact that apart from Alexandrus no upper-class slave-trader is as yet known to us. The same seems true of merchants as a whole, though perhaps less so than for shippers. They must have been either small independent merchants or slave or freedmen agents. The latter operated with upper class money. The former, like the shipper, may have been indebted to members of the urban elite, though inscriptions, of course, do not mention such details. An interesting example which may point to the dependence of a trader on a member of the urban elite comes from Smyrna and concerns a certain Attalus, son of Gaius, nicknamed Gaius (*C.I.G.* 3288). Boeckh gave him the cognomen 'Helemporos'. Attalus had bought and repaired a vaulted tomb (*kamara*) for himself and his family, and in the usual manner proclaims that none of his heirs will have the right to sell that tomb; this prohibition is explained by the unusual addition 'because it is the possession of a president (*prytaneus*) and councillor'. G. Petzl, who republishes this epitaph in the first volume of his forthcoming corpus of inscriptions from Smyrna, suggests reading *elemporos*, 'oil-merchant'. I assume that Attalus wanted to deter future evil-doers by explicitly adding that the entire tomb, of which his *kamara* was only part, belonged to one of the top citizens of Smyrna. It is (on onomastic grounds) less likely that he was referring to himself than to someone on whom he depended and for whom he worked, perhaps by selling products of his estate on the market, local or otherwise.

C. P. Jones has recently listed a number of inscriptions, mostly epitaphs, in honour of merchants. Most are undistinguished, but there are a few exceptions. A Greek inscription from Lyon records a certain Thaimus Iulianus, a merchant who operated a large general store in that city and styled himself councillor of the Syrian city of Canotha in the Hauran. Another Syrian merchant, also called Iulianus and similarly buried in Lyon, was called 'honourable on his father's side'. Against those who hesitate to consider this Syrian from Laodicea a merchant, Jones observes 'it is clearly no difficulty that he was of high social rank'.[37] In Moesia another Syrian is on record, Aur. Sabinus, who is both priest and wine-merchant, (*oinemporos*) and together with a *town-councillor* of Porollissus dedicates a temple of Dolichenus (*I.G. Bulg.* III 1590=1678). This is not to deny that most merchants belonged to the common people, especially those who personally bought and sold their goods; they enjoyed little prestige in their cities. When the Roman jurist Callistratus writes that such people should not be scorned as low persons, and in support of that admonition points out that it is not forbidden for them to seek the decurionate or some magistracy in their city, the obvious inference is that in general these merchants enjoyed low social prestige, and were only enlisted as town-councillors when more appropriate candidates were lacking.[38]

This being said, it is reasonable to emphasize that merchants, at least some of them, had a better chance than shippers of rising in the social scale. Jones ((1964), 866–71) registered several examples of reasonably well-to-do merchants in the Greek East in the later imperial period. We hear of merchants engaged in trade in luxury items on both sides of the frontiers of the empire. Others are said to have owned one or more ships which were operated by agents or relatives. The less emphasis there is on actual selling, the better the chances are that we are dealing with someone of respectable social status. Jones stresses the fact that some of these merchants aspired to posts in the office of the provincial administration (*officium*) and that the attested size of fortunes of merchants was modest beside the fortunes of great senatorial landowners. That is true, but it does not prove that far from Rome, on the level of the innumerable cities in the empire, such merchants also made a modest showing. P. Veyne ((1981a) 343) has recently shown that in the third and fourth centuries AD *curiales*, veterans and *officiales* were considered to be on the same social level. One wonders where the difference lay between the wealthy Alexandrian merchants who in one case had 'a great fortune in ships and in gold' and in another left 500 solidi in cash (300 lbs gold) plus slaves and clothes (and, I presume, houses), and the well-to-do merchants from later pre-industrial harbour-cities.[39]

The nature of the ancient historian's sources is often such that detailed data about the size of trading operations are not to be expected. Consistent indirect involvement through slaves, freedmen and indebted free persons enabled many members of the urban elite to gloss over their commercial activities in their honorary inscriptions and epitaphs. Who knows how our theories might be affected by the discovery of a business archive comparable in size to the Murecine-archive from Pompeii, which shows that sizeable sums of money were handled by freedmen of well-to-do families in the grain-trade?[40] With so little known about non-agrarian activities, it is the more significant that we have evidence for a number of merchants having respectable fortunes and corresponding social status, men like M. Aurelius Alexander Moschianus from Phrygian Hierapolis, who on his sarcophagus is called 'purple-seller' and 'town-councillor'. He was presumably a merchant not only in purple dye but also in purple wool and cloth.[41] Hierapolis – Laodicea was famous for its luxury wool and linen and it seems reasonable to suppose that this merchant ('Grosshändler und Exporteur')[42] derived considerable wealth and corresponding social status from this business. That purple-dyers were an important association in Hierapolis is suggested by the regulation that tomb-violators had to pay fines to their board.[43] This is not to deny that in most small communities, towns or villages, vendors are mostly undistinguished people. A quick glance at E. Patlagean's analysis ((1977) 156–81) of the numerous professions on record in the epitaphs from the Cicilian city of Corycus underlines this point. One may wonder whether it was otherwise in *comparable* communities in later pre-industrial Europe.

In the epigraphic evidence (leaving Corycus aside) no wool-seller or linen-seller of a social status comparable to that of Moschianus from Hierapolis comes to light. The explanation is that wool and linen were primarily the concern of the owners of estates and flocks. They were the people who derived profit from the wool trade by selling to small traders either directly or through their own agents.[44] Purple, however, is a very expensive 'industrial' product (cf. *ed. Diocl.* 24) requiring considerable capital outlay and bringing in attractive profits in view of the high prices paid for finished garments. Small wonder that it was precisely purple-merchants who managed to penetrate into the town councils.[45] This is corroborated by what we know about trade in another luxury item, silk. According to Jones, the late Roman silk-merchants from Berytus and Tyre, Constantinople and other cities 'handled the whole business from the purchase of the raw material to the sale of the finished product' and 'were men of substance' who were 'in the habit of buying court sinecures for themselves and their sons'.[46] They provide a nice parallel to late medieval textile merchants who similarly pulled the strings in the wool business.[47] Just as silk had to be procured from beyond the frontier, that is, from the Persians, and transported to the production-centre, similarly there was a flourishing transport of wool in late medieval times from England to Flanders.[48] This gave the merchant the opportunity to occupy the position of the spider in his web. As far as I know, there is no evidence for a comparable position of wool and linen merchants in the Greek East. Wool and linen were fed into the textile production process in the area in which the wool was produced. It was the flock-owners who dominated the scene and, as said above, made the crucial profits. From Diocletian's price edict it seems clear that the raw material is the most expensive item. The value added in the various stages of production is comparatively small. Even so, at least some dealers in expensive items – purple – managed to acquire a respectable social status.[49]

Reasons of space prevent us from discussing some further problems concerning the production and sale of textiles. Instead we conclude with a brief comment on possible interregional trade in bulk goods like grain, oil and wine. My impression is that in normal situations and with normal harvests the grain trade was a local affair, dominated by the grain-producing estate-owners of the cities, who either sold the surplus of their harvests to local traders, somewhat in the way the younger Pliny (*Ep.* VIII 2) in Italy is known to have sold his wine-surplus to independent *negotiatores*, or used their slaves and freedmen for that purpose.[50] Interregional trade would only be feasible by sea or river, since the cost of land-transport of relatively inexpensive bulk goods would have frustrated the entire business. Hopkins (1978) recently suggested that the regularity of famines must have necessitated transport of corn in quantity.[51] This may be true, but the little evidence we have does not point to the existence of an institutionalized class of professional corn-merchants, wealthy enough to handle large-scale imports. I have in mind a number of inscriptions from Ephesus and Tralles showing, first, that export of grain from Egypt to cities in Asia Minor was a privilege to be awarded explicitly by the emperor, and second, that if permission was granted in case of severe local shortage, it was not Ephesian or Trallian *merchants* who took up the business, but well-to-do and prestigious local citizens who could afford to advance (or give) money to the city for the buying and transporting of the grain from Egypt.[52] It is surely significant that even in Ephesus, a flourishing harbour-city, local merchants were not available for such transactions. Such merchants as there were obviously serviced the local market in normal conditions, but were not financially capable of handling the import of, for example, the 60,000 modii of grain which a Trallean benefactor is said to have had imported into his city from Egypt. I do not know whether the transport of fiscal grain to Constantinople had the same spin-off for the free market as was the case in Rome.[53] But I know no parallel in the Greek East to well-to-do Western grain-merchants like the Aufidii, who owned estates in Africa, occupied curial positions both in Ostia and African cities, and were corn-merchants in Ostia.[54] Nor did the important Western traders in oil and wine have Eastern counter-parts.[55]

One thing is certain: the sources for ancient economic history will always remain grossly deficient. We do not have the archives of the wealthy. But when we find tablets in Pompeii we see slaves and freedmen, with family names that recur among the urban magistrates, lending sizeable sums of money to grain-merchants who themselves have a fair chance of being freedmen (or their descendants). The crucial difference between the Roman Empire and the Ancien Regime lies in slaves and freedmen, and in the vast possibilities opened up by their existence to landlords to control manufacture, commerce and banking, while despising it.

It is not irrelevant that in the late Middle Ages successful merchants and entrepreneurs began to invest in real estate. This gave security to their acquired riches and assured a regular income. The Fuggers owned in Swabia alone about a hundred villages with an area of 230–50 sq km.[57] How are they different from Roman senators, who owned comparable estates[58] and are known to have invested in brick and tile-production,[59] used slaves and freedmen as bankers, profited from the marketing of grain and oil on urban markets, and with other urban landlords of comparable (though not identical) wealth, controlled non-rural industry? The difference between members of the urban elites of large cities in antiquity (shipping-centres or possibly even large weaving cities like Tarsus, with which I hope to deal elsewhere) and the great merchants of Flanders and Italy perhaps lies in the availability of middle-men. That is, it lies in the social structure of their respective societies, rather than in the dimensions of their trade.

[12]

Pottery and the African economy[1]

by ANDREA CARANDINI

An index for measuring the prosperity of the North African provinces in the imperial period.

Terra Sigillata Africana[2] can be defined as pottery

1. manufactured in several areas of production and workshops of Africa Proconsularis and Mauretania (from Algeria to Libya, with the nucleus in Tunisia)
2. belonging to a single craft tradition which develops between the first and seventh centuries AD
3. which is related to the regional needs of Africa and above all to the great Mediterranean market (and beyond)
4. of more or less fine quality, covered entirely or in part by a reddish-orange slip, which is more or less smooth and shiny and decorated in various ways (barbotine, wheel-turned, stamped, with moulded and applied relief).

The production of this sigillata has been attributed convincingly to Africa through a series of indications and proofs, which it is useful here only to summarize:

1. It appears initially in the West and only later in the East, so that there can be no question of a Levantine source.
2. It belongs to a craft tradition which has nothing in common (apart from certain imitations) with the working practices of Italian, Gallic or Spanish potters, so that one must look for the area of production in the western provinces of the African continent.
3. The earliest vessel types occur only in the Maghreb where they replace, from the 70's of the first century, the other western fine wares which appear there previously as imports – as subsequently occurs in Italy, Gaul and Spain, but only in the course of the second century (especially in its second half).
4. Some types of open forms and particularly closed forms are known

only in North Africa and often have parallels in the contemporary or earlier local coarse wares.

5. On the pottery decorated with applied relief of 'fabric' C^1 and C^2 there are inscriptions and scenes represented which refer to customs of Africa and in particular Byzacena (for example, the institution of the *sodalitates*, which were the 'Mafias' of their time).

6. The motifs of the stamped or relief decoration fit perfectly into the repertory and figurative language of African art (e.g. the representations of the personifications of Mauretania, Africa and Carthage).

7. On the pottery of 'Navigio' type there are the signatures of potters who are certainly African, and the same vessels in the shape of the human head recall by their physiognomy and certain antiquarian details indigenous African representations of the period.

8. We know of some centres of production (whose number is growing) such as Oudna (Uthina), Henchir el Biar (near Thebourda), Henchir es Srira (in central Tunisia), Sidi Khalifa (Pheradi Maius), Sidi Aich (Gemellae).

9. Some potters' tools are known, such as the punches for stamped decoration, which have been found at Thysdrus, Cirta and Timgad.

The distribution of the pottery must have come about principally, even if not exclusively, through sea transport, and it extended to the most diverse urban and rural settlements and the most varied levels of society (at least up to the fifth century). It penetrated the interior of Africa to the Fezzan, it reached Spain, above all the coastal settlements, Portugal, Southern France, the Balearic Islands, Corsica, Sardinia, Italy, Sicily, Malta, Dalmatia, Greece, the Aegean, Asia Minor, Syria (including Dura Europos), Cyprus, Palestine, the Nile Valley (up to Nubia) and Cyrenaica. A fragment is even known from Axum in Ethiopia; it is rare in the north European provinces (in Austria, Switzerland, the Rhineland, Holland, England and Scotland); finally it is even attested in the Black Sea. Such a distribution, 'worldwide' for those times, is unparalleled by the other centres of production of the period in Narbonensis, Spain, Asia Minor, Cyprus, the Aegean, Palestine and the Greek peninsula (Hayes (1972) 1–18, 428ff.). We can therefore say that we are dealing with the most widely distributed pottery of the Mediterranean in the whole of classical antiquity. (Archaeologists will be amused to note that it is never mentioned in a literary source).

The real significance of African sigillata is only understood if we place it within the general conditions of the North African provinces, especially Proconsularis: that is, we must think 1) of how the colonate was developing from the Flavian period; 2) of the production of oil and other foodstuffs and of their containers, which also reached overseas markets from the Flavian period onwards; 3) of the latest exports of flasks for perfumes and of lamps; and above all 4) of the extraordinary phenomenon of cooking wares exported to far distant places, as if they were luxury goods (there are still historians of the ancient economy who maintain that overseas trade in the Roman world was solely of luxury goods).

The earliest ware is A (Waagé's 'Late Roman B, early phase')[3] whose source is traceable to the Carthage area. In the first two centuries of the Empire it appears very much under the domination of the Italian and Gallic craft tradition (to the extent of producing some crude imitations), even if forms are present which recall the most primitive local productions. This ware begins, as do many other products of African workmanship, from the Flavian period onwards. The first imports into Italy (it would seem, of closed forms) are perhaps found in the 'Vesuvian centres' (destroyed by the eruption of 79 AD), but the first real, even if limited, distribution begins in the Domitianic period (as is convincingly demonstrated by the stratigraphic sequences of the Terme del Nuotatore at Ostia). Under Trajan and Hadrian the importation of the ware is intensified, but in Italy it has still not achieved dominance over the plain Italian and Gallic wares. However, in North Africa imports from the west and north of the Mediterranean cease from the 70s, except for the Italian lamps, which were imported and imitated (in secondary centres?) in the Maghreb up to the third quarter of the second century approximately. The greatest distribution of sigillata A is evident between the mid-second and third centuries – from Portugal to Palestine, and exceptionally also in central Europe – established at the moment when Italy ceased to exist as a producer for major overseas commerce, never to revive in fact until the late Middle Ages (another truth which many historians are reluctant to accept, but which the archaeological evidence demonstrates clearly).

The high quality of the first African products served to establish them in the market of their province of origin (to the disadvantage of the imports) and then in the interprovincial markets. The standardization of the same products from the Antonine period onwards, however, gave them undisputed dominance of the western markets: in the first place the gigantic one of Rome, and so also of the other great urban centres, villas and farms. Then the forms of sigillata A, which had served the tables of millions (including the two metropoleis of the west) withdrew from the scene into the confines of their regional market of origin, subsequently to disappear or be lost in the sea of coarse wares destined only for local consumption. This was to be the morphological and economic destiny of many products, which should be studied case by case (one of these is the bowl, from Lamboglia 21).[4]

But let us return to the end of the second century when Africa overcame its inferiority to central Italy or Narbonensis. The imported skills now became reabsorbed into the local craft tradition and (as often happens) the vanquished became victor. Sigillata A wares were dominant in the Antonine period in the heart of the Empire itself – in the throes of a deep crisis, far from a golden age! – to the benefit of the other shore of the Mediterranean. A little later we have the decline of this 'fabric', which had first symbolized the move of productive primacy from the northern to the southern provinces of the Western Mediterranean.

The fields of the province of Proconsularis were now inhabited by peasant smallholders who owned the land – protected in some cases by agricultural agreements which were more secure (established by the state), and perhaps to some extent more favourable, than those traditional to the area – and they now found the material and social conditions to revolutionize the agrarian scene of many areas of the Maghreb which now became a real tree-clad garden, with olive trees dotting the great plains as far as the eye could see. African oil was exported into Italy from the second half of the first century AD (as is shown by the 'Tripolitanian' and 'Tunisian' amphorae).[5] Cities, roads and ports multiplied at the same time. Between Hadrian and Septimius Severus African oil became more and more essential for Rome, Italy and many provinces of the empire. The success and the central position of Proconsularis were established and celebrated by imperial propaganda in the year 192, when Carthage was raised to the rank of 'Alexandria togata'. When the new Commodan corn fleet reached Carthage, it was received within a new harbour system, which was as functional as it was monumental, as the recent British and American excavations have shown (the preliminary reports of these are now being published). This and many other signs point in one direction: Africa as the focus of the Mediterranean. We have here a new situation, a break in the continuity of the earlier historical development, giving a sharp change of direction to the social and economic productive system of the empire. (The modern age had even greater surprises in store when the cities of the North Sea took the lead and the Mediterranean came to seem like one of many corners of the world). On the other hand, there are precise reflexions of this novel situation, even down to the composition of the leading social sector in the state: in the senate and in the equestrian procuratorships Africans now predominate among Latin-speaking provincials. Literature, mosaics and many other arts flourish in a culture that is at once Roman and African. Individually these are well-known facts, but they assume their dimension (their historical weight) only if placed side by side: that is, when we can assess the magnitude of the change by looking at the whole of the material culture. It is plausible that the displacements in the ruling class reflect wider changes (and thus that the ruin of the Italian peninsula can be linked to that of its aristocracy).

With the Antonines and Severans (African emperors, these last), the movement of the productive forces towards the south, already seen within the general frame of the Mediterranean, is repeated in miniature within Proconsularis itself: from the Carthage area to that around Hadrumentum. Rich Byzacena was crossed by two great 'oil roads', which lead from the heights of the Dorsal (from the centres of Thala and Cillium) to the sea (to the ports of Hadrumentum and Sullectum). It would seem that political and economic change is being expressed as geographical transferences. This is the time of the production of the A/D wares – also destined for export – and of the much better-known sigillata C (Waagé's Late Roman A). It is no accident that from this time or a little later we begin to recognize the first amphorae produced to contain and transport oil (and other liquid commodities), manufactured at Neapolis, Hadrumentum, Leptis Minor and Sullectum (that is, the ports of the eastern coast of Proconsularis). The amphorae called 'africane piccole' (Smaller African) begin to be diffused around 160–180 AD and the 'africane grandi' (Large African) a little after, between 190 and 200.[6] The greatest distribution of these containers is reached around the middle of the third century. Apart from these, the first lamps with a polished slip – these also with ambitions towards, if not yet with success in, the market – begin to be made (but not yet exported) around the years 230–40. Between the last quarter of the second century and the first quarter of the third, workshops independent of those of central Italy started producing lamps and phials for perfumed oils in pottery of good quality, but with no surface polish. Thus it is evident that the various phenomena move to a certain extent in parallel. It is no accident that we see at the same time a new dimension in the political weight of Carthage, due to the fragmentation of the *pertica Carthaginensium*. But research in this direction should be intensified, and caution is needed when one passes from the work of objects to that of institutions.[7]

The C ware (starting from that with dull polish, or C2) is the first African ceramic product to be really 'universal', in the sense that it is now dominant in the Eastern Mediterranean also and remained quite distinct for at least two centuries (from the mid-third to the mid-fifth). In the first half of the third century this pottery reached Dura Europos and in the fourth, sporadically, central Europe (it is rare in Mauretania). Thus – though not only because of this specific evidence – the old myth, which is also held by some Medieval historians, of the permanent dominance in antiquity of eastern over western products, is destroyed. (The vice of commerce was supposedly a characteristic only of the Levant). With the workshops of C ware the characteristic, which in terms of political economy would be defined as 'exchange value', is finally accentuated to such an extent that the closed forms (which had been produced in the A workshops) disappear almost totally, since they were more difficult to stack in the hulls of ships and more fragile. (Metal, glass or local coarse ware containers were used instead). Characteristic of C ware is the simplicity of the cups and plates, which have the appearance of extraordinary fineness, often even to the extent of surpassing the quality of well-known older Italic and South Gallic products, and of resembling vessels made of metal in their hardness and thinness. These technical achievements were obtained principally (according to Hayes) by the use of moulds even in making undecorated forms. It is noteworthy that at this time plates (the form now in fashion) and bowls reach enormous dimensions, so much so that they suggest a change in the way of serving and eating (towards collective eating).

Between the end of the third and beginning of the fourth century we have a vigorous revival of the northern Tunisian workshops which previously seemed to have disappeared altogether. The production of A ware is reborn, as if from its ashes, under the revival of Sigillata D (Waagé's 'Late Roman B, middle-late phase') which continued until the seventh century. The vessels are probably made with moulds even in the case of the undecorated types, which now seem to be more and more enriched by systems of stamped decoration. Previously, stamped decoration was present but rare in A, A/D and C wares. But now it is diffused with a taste for *horror vacui* which we find also in arts of a different type.[8] For the chronology of D (especially of its 'late phase') credit is due to Hayes who has made use of associations with eastern wares and of the stratigraphy of the dated churches of Constantinople. The British, Italian and Canadian excavations of the wall of Theodosius II at Carthage, dated to 425, have supplied another key dating context.

Passing to the other ceramic markets, it is noteworthy that the lamps of central Tunisia, which were widely exported from the middle of the fourth century, are overtaken by the so-called 'classical' lamps (lucerne classiche), attributed to the north of Tunisia or Zeugitana. Although these lamps enjoyed an extraordinary success in the western Mediterranean, in the East they do not reach the levels achieved by the table wares (except in Egypt, where they have a large distribution). The revival of production in the region of Carthage after the crisis of the third century is confirmed by other indications, such as the development of building in Carthage, which reached its peak in the periphery furthest from the harbours (and so in the most significant area) just at the end of the fourth century (as the Italian excavations have shown), and of the appearance at the same time of a new type of amphora called 'cylindrical late imperial', whose kilns have been found in a suburb near the city. It has a fourth and fifth century *floreat*, after which amphorae of the 'spateia' form take over, with a *floreat* of the fifth to seventh centuries (*Ostia* IV).

The greatest diffusion of D wares, both vessels and lamps, is to be placed between the mid-fourth and mid-fifth centuries, when it reaches the northwest of the empire and has various local imitations. Under the Vandals, exports appear to decline in the East (apart from Egypt), where Pergamene, Cypriot and Egyptian products predominate. The central position of Africa and the unity of the Mediterranean under its standard was never greater, and is now for the first time a matter for discussion. Its position is at once clearly reflected in the artistic and craft quality of the products. Less clear is what happens in the West, where the archaeological levels of late antiquity have rarely aroused the interest of the archaeologist (intent on the pursuit of 'better quality' or 'archaic' remains). We can perhaps presume a crisis for this area also, but it awaits confirmation and assessment of its severity. At all events there are clear signs of a revival after the Byzantine reconquest (Hayes (1972)). D wares reach the Rhineland centres in the fourth century, Scotland in the sixth century and Lombard cemeteries in Italy in the seventh century (but it is now treated as an exotic and luxury item). Between the mid-sixth and the mid-seventh century we have an unquestionable decline in production, to which the Arab invasion perhaps adds no more than the words 'The end'. Pirenne was by no means wrong in sustaining that the ultimate end of the ancient world was marked by the lighting of the first candles, through lack of African oil (Oil was the coal of the classical period). In this sense, the end of the great export of African oil marked the end of what was no more than a simple accompanying product – African Red Slip pottery. As it was heaped up in the holds of ships, probably in the gaps between the functional small and large African amphorae (for oil and fish sauce), it gives a most valuable indication not only of its own presence, but above all of the productive and distributive arrangements which in the ancient world operated for the exchange and the forced movement of foodstuffs.

Around the middle of the fourth century we encounter a last southwards shift in the production of African pottery (with all that that implies): as though there were a southwards progress of the commercial capital (also to be noted is a production of olive oil amphorae at Thaenae, well into southern Tunisia). A new 'fabric' distinguished by Hayes (which we call E, preceded perhaps by forerunners which we have called C/E) is in all probability to be located in southern Tunisia.

This ware also makes use of moulds for undecorated vessels and is exported in Tunisia, Libya, Greece and Egypt. As far as we know, it is absent in the western Mediterranean, which helps us considerably to understand the logic of the Mediterranean commercial routes at this period. Products loaded on to ships in the ports of central and, above all, southern Tunisia in fact had the greatest of difficulty in reaching the western coasts of North Africa and the west end of the Mediterranean.

The contemporary successes of E, C and D wares do not therefore all have the same character and weight although they all belong within the same productive framework. The fortunes of a ceramic ware would seem nevertheless to depend not so much on the coastal positioning of kilns as on their proximity to the outlets and handling centres of liquid foodstuffs destined for the overseas market, and on their nearness to the ports serving the most used trade routes.

In the fourth century many other terra sigillata wares with regional distributions are found, which cannot here be dealt with in detail. They imitate the most widely exported products of the coastal areas. They are in some ways the echo of these latter (a sign of their expansive force) into the interior of the provinces to their most backward areas. At all events it should be evident that African pottery, however varied its characteristics and irrespective of the degree to which it was commercialized, or of its functional purpose and the complexity of its decoration, is a productive phenomenon as remarkable as it is largely uniform, and it should be studied in its totality.

From techniques of production, typologies and distribution maps it is possible (and necessary) to move up to aspects of artistic treatment of these same pots, even if the fortune of their production centres is primarily based on undecorated wares. We can say that in the second century there are rare moulded imitations of some traditional decorative motifs (Dionysiac and genre scenes) of Italian pottery. The applied relief decoration of the third century on A ware vessels and C ware lamps show, as has been said, the assimilation and overtaking of knowledge gained from western imports and thus the end of cultural subordination to the centre of the Empire. The decorations show for the first time a crude realism in their content and a fresh naturalism in their style. The figured representation, which are lively and simple, are realized by means of the free assemblage of single motifs chosen from a rich repertory (of around two hundred items). More familiar iconographic material, such as the idyllic landscapes of the Hellenistic-Roman tradition, are now replaced by the realistic representation of local and everyday events and surroundings (such as the amphitheatre scenes of Thysdrus). The phenomenon is at least as revolutionary in the field of art history (but is a trace of something else too) as the discovery of the naturalistic landscape in the Hellenistic period, and it finds only rare precedents in the 'plebeian' art of Italy and of the northern provinces (but there are no proofs of 'contact' between these various efforts at figurative realism). In the Middle Ages – with the olives burnt by the nomads – the sands were to recover these figured representations of the urban and rural landscapes of Roman Africa. Europe was only to rediscover them when the cavalry and ploughs of French colonialism turned these soils, in step with the demands of 'private ownership'. To find a realism of comparable intensity within the European context, we have to await the art of the Mediterranean and European commercial bourgeoisie of the Renaissance, who were certainly ignorant of the earlier accomplishments of North African craftsmen, which were then still buried.

The pottery itself was first destined mainly for regional markets (for example the small jars of El Aouja and the corresponding lamps in C^1 and C^2), but later (from *c.*280) became a product for what was then a world-wide market (C^3 and C^4 wares, for example). An immediate comparison can be made between the figural decoration of the pottery and the major applied art of the mosaic, which now reaches its peak. At this moment (as in so many others of classical antiquity) there is a close correspondence between the major arts of architectonic decoration and the minor arts of expensive or cheap household articles. It is no coincidence that in precisely these years the technique of ceramic decoration reaches its highest level.

The end of the third century and the first decades of the fourth mark the moment of greatest diffusion of African figural arts in the west Mediterranean (in the ancient world art was not diffused as easily as goods of more everyday use). The masterpieces of the mosaic workshops established in the great African urban centres now travel around, and the luxurious and at the same time official residences of the great latifundia-owners now arise: this is the moment of the villa of Piazza Armerina, which serves as a characteristic example for all its unusual magnificence.[9]

The greatest success often precedes the first stage of decline. With the second half of the fourth century, applied relief decoration on vessels and lamps falls into decline and moulded decoration takes a clear lead (but the vessels of 'Navigio' type, datable between 290 and 320, already had moulded decoration). The collapse of the African form begins now, just as had happened with the Roman form around two centuries previously. Figured representations on vessels are now more complex, unitary, hierarchical and grandiose – as if to obtain a great effect at minimum expense – but they appear without doubt to be colder, less coherent and more repetitive and conventional, subordinated now to the more major arts from large scale painting to mosaics (from this moment onwards, the iconographic material includes Christian New Testament subjects). It is now, and not earlier, that we should place the start of late antique figurative language in North Africa. Every province has its own moment for this beginning and the first to start the series was late antique Antonine art (no contradiction) in Rome. The decay of realism and of figurative art of the Hellenistic-African tradition is to be seen most clearly in the 'monumental' architectural decoration of the great coastal cities of North Africa. (Inland the antinaturalistic language was always present; thus it is possible to speak of an endemic condition of late antiquity in the figurative arts, if by this term we mean the loss of hegemony of an art which was turning towards the end of the ancient world, rather than a condition of cultural subordination). The crisis is reflected in Sicily also, in the villas of Tellaro and of Patti, which seem later than the country palace of Piazza Armerina. Work in the various arts is no longer done for a leisured class of officials and local magnates but now rather for a limited group of *honestiores*, all the time becoming more detached from the lower classes. The tendency towards greater rigidity of artistic style reflects that of the classes and of *status* (the more privilege, the more severe the exploitation). The sphere of action of the dominant culture shrinks, as had already happened in the Late

Republican period in Italy, but without any more of that secure confidence in the Hellenistic and classicizing culture, which originated in Asia Minor and Attica and then became Roman. Now there is only a slow decay, an ossification also of the earlier formal conventions, a 'passive revolution'.

Et paene ipsa (Africa) omnibus gentibus olei praestat, states the *Expositio*. The material remains show that this is no rhetorical phrase (and oil, we now know, stands proxy for many other products also). African goods (foodstuffs and others) certainly help us to see the structure of African productive development (both economic and artistic) through a mesh of evidence which is continuous in space and time, so that we can classify (reassemble) various phenomena, which would otherwise appear like disjointed limbs, from which it would be difficult to extract any meaning.

But we have not yet succeeded (for the moment) in extracting from these same products the most precious secret – the 'social mode' in which they were produced. On the character of slave-based production in Italy we are now starting to have some clear ideas.[10] The slave-based organizations of the villa and of urban workshops succeeded in making many men work together in forced conditions, bringing returns from commercial capital and producing goods for major markets. But we know little indeed of the condition of African craftsmen (probably not slaves as emerges from the studies of Kolendo and Whittaker),[11] of their degree of freedom from the countryside and of their actual working arrangements (it would be necessary to excavate more often in the peripheries of cities in search of artisan quarters). But one thing is clear – and at the same time it constitutes the major historical problem – that not only the classical slave-based system (as applied for example to the production of Arretine pottery) succeeded in the ancient world in producing goods exported on a large scale. In short, the production of exchange values is not inevitably bound to the phenomenon of slavery: it can be remembered, among other examples, that South Gaulish pottery was produced by peasant craftsmen of free status, even if aided by slaves.[12]

Italy and Africa: two different worlds, two principles of unification and economic domination of the Mediterranean that differ profoundly. Africa's fortune succeeds, perhaps presupposes (though it is not clear how) the decline of Italy. These two moments nevertheless symbolize in the most effective way the two major directions of the history of the Roman Empire (above all if seen with Latin eyes). With the third century, as has been noted, the fortunes of the Peninsula had already been in decay for some time. The decadence of the African provinces is another, later phenomenon – the last act of a drama begun long before. This is the major significance of the confrontation between the two principal parts of the West Mediterranean. It should also be remembered that Italy and Rome itself were now only a fraction of the zone penetrated by the African productive centres. The sufferings caused by the Italian economic miracle are thus followed by those of the African economic miracle. In establishing this bi-polarity the other provinces must not be forgotten. But we must start from these basic facts of history over a long period and then descend to details and variations.

The *lex Manciana* once used to be interpreted as a measure designed to stimulate agricultural production in certain areas of North Africa, by the creation of a broad stratum of free peasant farmers. A contrary view has now gained weight, which tends to deny any transformation of the mode of production in the African provinces during the imperial period. The changes of ownership (which are impossible to deny) would have been carried out at such exalted levels as to make no difference to the working population. This presumed continuity in the system of production certainly has the advantage of explaining the lack of a generalized development of rural slavery in the Maghreb: 'the Romans left farming much as they found it' (Whittaker (1978) 355). This thesis does not exclude the possibility that the commercialization of agriculture may have modified the social situation within certain limits, but without altering the basic productive relationships – and this is the point – at least before the end of the third century AD: 'it was not until the later third century AD that export of a cash-crop in olive oil developed on any scale' (Whittaker (1978) 359). In brief, a limited and late commercialization of certain basic foodstuffs is admitted. Hence the prevalence of continuity in the structures of the rural African population and a reductive interpretation of the *lex Manciana*, which – continuing with this same argument – would have been passed for no other reason than to recognize formally (at the time of Vespasian) local labour practices whose tradition would seem to extend out of sight in the 'long' history of rural communities.

This is not the place, nor does this writer have sufficient competence, to criticize this point of view. But a first impression arises from the archaeological evidence, as we now know it, that we have thus passed from a *modernistic* vision of the state of Africa (the *lex* as an instrument of economic control in a virtually capitalistic sense) to a strongly *primitivistic* conception (in which we can hear the battle cry of the Cambridge historiographical school against any significant flowering of commercial capital in the ancient world). In what has been written above, we have seen, albeit summarily, that *everything* changes in North Africa from the Flavian period, but we are to believe that the peasant's way of life remained the same, that is, basically still immersed in a state of community existence, in a situation of almost 'Asiatic' immutability. But if the possession of the partiary colonate, in this critical period and in key areas of the economy, was not made more individual, defined and guaranteed by the state, if the forms of subordination (the agrarian pacts) were not transformed – perhaps, indeed, towards arrangements which were hardly more advantageous than the earlier ones – if we cannot presume a better co-ordination of work done between different peasant families, if the collection of rents and taxes did not become more efficient (contributing towards a more efficient rationalization of production), if agrarian technologies or systems of water use were not changed, if life in the countryside was not modified by the extraordinary development of urbanization (which must have absorbed a good number of craftsmen), if, in short, the countryside was not transformed in both its agricultural and human aspects in certain limited and key areas of the Maghreb, how are we to explain the African 'boom' (the term is deliberately provocative), which is shown incontrovertibly in the material remains, precisely from the period to which (incidentally) the *lex Manciana* is dated? The suspicion thus arises that the changes in proprietal relationships, the commercialization of foodstuffs, the collection of the *annona* and the development of employment in the cities modified productive relationships in certain key sectors of the economy. This does not exclude the possibility that over large areas (even geographically dominant, but structurally subordinate) aspects of working practice that were much more ancient and primitive were conserved.

In short, distinctions have to be made area by area and period by period, and we must not interpret the mode of working in too restricted a way (in its economic aspect) to fit it into the overall picture of social life in Roman Africa and the Empire: only thus is it possible to understand the novelty of this story. If there were not certain peculiar and favourable aspects in the agrarian pacts of certain great estates, how are we to explain the fact that in the Antonine period the *coloni* of the imperial estate of the Bagradas were calling not for other agrarian agreements but for the observance of the existing ones, which the *conductores* were tending to violate, thereby aggravating the burdens suffered by the peasantry? The whole question is summarized by asking if it is possible that Roman colonialism (which irrespective of its precise character was still the most formidable exemplar before the modern period) was so idyllic in Africa as not to upset the key points (with some major exceptions) of the ancient traditions of productive life? The inappropriateness of the primitivistic model described above is revealed when one is obliged to postpone, against all specific evidence, the commercialization of oil and fish sauce (pushed back by Whittaker to the end of the third century). Let us rather pursue African goods to their place of deposition on land or in the sea with the aim of uncovering the reality of Africa outside Africa itself, and then we will conclude that the African 'economic miracle' is at least a century earlier (to speak in terms of market dominance and not in terms of the formation of a market, for which we would have to go back further in time).

If this survey of Roman pottery serves to make the historian of ancient society reflect, to make him pose new questions and raise new uncertainties toward the end of revising our ideas of continuity and change, of space and of time, then this work will have achieved its principal aim, which is not only to provide a useful tool to the field archaeologist but also to break down old barriers, in widening the field of source material (to take in even discarded pottery) and in fitting the range and the quality of the evidence to the complexity of the various worlds which made up the Roman Empire.

On the other hand, the remains of this world are not hidden on the other side of the moon, but lie stratified beneath our feet and are recoverable by our hands and our intelligence. We can no more pass them by than human science can ignore the existence of the unconscious. Archaeology performs in historical studies the same function as psychoanalysis performs in the human sciences – and it is no coincidence that both make use of the stratigraphical method.

APPENDIX: The historiography of African sigillata

The first fragment of sigillata africana was published in 1833. The first workshop (Uthina, in northern Tunisia) was published in 1897. The first division of the pottery into 'fabrics' was the work of the British scholar Waagé (1933), with his 'Late Roman B' (equivalent to Lamboglia's 'sigillata chiara A' and 'D'). Beside these wares and, as he considered, different from them, he placed 'Late Roman C', 'Late Roman D' and 'Late Roman E', which are Pergamene or Cypriot products. Waagé was thus the first to make the mistake, repeated by Lamboglia, of placing in a single series pottery from very diverse sources (but this is in no way to detract from the achievement of these first summary groupings of the 'founding fathers' of Roman ceramic studies). Waagé in any case is to be credited with being the first to have guessed the African identity of his two 'fabrics'. The initiator of these studies in the West (although he tends sometimes to be forgotten) was Nino Lamboglia (1958) (1963). We are indebted to this scholar, whom we can call a dilettante in the best sense of the word – although an ally of official Italian archaeology, he was never really a part of it, and perhaps because of this succeeded in filling its serious gaps (from stratigraphical excavation to the systematic classification of finds to underwater archaeology) – for the first classification of the forms of what we call African sigillata by 'fabrics', and for the basic outline of their chronology from the 1st to 4th centuries, built up on the base of stratigraphical sequences in the West (particularly that of Albintimilium, the first centre of Roman Italy to be examined scientifically).

There were for a time clear divergences between the schools of ceramic studies for the West and the East, which respectively did not recognize and were ignorant of each other. The Western school (especially in Italy) had for its part a limited idea of 'Latinity', which was based on ideological 'Nationalist-Fascist' assumptions rather than objective historical realities. The Eastern school (especially its British part) showed on its side a presumption, perhaps born of an 'imperial' tradition, which tended to ignore scholarly studies in languages other than English. With the passing of time the old barriers have happily been broken for ever and new scholarly links have been established between different nations and traditions in this field of studies as elsewhere. Thus it has come about that scholars of the Eastern school have begun to recognize the scientific merits of the Western school (even if a real exchange of views is still some way off in the field of scholarly publications). On the other side, scholars of the Western tradition have finally recognized the possibility a) of the African production of 'sigillata chiara' A, C and D (in which they did not believe for a long time); b) of recognizing new fabrics of African sigillata, less significant individually than the above, but because frequently exported important in their contribution towards a full understanding of the production of African pottery; c) of understanding the diffusion of the various products in the East also (hence the necessity of coordinating the British and Italian classifications); d) of lowering by several centuries the end of African sigillata pottery.

In this connexion mention should be made of the important studies of

Jan Willem Salomonson (1968) (1969), who was the first to correlate the classifications of the two different traditions and therefore to give to the African products their true global and cosmopolitan dimension. He also gave a new impetus to studies of the relationships between African sigillata and the products of the other African arts, both minor and major. In addition he made an excellent study of the moulded and applied relief decorations (on vessels and lamps) between the Severan and Vandal periods, in which he was able to distinguish new aspects of African ceramic craft skills in the pottery of El Aouja, of the 'Navigio' type and in the contemporary slip-coated lamps. With the publication of the Raqqada cemetery (in central Tunisia) he made, finally, a notable contribution to the chronology of the different wares and of individual forms.

At the same time Italian research was developing, particularly that linked with excavations at Ostia and in Africa (carried out mainly by pupils of Lamboglia). An African sigillata workshop was recognized at Pheradi Maius. The new A/D fabric was distinguished. Detailed study was established of the pottery 'a patina cenerognola' ('with ashy grey surface') and of that 'a orlo annerito' ('with blackened rim'), as the African 'cooking wares' then used to be called, with particular attention being paid to what was called at that time 'A a strisce' ('A with stripes'), now defined as burnished cooking wares. The relationships were clarified between African sigillata and the most widely distributed cooking wares, which themselves began at that time to look like African products. Refinements were made to the chronology of individual wares and forms. A geographical identification was attempted of the wares and an analysis of the relationships between ceramic production (including lamps), agricultural production and artistic production (Carandini (1970)). The Ostia volumes I–IV[13] and the combined and individual studies, which were developed alongside and out of the excavation of the Terme del Nuotatore at Ostia, meanwhile became important for advancing knowledge of North African material culture (we would mention particularly the study of *L'instrumentum domesticum di Ercolano e Pompei* (Pompeii, (1977)).

John Hayes' volume, *Late Roman Pottery*, the product of five years' research, was published in 1972. In many points it agreed with the results of the research at Ostia mentioned above, adding precision and amplifying it in a convincing way. It takes into consideration all the fine wares of the middle and late Empire: no small undertaking. The documentary base is given mainly from excavations in the East (Abu

Mena, Alexandria, Antioch, Apollonia in Cyrenaica, Athens, Ballana, Constantinople, Corfu, Corinth, Cyprus, Dura Europos, Emporion at Chios, Jerusalem, Pergamum, Salonica, Tarsus, Tocra). But Hayes is familiar with the sites and museums of the West (among other things he followed closely the American excavations at Carthage and the topographical work of the British School at Rome in Southern Etruria). In addition to placing African sigillata for the first time in the context of the ceramic outpoint of both parts of the Mediterranean, he is to be credited with the definition of another relatively important fabric (which we call E) and with recognizing the continuity of C throughout the fifth century and of D up to the seventh century. Finally, he also made a systematic study of the stamped decoration, proposing a dated development (even if preliminary) of the 'styles' of this simple way of enriching late antique ceramic table ware. Hayes also dealt with African wares which only had a regional distribution ('Tripolitanian ware' is that covered most fully). On the other hand he does not distinguish in his study between terra sigillata and the cooking wares that were exported, although they should have been differentiated by function and value from the fine table wares. Nor does he deal with other wares such as the 'Navigius' type and he makes only short references to lamps. Further, in the catalogue of forms, the various fabrics are only defined along general lines and by means of empirical descriptions, which are as precise and informative as they are unsystematic and unsynthetic (as a result of which it is difficult for the non-specialist reader to relate an individual example to the class of wares to which it belongs). Finally, the brevity of the stratigraphical dating references, if not weakening the general results of the study, certainly makes some dates look arbitrary and in need even of major correction. But these criticisms in no way detract from the breadth of Hayes' study and from the fundamental value of his manual. It offers indeed a chronological framework to the Roman archaeology of the Mediterranean. It is therefore a classic work, as was that of his British predecessors Felix Oswald and T. Davies Pryce on the Italian and above all Gallic Terra Sigillata, published in 1920. At this point it must be said that the technical basis of Roman archaeology (treated not simply as 'art history') owes most in the last fifty years to the achievements of British scholarship. And while many Italians tore Rome apart (as Antonio Cerderna recounts in his *Mussolini urbanistra*, where the intellectuals come out worse than the Duce) and then allowed, so to speak, the marble reliefs of the greatest empire of antiquity to be turned into lime – the Fascist destruction and the economic miracle were both the servants of property speculation – it was from those who were called the plutocratic western powers (particularly England) that we received the main tools for understanding the history of our peninsula from the study of its material remains – humble tools given to us who had been such lovers of art as to have destroyed alike the artistic and non-artistic heritage of what was once known to all as the 'bel paese'.

[13]
Late Roman trade and traders
by C. R. WHITTAKER

'Le commerce et les échanges ont existé à toutes les époques. Ce qui est en question, c'est leur importance et leur nature.'
(H. Pirenne, *Mahomet et Charlemagne*, p. 219)

The medieval model

It is not the existence of trade and commerce which requires examination, but, as Pirenne said, their scale and nature. His thesis of the continuity of trade from late Roman to Merovingian times is still[1] – despite some dissent – largely supported by modern research.[2] Indeed, even the Carolingian period is now thought to have been less barren of exchange than Pirenne himself believed.[3] The implication is that some of the trading institutions of early medieval Europe must have had their origins in the Roman Empire.

One such possibility lies in an institution examined by a Belgian successor of Pirenne, Henri Laurent,[4] who argued from a Carolingian text, the *praeceptum negotiatorum*, included in the imperial formularies of the court at Aachen,[5] that in the Merovingian and Carolingian periods *negotiatores* were frequently to be found attached to the royal court or to an ecclesiastical foundation, where, in return for fiscal privilege or immunities, they were tied to the service of the institution. The task of the palace agents, for example, was to keep the imperial household regularly supplied with exotic goods and staple produce of the imperial *villae*.[6] In the formulary there is also mention of Jews, who are compared to the palace *negotiatores*, with a duty to serve the palace, although neither group was entirely excluded from private transactions – *pro nostris suorumque utilitatibus negotiandi gratia*.

The agents operating for the massive abbey domains, such as those of St Denis or of St Germain-des-Prés, do not seem to have had even that much freedom, since they were usually either tenants of, or themselves members of the clergy and referred to as *nostri mercatores, nostri negotiatores*.[7] We have quite a lot of examples in addition to those quoted by Laurent, showing them at work. Each year a monk from the abbey of St Bertin at St Omer was sent to supervise the transport and supply of wine from the abbey lands near Cologne.[8] In 615 Bertrand, Bishop of Le Mans, bequeathed his house at Boulogne to his nephew on condition that he lodged the agents of the church sent there *pro piscibus ad negotiandum*.[9] The interest here lies in the fact that much of the produce of the estates was interchanged between properties, often going to support the huge bands of dependants and poor. That was the virtue of the large wheat barns built by Remigius, Bishop of Reims.[10] But at the same time the agents or monks were often instructed to commercialize their surpluses, as can be seen in the arrangements made by the monks of St Germain-des-Prés.[11]

Although both local and long-distance trade existed, therefore, for genuinely entrepreneurial activity – and we have plenty of references to men like the corn merchants of Mainz or the independent dealers in Sicily who sold corn to the papal agents[12] – the evidence gives the impression that a large part of the economy and perhaps the bulk of long distance exchange was controlled by the landholders and regional producers.

Laurent also argued that the appearance of these types of attached merchants or 'pseudo-*negotiatores*' was a sign of reduced trade, since the court would not have needed them had it had access to regular supplies on an open market. Agents, he believed, operated only where landed estates were virtually autarkic and where regular exchange had entirely ceased or had been reduced to 'une petite économie en circuit fermé'.[13] By 'closed' economy is meant the movement of goods which entirely by-passed the market place. Such a condition, said Laurent, had been inherited from the later Roman Empire, or, to be more precise, from the third century AD. In this respect he challenged Pirenne's portrait of a vigorous economy in the fourth century AD, although he was at pains to dissociate himself from nineteenth-century liberal views that 'l'étatisme économique' and 'dirigisme' were synonymous with stagnation.[14]

Since Laurent, however, 'new archaeology' together with the contributions of economic anthropologists has stressed for medieval historians the importance of non-commercial and social exchange. Neither the movements of goods, nor even less the distribution of coins, are now attributed wholly or even largely to trade in a society which attached social importance to the exchange of gifts.[15] The term 'commerce' does not begin to cover the basic notion of reciprocity or dependent obligations.[16] Long-distance trade, far from acting as an economic indicator, often followed no obvious marketing principles, since the goods were an essential part of the ruler's prestige.[17] Of the ten different 'modes of trade' listed by Renfrew, only one involves 'middlemen' or 'free lance' trading.[18] A self-regulating system of price-making markets within a society such as Laurent described could not have existed and therefore, in principle, it could not have been the dominant form of integration.[19]

It follows that the opposite of a market economy is not a 'closed' economy of consumption, since exchange can be carried out by non-market mechanisms. In the medieval world villa autarky and a purely domestic economy have proved to be an illusion, in any case, even in the Carolingian period.[20] Nor did long-distance trade necessarily cease when under state supervision. On the contrary, royal control of the ports of trade (or *Wiks*) and the desire for prestige goods and wealth positively stimulated activity beyond the *limes* and overseas.[21] If wealthy monasteries or landlords put the burden of transport on tenant corvée, entrepreneurial trade could not have competed in strictly economic terms.[22]

Tied trade in the later Roman Empire – the emperor

Assuming, then, that the institutions found in Merovingian Europe aped those of the later Roman Empire,[23] it is impossible to doubt that the general features of the supply and control of essential goods were inherited in this way.

The most obvious of controlled institutions were the manufacturing centres for the supply of state cloth and weapons listed in the *Notitia Dignitatum* and the imperial estates of the *res privata*. Both of them, as is well known, developed dramatically in this period. Terms like 'factories' and 'state supply', however, give an impression of size and centralization which is not really justified by the archaeological or literary evidence.[24] The organization of production, in fact, seems to have remained much as it was before, based upon the home economy that was characteristic of private estates.[25] The same 'private' character is observable, also, in the state *annona* system, which, despite close controls,[26] was never organized in the late Empire as a state *militia* service. Contracts were still issued *ex locato* (*C.J.* IV. 65.4) and the *annona* was often mixed with non-state cargoes (e.g. *C.J.* XI. 1.7–8, *C.Th.* XIII

5.26). Nor is there any obvious reason why this system should represent a decline in exchange.[27]

Less well studied than state industries and transport are the palace businessmen and merchants in the later Empire, for whom we possess quite a large body of legislation.[28] They appear strikingly like those whom Laurent found at the Carolingian court. A law of 364, for instance, forbade *negotiatores* 'who are attached to our household and those who belong to the powerful' (*si qui ad domum nostram pertinent, potentiorum quoque homines*, *C.J.* IX 63.1 = *C.Th.* XIII 1.5 and I 4.1) from contravening the law of commerce (*modum mercandi*) unless they paid the lustral tax. In the Theodosian Code version of the law, incidentally, *clerici* are included. In 409 a piece of legislation *de commerciis et mercatoribus* limited the number of *collegiati* who could gain immunities to 563. I assume these were the men at court (*C.J.* IV 63.5).[29] Tax exemptions for traders and transporters were granted 'to persons in our imperial service or to those who serve in our palace' (*C.Th.* XI 12.3 (365)). Apparently other members of the imperial family tried to cash in on this benefit for members of their own households (*C.Th.* XIII 3.12 (418)). But, as later, state service did not exclude private business at the same time (*qui in privatis negotiis occupantur quibus iure militiae servientes obsequiorum praemiis gloriantur*, *N.Th. II* VII I (439)).

It is tantalizingly difficult to discover just what these *negotiatores* actually did. One may assume a good deal of their energies were devoted to the supply of staples. A later law of Justinian seems to be saying that compulsory purchases of corn (*coemptiones*) were to be carried out *per negotiatores* (Justin. *App.* VII 26 (554)). And it is not unreasonable to suppose that the court was involved in the transport and sale of produce of its own estates, as were the clergy and nobles. Severus Alexander is said to have encouraged *negotiatores* to come to Rome at the time when he was purchasing grain privately (H.A. *Alex.* 21–2). A large part of the emperor's revenue, in any case, came from imperial domains, which the emperor used to maintain his retainers and guests, just as any other landowner would have done. Julian's *horrea* on the Rhine, for instance, which were stocked with British corn, were separate from the supplies brought up by his arch-enemy, the praetorian prefect Florentinus, who had charge of the official state *annona* (Amm. Marc. XVIII 2.3–4). Constantius II offered supplies of *annona* and *cellaria* to a council of bishops (Sulp. Sev. *Chron.* II 41.2). The imperial *negotiatores* presumably fitted somewhere in this supply system. At Constantinople money changers were classed as *negotiatores* and were used to finance arms contracts, as were the supervisors of the weapon-making establishments themselves, in return for which they were given *militia* privileges (*C.J.* XII 34(35).1 (528/9)).

Apart from supplies within the empire, there was also long-distance trade or exchange. The pretender Firmus (whether a historical person or not does not matter here) is said to have 'kept up a close *societas* with the Blemmyes and Saracens; and he also often sent merchant ships (*negotiatorias*) to India' (H.A. *Firm.* III 3). Contact with the barbarians beyond the frontiers was controlled by the *comites commerciorum* at the ports of exit (*C.J.* IV 40.2) and although the *negotiatores* and *mercatores* who passed through were not necessarily imperial agents, legislation of Honorius and Theodosius assumed that *mercatores* between Persia and Rome were often *legati* of the emperor (*C.J.* IV 63.4). Vice versa, the Greek trader from Viminacium whom Priscus of Pannium found at the court of Attila had by then become a servant of the Hunnish king (Priscus VIII (p. 86)).

And there was the commerce in slaves who had been taken as prisoners-of-war, a form of long-distance trade which became hyper-active in the later Empire and in the medieval period. Again it is not absolutely clear that the traders involved were commissioned agents of the court. Many of them were Jews and Syrians who, despite the condemnation of churchmen like Pope Gregory, were too useful to their rulers and, in the Merovingian court at least, enjoyed their protection.[30] Gregory of Tours, for instance, records the Jew Priscus who was on close terms of intimacy with Chilperic as 'his agent who had acted for him for some purchases which he had made' (Greg. Tur. *Hist.* VI 5). A complete title in the Theodosian Code *ne Christeanum mancipium Iudaeus habeat* (*C.Th.* XVI 9) is not necessarily an indication of court control nor are the privileged exemptions from municipal duties accorded to Jews at Cologne (*C.Th.* XVI 8.3(320)), but the possibility seems quite high.[31]

Tied trade – the Church

In contrast to the vagueness of the sources describing the organization of the court, the Church is constantly before our eyes in the epoch of growing wealth and accumulating privilege. Whatever the political transformation from later Roman Empire to medieval periods, the Church enjoyed a continuity and progress unbroken by the replacement of Roman by barbarian rulers. The *patrimonium Petri*, which the correspondence of Pope Gregory has done so much to illuminate in the twilight of the Frankish and Lombard regimes of the late sixth and early seventh centuries, contained the massive property which the Roman church had been acquiring since the donations of Constantine in 321.

The Church's property, of course, was the instrument by which it maintained its army of officials and by which it fed the poor. In fulfilment of its social and administrative role, therefore, close attention was given to the transfer of produce between its estates as well as to the commercializing of its surpluses in order to produce the huge treasures of gold for which the Church was celebrated. The private granaries of Peter's Patrimony on the Tiber, which were large enough to feed the whole of Rome in emergencies, were replenished by corn from its Sicilian estates. The corn was normally for distribution to the poor, although sometimes also sold on the open market.[32] In Sicily itself the *coloni* on Church estates sometimes had to market their own produce to pay cash rents, although the existence of accounts computed in gold was an administrative convenience and not necessarily proof that the peasants themselves carried out transactions in the market.[33] Gregory is said to have 'turned into money the revenues of all the patrimonies and estates according to the *polipticum* (ledger) of (Pope) Gelasius' in order to pay 'his officials of the Church and palace' (Joh. Diac. *v. Greg.* II 24). But on the other hand it is also recorded that 'on the first day of every month he distributed that part of the Church revenues which were paid in kind,' which included items like bedclothes, grain, beans and wine (Joh. Diac. *v. Greg.* II 26; cf. II 28, Greg. *Epp.* I 44, 65, IV 28). And so on. From many examples one can get some idea of the variety of the Church's economic activity both within and outside the market.

For this activity, hardly surprisingly, a great staff of servants and agents were required, among whom were shippers, traders and *negotiatores* who were tied to the services of the Church. John the Almoner, for instance, who headed the church at Alexandria in the early seventh century, possessed a fleet of large transport ships manned by agents (*pistikoi*) and captains (*pronaukleroi*). One of them is recorded as taking corn to Britain in time of famine which we can assume came from church estates in Egypt, since a papyrus of 390 mentions church ships bringing corn from Hermopolis to Alexandria (Leont. *v. Joh. Eleem.* IX; Mitteis-Wilcken, *Chrest.* no. 434).[34] Bishop Patiens of Lyon on one occasion when bringing famine relief to cities in the south of France 'fitted out not two ships but two rivers' (i.e. the Saône and the Rhône) and 'jammed the roads with grain', according to Sidonius (*Ep.* VI 12).

Clerics, who were technically banned from open market activity as *negotiatores*, could undertake *mercatura* if it was for the benefit of the poor or if the profits of their workshops (*ergasteria*) and shops (*taberna*) went to the Church (*C.J.* I 3.2 (357)). There are plenty of examples of such persons, men like Theodosius, the founder of a monastery near Rhosus in Syria who built his own ship to market the produce (Theodoret, *H.R.* = *P.G.* 82.1389). Monks had a reputation for petty market activities – *emere aut vendere, ut plerisque monachis moris est* (Sulp. Sev. *v. Mart.* X 6; cf. Jerome, *Ep.* XXII 34). The canons of the Church Councils are also full of vain prohibitions attempting to stop the clergy acting as *procuratores* and *conductores* for rich secular patrons or carrying out *negotiatio* for filthy lucre while engaged in business for the Church.[35]

State legislation reflected this wide range of business activities of Church agents. Apart from dispensation from the lustral tax in the running of stalls and workshops, they were also given immunities for long distance trade (e.g. *C.Th.* XVI 2.10 (320)). The proviso that this should be for charitable purposes – *alimoniae causa* (*C.Th.* XVI 2.8 (330)) – obviously failed to work and a limit of ten to fifteen solidi worth of exemption capital was substituted (*C.Th.* XIII 1.11 (379)). But this too apparently did not work (*C.Th.* XIII 1.16 (399)). All of which indicates that a great number of tradesmen or *negotiatores*, even when participating in market activity, did so in conditions quite unlike those faced by their free enterprise cousins. Whether the church at Marseilles paid cash for its oil, papyrus and other cargoes or imported the produce from its own estates and related properties in its own ships (Greg. Tur. *Hist.* V 5), there is no reason to think normal commercial principles applied to the transactions. The sometimes crooked deals of the *mercator* Amantius, who operated between Marseilles and the Auvergne, were vastly assisted by the canonical letter he carried from Bishop Sidonius and by his admission as a *lector* to the Bishop of Marseilles, which must have given him tax immunity and in return for which he appears to have acted as church purchasing agent at the docks (Sid. *Epp.* VI 8, VII 2 and VII 9.4).

Tied trade – the landowners

In the later Empire, as in the medieval period, rulers and churchmen behaved precisely like noble estate owners, whose properties they had inherited, in so far that their land surpluses attracted and fed supporters while providing for prestigious displays and rich gift exchanges. Gregory's gift to Bishop Zeno of 2,000 modii of wheat (Greg. *Ep.* VI 4), is typical of the way, if not the scale, such wealth was manipulated. In Gaul, at least, and perhaps elsewhere, the bishop was regarded as legal owner of church property.[36]

Gregory's close interest in the fifteen separate patrimonial accounts and the organization of the church estates was the result of his experience as an aristocratic landowner before his elevation.[37] Some of the enormous estates of nobles, like those of Pontius Paulinus of Bordeaux, were indeed considered little 'kingdoms' (*regna* – Aus. *Ep.* XXVII 115–16), which, in the case of this particular property, did subsequently become the church property of Bishop Pontius Leontius, who was *dominus innumerabilium praediorum* (*Chron. Min.* I p. 650).

The behaviour of nobles, therefore, and their relationship to *negotiatores* and trade illustrates some of the obscurer aspects of imperial and church affairs. The multiplicity and size of these domanial estates, some of which individually are described as larger than town territories in the fourth century, as in earlier epochs,[38] supported private armies of servants and dependents. The management of these important depots of power, therefore, was not a matter of indifference to the wealthy, to whom it qualified as *negotium*. The future emperor Theodosius, for instance, retired to his estates in Spain to build up his support by *beneficia*, which the panegyricist describes with the words, *negotia adsiduitate, consilio, re iuvabas* (*Pan. Lat.* II (XII) 9). And to this political end especially the worth of the estate, which meant its produce, was of direct concern.[39] Most obviously the noble needed gold as a means of thesaurizing his wealth and for the purchase of goods he could not produce himself – whether to obtain foreign gourmet delicacies from Augustine's *negotiator* (*Serm.* XXVIII 2) or to buy special shoes from Sidonius's *krepidopoles* (*Ep.* XXXII). As with imperial taxes or church property, it is reasonable to assume some of this cash was supplied by peasant farmers themselves (in this case, tenants) when they had access to a money market. But legislation recognized reality when it forbade the *domini praediorum* to demand money instead of kind as rent under normal circumstances (*C.J.* XI 48.5 (365) – to the governor of Tripolitania). Even in exceptional circumstances, like a rent dispute over the produce, the *officium* of the governor, not the tenant, took the initiative for sale of the *reditus* (*C.J.* XI 48.20.1–2 (529)). Other legislation required Roman senators to pay the *aurum oblaticium* in Rome, even if they had possessions in far away provinces, 'because their income (*reditus*) is brought to the city by their procurators and agents (*actoribus*)' (*C.Th.* VI 2.11 (395)). *Reditus* was in kind and some of it was sold in Rome or nearby. This at any rate is what Symmachus did with the produce from his estates in Apulia (Sym. *Ep.* VI 12).

The massive gold incomes of Roman nobles in the later Empire are well known,[40] and make nonsense of the notion of autarky or of a closed domestic economy. The production of estates such as that at Morville near Anthée (Namur), which possessed its own metal mine, six furnaces with forges and thirteen workshops, could not conceivably have been limited to its own needs.[41] The 'industrial' activity of Belgian villas in addition to their agriculture continued into, but did not begin in, the fourth century.[42] The organization of the workshops of the villa of Anthée itself must preclude any idea that the distribution of the enamel ware was carried out by the tenants.[43]

Not all surplus produce, however, was turned to gold or used to feed the retainers of the estate. A major part of the correspondence of rich landowners like Ausonius or Sidonius was devoted to rendering obligations towards guests, friends and supporters, either by entertainment or by gift exchanges – (*mensa non minus pascens hospitem quam clientem* – Sid. *Ep.* IV 9). The astonishing network of villas held by various branches of the families of the Pontii Paulini, the Syagrii and the Sidonii, not to mention those of Ausonius's descendants, in Aquitania, were units in a relationship assiduously maintained by exchanges. Pontius Paulinus sent Ausonius a gift of oil and *garum* from his estates near Barcelona (Aus. *Ep.* XXV); Ausonius sent thrushes and ducks to Hesperius (Aus. *Ep.* XVIII); Paulinus gave wild fowl to his friend Gestidius and in return received fish (Aus. *Ep.* XXXIV); Sulpicius sent Paulinus corn oil from the Midi (Paul. *Ep.* V 21). These may sound trivial until one hears how Munderic, priest at Langres, was accused of treachery for having 'brought provisions and gifts' to King Sigibert to use against King Chilperic's brother (Greg. Tur. *Hist.* V 5), or how Faustus, Abbot of Lérins, was sent with gifts to the Britanni (Sid. *Ep.* IX 9); or how the munificence of Bishop Patiens saved half the Midi. Then the scale of the *beneficia* carried political power.

Huge stores were constructed to house this currency, like the immense *horrea* at *Burgus*, the chateau of Paulinus on the Garonne (Sid. *Carm.* XXII 169). Ausonius's 'little estate', one of many, stored enough grain and food for two years (Aus. *de hered.* II 27–8). A good deal of the produce was moved internally, as it were, between domanial estates.[44] Ausonius moved wine by cask from his Garonne estate to another of his estates at Saintes (Aus. *Ep.* VII) just as Gregory transported timber to Rome from his papal estates in Bruttium (Greg. *Ep.* IX 124–7).

It is here that the status of *negotiatores* and traders of various types has to be taken into account. For, while undoubtedly there were entrepreneurs with whom rich estate owners had dealings, much of the 'business' just described was carried out by tied agents. We may sometimes detect a difference between directly employed agents (*actores*, *procuratores*, or *pragmateutai*) and entrepreneurial *mercatores* or *negotiatores*, but most references obscure the distinction for the good reason that a single person might fill both roles. The direct sale of the produce of land by agents or *coloni*, which included industrial products of the estate, was not subject in law to the lustral tax, but it evidently sometimes became mixed with the taxable 'business of commerce' (*C.Th.* XIII 1.3 (361)), or elsewhere *mercandis distrahendisque rebus* (*C.Th.* XIII 1.10 (374)).

Philo, former *procurator/vilicus* of Ausonius, looks like one such person. 'He had stored up at the estate of Ebromagus the *merces* which he had bought on various lands', says Ausonius, which included exchanging salt for grain, etc. (Aus. *Ep.* XXVI *passim*). Philo however was not an independent colporteur, as Jullian alleges,[45] but firmly tied to Ausonius's service still. He was commissioned by Ausonius to procure grain for Ausonius's Lucaniac estate, financed by Ausonius (whose books he fiddled) and above all protected by the *hospitium* which Ausonius could command from friends with estates along the Tarn and Garonne. These are the sorts of transactions which Libanius also described when he dispatched wine to Cilicia (*Ep.* 709) and sent servants there to collect wood (*Ep.* 568), perhaps in direct exchange or through a special arrangement of the type he made with his councillor friend, Severus, who had property in Lycia (*Ep.* 1191).[46]

One aspect of the more general phenomenon of patronage in this age was that smaller shipowners tried to gain exemption from requisitioning by claiming to be the agents of *potentes* (*C.Th.* XIII 7.1 (379) 7.2 (406)). The enterprising *mercator*, Amantius, mentioned earlier, who cashed in on the power of the Church, was at one stage also the *cliens* of the *comes civitatis* at Marseilles (Sid. *Ep.* VII 2.7). Similarly, Libanius used his influence with Themistius, the administrator, and with other contacts at Sinope to obtain protection and facilities *kat' emporian* for the agents (*paides*) of his friend Lollianus (Lib. *Epp.* 177–8).[47]

The landowning class frequently, probably normally, owned ships or other transport for the distribution and exchange of their estate produce. That is simply assumed by Libanius (*Or.* VIII 3; cf. *Or.* VII 9, VIII 1). The *functio navicularia*, as is often noted, was linked to land just because landowners, both rich and poorer, were often *domini navium*.[48] Private ports on the rivers or on the coast were a regular feature of the great estates, like that of Paulinus at Ebromagus, noted above, on the Garonne, which Philo used. Later Sidonius says there was a private 'fleet of ships' to be seen there (*Ep.* VIII 12).

Summary of the nature of trade and traders in the later Empire

The nature of what we loosely class as trade in the later Roman Empire, conducted by men whom we, like the Romans, loosely call traders, turns out frequently not to be either entrepreneurial or strictly commercial. What has been described was more exchange and distribution, sometimes through the medium of the market place, frequently directly between supplier and consumer.

Even the market however was frequently not free to find its own price levels, since distortion was created through discriminatory taxation, privilege and protection. Traders, though sometimes combining their other activities with entrepreneurial enterprises, were fundamentally agents, dependents or clients of the rich, whose requirements, not abstract economic forces, dictated their activities.

The idea that rich landowners were not involved or interested in the profits from the produce of their land – or that we should be surprised when they were involved – is quite simply absurd. 'Business' of this sort, that is, the direct disposal of surpluses and the acquisition of necessities or luxuries (which are, after all, necessities for the rich), whether through the market or not and whether through agents or not, must be sharply separated from 'living on the *profits* of buying and selling', as Roman legislators tried to define it (*C.Th.* XIII 1.13 (384) – *emendi vendendive compendiis ultro citroque quaesitis*).

The importance of tied trade and traders in the later Empire

It is much more difficult to assess the relative importance of this type of tied trade within the whole sphere of economic activity and exchange of the later Roman Empire. Not only is there the perennial problem of a lack of statistics, which produces pseudo-statistics (e.g. figures for corn and pottery distribution, shipwrecks, production and productivity etc.), but there is the basic question of the purpose of the market – whether it existed primarily for economic profit or for social exchange – the sort of problem noted at the beginning of this paper which is being increasingly discussed by medievalists.[49]

To start with, we need not doubt the widespread existence of traders as genuinely independent middlemen in urban markets and rural fairs, whether as local shopkeepers, long-distance traders on trampships or colporteurs travelling from town to town. There are plenty of references to all of them. No-one for instance would have tried to exclude Greek *pantopolae* from Rome on the eve of the Vandal invasions, who had congregated there 'in the greatest number' and with 'enormous diligence to buy and sell' (*N. Val.* V 1(440)), if there had been a shortage of traders. Salvian (*de gub. Dei* IV 14) says that, even in the midst of the political upheavals of the fifth century, 'crowds of Syrian merchants occupied the greater part of nearly all cities'. But none of this gets us very far.

There are however three observations to make about this type of entrepreneurial activity. First are the points stressed by Jones, which need no elaboration, that the *collatio lustralis* which was levied on such trade and even the greatest mercantile fortunes of which we have record were never significant in terms of the general economy or the wealth of the landowning classes.[50]

Second are Finley's arguments for the reduction of the urban commodity market with its effect on the sale of slaves, due to a decline in the cities themselves.[51] The decline of the urban market can be observed by a reduction to some extent in the money supply in the later fourth century.[52] We need to be careful, perhaps, not to exaggerate the measure of the urban decline[53] and not to ignore the extent to which a reduced urban market was compensated for by rural *nundinae* and fairs (see e.g. *N. Val.* XXIV (447)). But more important is the fact that Finley is talking about a decline in the purchasing power of the mainly entrepreneurial shopkeepers, petty suppliers and middlemen, who were in any case relatively insignificant.

Third are the points already made in the case of Ausonius's ex-steward, Philo, who on closer examination turns out to be not totally entrepreneurial but still tied to the service of the *dominus*. Philo's name might suggest he was of Greek extraction, but the many other references to Syrians, Jews, Greeks in the later Empire normally occur without any clue as to what attachments, if any, they had.[54] Their services to the court or Church have already been documented. Many were probably former slaves with Greek-sounding names who continued to serve their former masters. But some were not.

Finally, there is the question raised by Laurent that the existence of pseudo-*negotiatores* was an index of economic decline. This is a large and complex question without any quantitative data, which finds no common response among historians of the later Empire. There are plenty of arguments in favour of prosperity. Rougé, for instance, concludes that there was a breakdown in trade in the third century, but detects an economic revival in the fourth.[55] In the East which faced no military crisis, even the cities seem to continue to enjoy affluence and vigorous exchange.[56] Egyptian historians argue that the large estates of the later Empire implied a redistribution of wealth but no diminution in the cloth trade.[57] Recent excavations of the Bourse in Marseilles show no apparent reduction of commercial activity in the fourth and fifth century, while the distribution of rich marble sarcophagi, including imported Carrara stone, in the late fourth and fifth centuries demonstrates the rich prosperity of the Midi.[58] For those who like numerical data, the references to Gallic cloth collected by Jullian to illustrate his volume on the high Empire (*NB* not the later Empire) include twenty-five from literary sources of the later third century onwards and only ten from the earlier periods. This of course proves nothing. But neither archaeology nor fiscal legislation can be used to prove a general decline in population or land cultivation.[59] There were, naturally, certain regional changes, particularly in Italy. But recent work on the farms in Picardy shows that, although many of the medium size villas were abandoned (not surprisingly) in the troubles of the later third century, actual cultivation of the land and many of the villages continued, suggesting once again that we are witnessing a reorganization of social relations but not an economic decline.[60] The same conclusion can be drawn from the polarization of wealth evident in the graves of Pannonia and in the growth of great villa estates throughout Africa.[61]

The reorganization of social relations can be seen in the growth of the patronage which directed the disposable surpluses of the producers, often away from the urban market place. Estate production in the West and to a lesser extent in the East took over from urban manufacture, if one is to judge by the legislation attempting to prevent *collegiati* and *ministeria* leaving the towns (*C.Th.* XIII 19.1–3 (400)). Many of the *nundinae* and *vici*, where exchanges took place, were located on the estates themselves, as the example of Philo at Ebromagus shows, to the benefit of the domanial lord. But desertion of the towns by *collegiati* would have had a limited effect, since rural estates had always controlled much of the specialist manufacture. Even in eastern provincial towns, such as Korykos in Cilicia during the later Empire period, a high proportion of the population was engaged in occupations of service and consumption; no more than a third were artisan producers.[62] In the West many rural estates, as we saw, were like medieval chateaux, incorporating whole communities and resembling towns – *nunc villae grandes oppida parva prius* (Rutil. *de red.* I 224). The rural *vici* of the later Empire were, as the name implies, ancestors of the medieval *Wiks*. These phenomena may imply an increase in control and 'decommercialization', increasing exploitation no doubt and a shift in the distribution of wealth from poor to rich. But they do not prove an obvious decline in production or exchange.

'Decommercialization' implies the growth of 'internal' supply and reciprocal exchange between the estates of the rich. That has been abundantly illustrated by examples from Ausonius and Libanius. Multiple ownership of estates, always a characteristic of Roman landowning classes, must have increased with the concentration of wealth in fewer hands during the late Empire. Ausonius had a network of estates around Bordeaux plus others in the Poitou, the Saintogne and the Gironde. His son, Hesperius, also had properties in Marseilles and in the East, to which his grandson Paulinus of Pella added others in Greece and Epirus – *complures sparsa per urbes* (Paul. Pell. *Euch.* 414). Melania the Younger's properties extended to Rome, Campania, Aquitania and the rest of Gaul, Britain, Sicily, Numidia, Mauretania, Africa and to the East (Pallad. *Laus. Hist.* LXI, *v. Melan. Graec.* XI, XIX, XX). They provided an enormous annual income, accounted as 12,000 pieces of gold, apart from moveable goods (*kineta*) which 'were so great they could not be reckoned' (*v. Melan. Graec.* XV).

Melania was not just a spectacular exception. Other members of the imperial elite, like Petronius Probus, Melania's cousin, 'possessed domains in almost every part of the Roman world' (Amm. Marc. XXVII 11.1). Flavius Rufinus likewise (Claud. *In Ruf.* I 137ff. esp. 193–4). Even quite ordinary senators are characterized by Ausonius and the Theodosian Code as having *patrimonia sparsa sub regnis* (Aus. *Grat. actio* VII 36) or *per longinquas provincias atque diversas possessiones* (*C.Th.* VI 2.11 (395)). Ten or twenty domains of 1,000 to 2,000 hectares, Jullian calculated, was not unusual for a Gallic noble.[63] Quite apart from great figures like the Symmachi or Caeonii, many undistinguished Roman senators had estates in one or other of the rich African provinces, which thereby constituted a vital part of their political influence.[64] Internal trade from these African estates provides a more satisfactory explanation than the development of new forms of production and economies of scale to explain the otherwise economically puzzling capture of Italian and South

Gallic 'markets' by African table and kitchen ware and the apparently irrational but widespread dispersal of African oil and *garum* to places like Spain and Gaul which produced their own. Pottery, according to the law, counted as rural production on the estates and was free from tax provided it did not get into the hands of middlemen (*C.Th.* XIII 1.10 (374)).

Internal supply of disposable surpluses and the redistribution of wealth by charity or largess was one of the major activities of the Church, as the letters of Gregory prove. There is no doubt that this is one explanation for the success of the institution. The consumer demand of many poor inhabitants of the cities, possibly as many as a tenth of the population (Joh. Chrys. *In Math.* LXVI (LXVII) 3 = P.G. LVIII 63)), was diverted from the commodity market to the open door of the Church. This sometimes caused not desertion from, but a drift into, the city (e.g. Lib. *Or.* XLI 6). That helps us gain some notion of the scale of one non-market activity. More spectacular was the charity of Bishop Patiens of Lyon who in a bad year fed with corn 'at his own expense' (*peculiari sumptu*) the people of Arles, Riez, Avignon, Orange, Viviers, Valence, Clermont and the Tricastini, not forgetting others 'throughout all Aquitania' (Sid. *Ep.* VI 12, Greg. Tur. *Hist.* II 24).

On the other hand market activity did not cease. Patiens's corn would normally have been sold, Sidonius says. About half the revenue from the partrimonial estates of the Ravenna church in the seventh century was accounted in gold; in the sixth century the proportion was probably rather higher, even allowing for the problem of accounting methods noted earlier.[65]

The scale of imperial redistribution and the size of the controlled, internal economy is best illustrated by the growth of the estates of the *res privata*. It was upon the *res privata* in Gaul that the Merovingian kings relied almost exclusively to maintain their court and army and to endow their supporters. Tracing the extent to which this was developing in the later Empire is a hazardous undertaking, but it seems clear that, regardless of what system of taxes prevailed elsewhere, a large part of the surpluses of the imperial estates were always collected in kind for extra-market supplies. The area of land of the *res privata* in some provinces, such as Africa, constituted a sixth of the province and a far higher proportion of the cultivable terrain.[66] If also, as the sources say, the *res privata* owed its greatest growth to massive confiscations from the period of the Severan emperors onwards (H.A. *Sev.* 12), the development must be linked to imperial management of oil production in Spain and Tripolitania first and subsequently in the other African provinces.[67] Again, this helps to explain the otherwise odd distribution and near monopoly of African amphorae in the later Empire.

One such obvious non-economic consumer was, of course, the army. The proposition put forward by Gren that the major, although not the only, function of imperial estates from Augustus onwards was to supply the army,[68] is impossible to prove and to some extent weakened by the haphazard way in which they were acquired.[69] Presumably regular army supplies came from standard taxation, the *officium* of the Praetorian Prefect in the later Empire. Nevertheless the scattered estates of the *res privata* must have aided a mobile emperor and his court to find supplies. What is not implied by the change is a fall in production or exchange, although there must have been a reduction in the entrepreneurial commodity market if soldiers and others received their pay in kind not cash.

Summary of the scale of trade and traders

Plentiful evidence of the existence of trade and traders in the later Empire exists and does not in any sense support the hypothesis of a closed economy. Entrepreneurial activity, which was of limited importance economically anyway, may have diminished to some extent as wealth became more concentrated in the hands of institutional proprietors such as the Church and State or of aristocratic elites.

The activity of the latter, however, in the interchange of commodities between their estates or in the marketing of their surplus produce was not obviously reduced with the decline of urban institutions. The Church's role as an agent of redistribution was frequently massive and always increasing. And the State's reorganization of its military and bureaucratic system was assisted by the steady growth of its own sources of supply. But from neither development can one prove there was an economic decline.

We must beware of supposing that a reduction in long-distance trade, as may have happened, is a symptom of absolute decline.[70] But in any case the presence or absence of markets and of a market economy is not necessarily decisive to the success of long-distance trade.[71] Almost certainly there was from the third and fourth centuries onwards a development of new axes of exchange or trade routes, between northern Gaul and Britain, for instance, or between the Rhine, the Danube and North Italy, which would not be reflected in statistics of Mediterranean shipwrecks.[72] It is also worth underlining the fact that, in long-distance trade beyond the German frontiers, an analysis of the distribution of a series of trade goods shows very little difference between the later and the earlier Roman periods.[73]

If there was a tendency towards regionalism, cabotage and local production which appears, for instance, in pottery manufacture, this is very different from villa autarky or stagnation.[74] If estates to some extent lost their incentive to produce for international exchange, they could still produce, as they did in the Merovingian period, to satisfy domestic or provincial demand. It is possible that there was within Gaul, for instance, a shift in economic activity – Argonne pottery, Rhineland glass, Belgic textiles – from the Midi to north of the Loire in the fourth century which the invasions of the early fifth century drove south again.[75]

In these conditions, the number of pseudo-*negotiatores*, tied to the services of those who did not make their living from the profits of buying and selling in the market, probably increased, to judge by the frequency of the references to them. This is particularly evident in the growth of the Church.

Conclusion

The aim of this paper was to follow in the footsteps of Pirenne and Fustel de Coulanges by showing that the institutions and even the practice of trade did not alter radically between the later Roman Empire and the Merovingian period. There are however many who, while conceding this much, would argue that the Roman Empire by the fourth century AD had already undergone a total transformation and was by now medieval in its institutions. It is worth concluding therefore by considering briefly where there may be parallels to be drawn and questions to be asked about the history of the earlier Roman Empire.

(a) Aristocratic trade. Has too much energy been wasted proving the self-evident fact that the rich sold or otherwise disposed of the produce of their estates for profit, whether directly themselves or through their own agents? Whereas what requires definition is the extent to which they made use of entrepreneurs also.[76] I suspect that few middlemen were used.

(b) State trade. Has too much been made of the theoretical freedom of *annona* suppliers and shippers or of army contractors, because one underplays the mechanism of state controls, tax privileges and requisitions, which rendered such services effectively compulsory and hence outside the normal entrepreneurial market? As suggested above, the existence of state 'factories' in the later Empire does not actually prove that the units and methods of production changed greatly.

Negotiatores and traders are ubiquitous in the evidence, but the references by themselves do not tell us whether a man was an independent operator or not. In some cases the term unequivocally denotes agents of households or those formally in charge of army supplies.[77] This is, then, the proper context from which to view the celebrated series of inscriptions from Gaul, whose distribution is limited to the main axes that lead towards the Rhine army.[78] Such men were more than just 'in der Interessensphäre des Staates'.[79] Many surely must have been commissioned as purchasing or collecting agents of the army or provincial governor. As for 'le "grande" commerce', that, says Goudineau, 'risque de constituer un mythe'.[80]

Dirigisme therefore and a closed economy were not just inventions of the later Empire and a distorted economic regime. If they did increase in the later Empire, as our sources suggest, it is not thereby self-evident that they were symptoms of decline.

Notes

KEITH HOPKINS: Introduction

1 – Austin/Vidal-Naquet (1977) 3f.
2 – W. Sombart, *Der moderne Kapitalismus* (Munich,[2] 1916) vol. 1, 142–3.
3 – W. V. Harris, 'Roman Terracotta Lamps: the Organisation of an Industry', *J.R.S.* 70 (1980) 126ff.

1 – PAUL CARTLEDGE: 'Trade and politics' revisited: Archaic Greece

1 – G. E. M. de Ste. Croix reviewing Finley (1965) in *J.H.S.* 87 (1967) 179–80. Other important reviews by E. Gabba, *R.F.C.* 94 (1966) 112–8; Ph. Gauthier, *R.Ph.* 41 (1967) 144–51.
2 – Finley (1965) 11, 13, 33, commenting on Hasebroek (1933) (1931).
3 – Now conveniently reprinted as Finley (1979).
4 – Of the books published in English within the past quinquennium the most useful for our purposes are Starr (1977), Boardman (1980), Snodgrass (1980), Finley (1981).
5 – de Ste. Croix (n.1); Bravo (1974) (1977); Humphreys (1978) 159–74; Mele (1979); Snodgrass (1980) 123–59. An earlier example is Gauthier (1972).
6 – O. Murray, *Early Greece* (London, 1980) 308; but he is of course wrong to state that Hasebroek's *Staat und Handel* began the controversy.
7 – Strictly, one should speak of his positions, since he conceded in the preface to his second book that *Staat und Handel* had been a one-sided and exaggerated polemic. Still, his fundamental theses remained unchanged and he sanctioned the corrected English translation of *S.H.* that appeared after the *Wirtschaftsgeschichte*; I therefore quote from the 1933 version. The passages that particularly concern archaic (as opposed to classical) trade are (1931) 29–33, 142–51, 255–91; (1933) 44–71.
8 – Ed. Meyer, *Kleine Schriften* (Halle, 1924) 118–9, repr. in Finley (1979). Cf. in the context of Meyer's view on slavery, Finley (1980) 46–7.
9 – M. Weber, *Economy and Society* (California, 1978; German original 1922) 1354, 1362, 1341, 1350.
10 – Yvon Garlan, 'Le travail libre en Grèce ancienne', in P. Garnsey (ed.), *Non-slave labour in the Greco-Roman world*, *P.C.P.S.* supp. 6 (1980) 19 n.4.
11 – K. Marx, *Pre-capitalist economic formations* (London, 1964); *Grundrisse* (Harmondsworth, 1973).
12 – Most notably in Finley (1978) (originally published in 1954); this filled an

admitted lacuna in M. Mauss, *The Gift* (London, 1954) (French original 1925), on which see also M. Sahlins, *Stone age economics* (London, 1974) 149–83.

13 – Hence the 'formalist-substantivist controversy', a bibliography on which is given by G. Dalton in Sabloff/Lamberg–Karlovsky (1975) 117 n.20.

14 – E.g. generalized, balanced and negative reciprocity, to use the terminology of Sahlins (n.12) 185–275.

15 – Polanyi's 'patterns of integration' was an unfortunate formulation, since it committed him to reifying 'the economy' as the object of the supposed integration while simultaneously denying its autonomous existence.

16 – This is one reason why Polanyi's tools have been taken up so eagerly by prehistorians (e.g. Sabloff/Lamberg-Karlovsky (1975); Earle/Ericson (1977); but these are not encumbered by the need to make the concepts fit the contemporary written evidence. For a more favourable assessment of Polanyi than mine see Humphreys (1978) 31–75.

17 – For some of my views on Starr (1977), see *Phoenix* 33 (1979) 354–7; on Murray (n.6) *T.L.S.* 13 June 1980, 675; on Snodgrass (1980) section V of this paper.

18 – Cf. A. Aymard, *Etudes d'histoire ancienne* (Paris, 1967) 329–30.

19 – See rather Hasebroek (1933) 19–20; Mele (1979) 42–3 and n.28. I am not convinced that an inscribed lead plaque of *c.* 500 BC from Kerkyra (Corfu) records a maritime loan, cf. P. Kalligas, 'An inscribed lead plaque from Kerkyra', *B.S.A.* 66 (1971) 79–94.

20 – Mele concedes that Hesiod's *phortos* is envisaged solely in terms of surplus cereals, whereas Homeric *prexis* deals in a far wider range of goods – metals, cattle, slaves, wine. But he reads between the lines of Hesiod's advice to use commerce as an escape from hunger and debt the implication that at least other products relevant to agriculture – slaves, animals – could have been involved. This strikes me as special pleading.

21 – For the concept of 'port of trade' see Polanyi (1968) 238–60.

22 – Cf. Humphreys (1978) 167: 'Little but an ideological hairline divided the noble who voyaged in order to come home loaded with valuable gifts . . . or to exchange iron for copper . . . from the "commander of sailors out for gain . . . , always thinking about his cargo".'

23 – On all aspects of the historical significance of Greek pottery see Will (1956), Cook (1959), Vallet/Villard (1963); cf., on early state societies generally, Renfrew (1977).

24 – In detail see my 'Sparta and Samos: a special relationship?', *C.Q.* 32 (1982) 243–65.

2 – A. M. SNODGRASS: Heavy freight in archaic Greece

1 – *Deutsches arch. Inst., Antike Denkmäler herausgegeben vom Kaiserlich Deutschen arch. Inst.* I 1 (1887) pl. 8, 3a; cf. II 3 (1898) pl. 29, 12.

2 – See H. Walter, K. Vierneisel, 'Heraion von Samos: die Funde de Kampagnen 1958 und 1959', *A.M.* 74 (1959) 10–34, at 11, fig. 1 and Tafel, squares M–N 11–13.

3 – H. Kyrieleis, 'Archaische Holzfunde aus Samos', *A.M.* 95 (1980) 87–147, at 89–94.

4 – See e.g. G. M. A. Richter, *Kouroi*, 3rd ed. (London, 1970), 6.

5 – G. Lippold, *Die griechische Plastik*. Handbuch der Altertumswissenschaft. W. Otto, R. Herbig (ed.). Handbuch der Archäologie III (Munich, 1950), 92 n.11.

6 – Richter (n.4) 154, no. 63a.

7 – J. Ducat, *Les kouroi du Ptoion: le sanctuaire d'Apollon Ptoieus à l'époque archaïque* Bibliothèques des écoles françaises d'Athènes et de Rome, 219 (Paris, 1971).

8 – Richter (n.4) 51–3, no. 15; J. J. Coulton, 'Lifting in early Greek architecture', *J.H.S.* 94 (1974) 1–19, at 17.

9 – Richter (n.4) 51–3.

10 – At least, this is how I understand the passage, with the relative clause *choris ho ti . . en* being dependent solely on *anathemata* and not on *agalmata* too; for if bronze and stone *statues* are excepted, then what sculpture worth mentioning is left? *graphe*, writing, points the same way: that is, to dedications in general, not to statues.

11 – B. Isserlin *et al.*, 'Motya, a Phoenician-Punic site near Marsala', *Annual of the Leeds University Oriental Society* 4 (1965) 84–131, at 129.

12 – N. Yalouris, 'Problems relating to the temple of Apollo Epikourios at Bassai', *Acta of the XIth International Congress of Classical Archaeology, London, 1978* (London, 1979), 89–104, at 91.

13 – P. A. Ålin, Review of A. M. Snodgrass, *The Dark Age of Greece* (Edinburgh, 1971), *A.J.A.* 77 (1973) 238.

14 – Whatever its remaining deficiencies, this paper has benefited from the criticisms of Dr P. A. Cartledge, Mr M. H. Crawford, Professor M. I. Finley and Dr R. G. Osborne.

3 – YVON GARLAN: Greek amphorae and trade

1 – The contents of Greek amphorae found in land or underwater excavations are generally impossible to determine. In certain cases, however, it has been possible to note that their sides were coated in resin, as in the shipwreck of Kyrenia: H. W. Swing, M. L. Katzev, 'The Kyrenia shipwreck: A fourth-century BC Greek merchant ship', *Marine Archaeology*, D. J. Blackman (ed.) (London 1973) 341, or to interpret a graffito as an indicator of the contents (e.g. V. I. Kac and S. Ju. Monachov, 'The amphorae of the Hellenistic Chersonese from the settlement of Panskoe I in the north-west of the Crimea' (in Russian), *Monde antique et archéologie* 3 (1977) 95–7: E = Elaion?). For oil, attempts have been made to analyse the microscopic traces which it can leave in porous vessels (J. Condamin, F. Formenti, M. O. Metais, M. Michel and P. Blond, 'The application of gas chromatography to the tracing of oil in ancient amphorae', *Archaeometry* 18 (1976) 195–201). But it must be admitted that it is often on the basis of arguments of simple probability (the reputation of local oil and wine) that we decide the purpose of particular amphora types. The great variety of foodstuffs transported in them is well attested; but I have some difficulty in believing that it extended to relatively light products like the nuts of Heraclea of Pontus (as is thought by Ju. G. Vinogradov and M. A. Onajko, 'The economic relations of Heraclea of Pontus with the north and north-east of the Black Sea in the Hellenistic and Roman periods' (in Russian), *Sov. Arkh.*, (1975) 86–93): almonds in any case were transported in sacks, or at least in perishable containers, in the shipwreck of Kyrenia (Swing, Katzev (above) 344).

2 – It seems improbable to me that Rhodes, for example, should have exported

empty amphorae on a large scale to Alexandria or the Black Sea as is imagined by Fraser (1972) 168, S. M. Sherwin-White, *Ancient Cos* (Göttingen, 1978) 241 or A. Sadurska, 'Timbres amphoriques de Mirmeki' in J. Irmscher, D. B. Shelov, *Griechische Städte und einheimische Völker des Schwarzmeergebietes* (Berlin, 1961) 110. Even in the great importing centres there should normally have been a local production of amphorae – in which little interest is taken, and which is very often difficult to identify: that does not, however, mean, that there were no *local* markets in empty amphorae, both new and used, as will be seen below (p. 31).

3 – On his personality, see the articles of A. I. Meljukova, D. D. B. Shelov and Yu. G. Vinogradov in B. N. Grakov, *The early iron age* (in Russian) (Moscow, 1977) 203–13. His key publication is his study of the stamps of Sinope (*The Greek potters' stamps in the names of astynomoi* (in Russian) (Moscow, 1928). But his thesis (1939) on *The stamped containers of ancient Greece in the Hellenistic epoch as source for the history of production and commerce* as well as his *corpus* of potters' stamps found in the Soviet Union (*I.O.S.P.E.* III) have unfortunately remained unpublished and are only known in the West through the use that his successors have made of them.

4 – See her most recent publication of the Greek amphora stamps of the Insula of the house of the actors: *Expl. arch. Delos* 27 (1970) in collaboration with M. Savvatianou-Petropoulakou, also 'Revisions in early Hellenistic chronology' *Ath. Mitt.* 89 (1974) 193–200; cf. Grace (1979). I owe all gratitude to this scholar who patiently introduced me to this type of research and has since continued to give me the benefit of her incomparable knowledge of the subject.

5 – High and low chronologies still exist, for example, for the stamps of Heraclea and Sinope, and the provenance is not yet known securely of the 'wheel stamps' (certainly not Thasos, perhaps Amphipolis?).

6 – The division of material between several countries (mainly Greece, Egypt and the Soviet Union) does not facilitate exhaustive collection of data, which is indispensable in this type of research – the more so since numerous publications (when there is publication) leave much to be desired through ignorance of the level of technical knowledge reached by the specialists.

7 – Cf. H. P. Isler, 'Bolli d'anfora e documenti affini degli scavi di Monte Iato, *Misc. E. Manni* (Rome, 1980) IV 1215. The situation in this respect will probably only worsen if printed *corpora* are sacrificed for computerized data-banks (this is not to exclude a good use of the latter).

8 – Finley (1973) espec. 33; 'Archaeology and History', *Daedalus* 100 (1971) 168–86 (= *The use and abuse of history* (New York, 1975) 87–101).

9 – I am indebted for the translation of certain works in Russian to V. Grace and for others to my wife.

10 – Consult now *B.C.H.* 106 (1982) 219–33, of which a first draft was kindly sent to me.

11 – 'Questions on the method of study of imported amphorae in the Black Sea in antiquity' (in Russian), *Krat. Soob.* 148 (1976) 11–15 (finds from the village of Pivdennoe on the bank of the Dniestr and of the settlement of Elizavetovskoe at the mouth of the Don).

12 – A brief summary of the excavations which I carried out there in 1981 will be found in the 'Chronique' of *B.C.H.* 106 (1982), as well as in an article on 'Les timbres thasiens. Bilan et perspectives de recherches', to appear in *Annales E.S.C.* in 1982.

13 – Garlan (1979) 228–9.

14 – Y. Garlan, 'Chronique' *B.C.H.* 102 (1978) 807.
15 – The calculation of J.-Y. Empereur (n.10) after deductions made by V. Grace, *Newsletter Amer. res. centre in Egypt* 57 (1966) 1–5.
16 – I. B. Brashinsky does not take account of this factor in presenting his data: he includes, for example, in a single statistic at Elizavetovskoe, fifth century Thasian production, which is unstamped or rarely stamped, and that of the end of the fourth century, where stamping seems to have had a wide distribution (which would at least partly explain the percentage of 80 per cent that I noted at the Gate of Zeus). One would have liked to know, among other things, the incidence of stamping at Elizavetovskoe in the 'House of the wine merchant' when the early stamps were coming to an end (around 370–350). A cause for greater regret is that almost all western archaeologists are completely uninterested in this type of problem: see most recently M.-L. Säflund, *Stamped amphora handles, Labraunda* II. 2 (Lund, 1980).
17 – This is the impression that one gains from the publications of Brashinsky or of I. B. Zeest, *The pottery containers of the Bosphorus* (in Russian) (Moscow, 1960) as well as a list (unfortunately not very explicit in this respect) of Thasian amphorae of the fourth-to-third centuries imported into Bulgaria-Rumania (M. Lazarov, 'Le commerce de Thasos avec la côte thrace à l'époque pré-romaine', *Actes du IIe congrès int. de Thracologie, Bucarest 1976*, II (Bucarest, 1980) 171–87).
18 – Shelov (1970) 155; (1975) 8–9.
19 – Brashinsky has shown convincingly that conclusions derived from a sample are generally not seriously undermined by further work. From my own experience, even simple surface finds are often representative enough of buried material.
20 – Shelov (1970) 18, 160; (1975) 6–8.
21 – These are always key dates in the history of the stamps of Sinope. But their significance varies according to whether one adopts the low dating of Grakov (1977) or a dating earlier by a half-century: cf. I. B. Brashinsky, 'The economic relations of Sinope from the fourth to the second century BC' (in Russian), *La ville antique* (1963) 132–45.
22 – There is no sign of a general reduction in the export of Rhodian amphorae after this date.
23 – I give a detailed account of it in *D.H.A.* 8 (1982).
24 – Glodariu (1976) 12, 66; C. Muşeţeanu, N. Conovici and A. Atanasiu, 'Contribution au problème de l'importation des amphores grecques dans le sud-est de la Munténie', *Dacia*, n.s. 22 (1978) 190.
25 – Shelov (1970) 159–60.
26 – I am very grateful to the many Bulgarian and Rumanian scholars who gave me, in the summer of 1979, every facility for studying all the Thasian stamps, published or otherwise, which feature in their collections – with a view to their inclusion in the *corpus* which I am preparing in collaboration with V. Grace and M. Debidour.
27 – C. Muşeţeanu *et al.* (n.24) 192–7.
28 – 'Stamped handles of commercial amphoras', *Excavations at Nessana* (*Auja Hafir, Palestine*), H. Dunscombe Colt (ed.), I (Princeton, 1962) 108–9.
29 – 'Stamped amphora handles from the Delian temple estates', *Studies D. M. Robinson*, G. E. Mylonas (ed.) II (St. Louis, 1953) 127–34.

30 – These workshops produced in addition to amphorae only common ceramic. Cf. the distinction established in Roman Egypt between the *kerameus oinikou keramou* and the *leptokerameus*: H. Cockle, 'Pottery manufacture in Roman Egypt: A new papyrus', *J.R.S.* 71 (1981) 88.
31 – Cf. above, n.13 (Koukos); Garlan (1979) 258–65; 'Chronique', *B.C.H.* 104 (1980) 741 (Vamvouri Ammoudia); above n.12 (Kalonero).
32 – Cf. R. Rosati, 'La nozione di "proprietà dell'officina" e *l'epoiesen* nei vasi attici', *Atti Acc. Bologna, Rend.* 65 (1976–7) 45–73.
33 – Cf. M. Debidour, 'Réflexions sur les timbres amphoriques thasiens', *Thasiaca*, Suppl. V to *B.C.H.* 103 (1979) 274.
34. – The question should be posed again in relation to certain stamps like those of Cos, where mention is only made of the 'manufacturer', it is thought.
35 – 'The pottery stamps of Heraclea in Pontus' (in Russian), *Num. i ep.* 5 (1965) 18.
36 – Cf. Ph. Gauthier, in J.-M. Dentzer, Ph. Gauthier, T. Hackern (ed.) *Numismatique antique. Problèmes et méthodes* (Louvain, 1975) 169.
37 – V. Canarache, *Importul amforelor stampilate la Istria* (Bucarest, 1957) 388–90; V. Eftimie, 'Imports of stamped amphorae in the lower Danubian regions and a draft Rumanian corpus of amphora stamps', *Dacia* n.s. 3 (1959) 206, 209–11; M. Gramatopol and Gh. Poenaru Bordea, *Amphora stamps from Callatis and South Dobrudja* (Bucarest, 1970) 144–6; I. Glodariu (n.24) 74–7.
38 – H. P. Isler (n.7) 1228.
39 – Cf. my account of the book of I. B. Brashinsky (above, n.23). It is easy, too easy, to find in the Greek world a system of measurements capable of accounting (with a certain degree of approximation) for the capacity of an amphora. This is not to say that ancient potters made receptacles of any dimensions: it is self-evident that they followed traditions, even obeyed certain regulations.
40 – Chr. Dunant, J. Pouilloux, *Recherches sur l'histoire et les cultes de Thasos* II (1958). Fr. Salviat kindly informed me of his own views on the dating of the lists of Thasian *theoroi* and archons.
41 – The workshop mentioned in the Egyptian papyrus of 243 AD is situated 'in the large farmstead of your estate round Senepta', H. Cockle (n.30) 87 l. 6–7. The most recent studies on amphorae-producing workshops in the Roman world produce a similar result. See e.g. D. Manacorda, 'The *Ager Cosanus* and the production of the amphorae of 'Sestius', *J.R.S.* 68 (1978) 122–31.
42 – Bravo (1974) (1977).
43 – See now Y. Garlan, 'Les acclamations pédérastiques de Kalami (Thasos)', *B.C.H.* 106 (1982) 20–1.

4 – PAUL MILLETT: Maritime loans and the structure of credit in fourth-century Athens

1 – By far the best account of maritime loans as an institution is de Ste Croix (1974).

2 – I list a few additional figures to give some idea of scale. The commonest rate of interest on landside loans in classical Athens was 1 per cent per month. The return voyage from Athens to Pontus and back took a maximum of three months and the rate of interest charged on the double trip was at least 30 per cent. The

median size for loans on the *horoi* secured by real property is 1,100 drachmae; a crude calculation based on all the loans in Demosthenes' private speeches gives a median value of 1,700 drachmae.

In these and other similar calculations, in order to give the appropriate statistical bias, I have excluded all dubious figures which are favourable to my case.

3 – A maritime loan contract preserved in full in one of the law-court speeches attributed to Demosthenes gives a good idea of the possible complexity of the agreements: [XXXV] 10–3.

4 – This is not the place to catalogue all the points at which I disagree with Erxleben's handling of the evidence. I content myself with indicating the methods by which he arrives at the figures summarized in the text.

The figure of 41 citizen creditors (as opposed to Hansen's 7) is achieved by stringing together a series of unprovable assumptions which are too complicated to summarize. In this way, Erxleben is able to identify any number of otherwise obscure people as both citizens and lenders in maritime loans (480–2). Erxleben argues that the term *emporos* can mean 'lender in maritime loans' as well as 'merchant' (473–7). This enables him to reduce the number of trader-creditors to 3 (Hansen's figure is 12). Finally, Erxleben refuses to accept Andocides and Leocrates as proper citizen *emporoi* (Lysias VI 48–9; Lycurgus, *Leocrates* 26–7), on the grounds that they only turned to trade as a refuge from poverty after their respective flights from Athens.

5 – For a restatement of the citizen-metic cleavage, see D. Whitehead, *The ideology of the Athenian metic*, *P.C.P.S.* Suppl. 4 (1977), 117.

6 – Hasebroek was apparently pushed towards these uncharacteristic statements by the earlier work of Preisigke on the papyri, where relatively sophisticated types of banking transactions do occur: F. Preisigke, *Girowesen im griechischen Ägypten* (Strassburg, 1910). His second thoughts on Greek banking were the result of criticisms by B. Laum: 'Kein Giroverkher bei athenischen Banken' *Philologische Wochenschrift* 41 (1922) 427–32. The evidence on giro and associated operations has been carefully re-examined by Bogaert, who scrupulously ignores the papyri: (1968) 30, 336–45.

7 – Hasebroek (1933) 86 n.1. Bogaert's arguments in favour of interest payments ((1968) 346–51) are rightly rejected by Thompson ((1979) 225–8). I would go further than Thompson and question whether Greek bankers anticipated the modern distinction between savings and demand deposits.

8 – Prohibition of grain shipments: [Dem.] XXXIV 37, [Dem.] XXXV 50; penalties for frivolous prosecutions: [Dem.] LVIII 10.

9 – Terms of contract: [Dem.] LVI 10; the death penalty for inadequate security: [Dem.] XXXIV 50; restrictions on lending on double journeys: [Dem.] XXV 51: LVI 6, 11.

Although the purpose behind this last law and all the other legislation on trade is clear – to keep Athens supplied with essentials – the mechanism of the law is uncertain. The best discussion of which I am aware is C. R. Kennedy, *The orations of Demosthenes* (London, 1892) IV 332–5.

10 – There is a very full discussion of this complicated question by E. E. Cohen, *Ancient Athenian maritime courts* (Princeton, 1973) 3–95.

11 – I despair of summarizing the dispute over the precise jurisdiction of *dikai*

emporikai, which all depends on the placing of a comma in Dem. XXXII 1. For a brief account of the debate and a solution which I do not understand: Vélissaropoulos (1980) 236–41. The exceptional *dike emporike*: [Dem.] XXXIII.

12 – Dem. XXXII (*c*.350 BC); [Dem.] XXXIV (327 BC); [Dem.] XXXV (*c*.345 BC); [Dem.] LVI (322 BC).

13 – Maritime loan transactions: Isocrates XVII 42; [Dem.] XXXIII 4; [Dem.] LII 20. Lenders in maritime loans: Lysias XXXII 6; Dem. XXVII 11; Hyperides, *Against Demosthenes* frag. IV col.17.

I have omitted all doubtful cases; for the fullest possible list, see Erxleben (1974) 462–71.

14 – Theophrastus, *Characters* 23; Diogenes Laertius VII 13; Scholion to Eupolis' *Marikas* (*P. Oxy*. 2741) with the commentary by F. D. Harvey: 'The maritime loan in Eupolis' *Marikas*' *Z.P.E.* 23 (1976) 231–3; Diphilus frag. 43 vv.15ff; Xenophon, *Poroi* III 9, with a possible parallel at Diogenes Laertius VI 99, if I interpret the text correctly: P. Millett, 'Note on a Greek text relating to credit transactions', *P.C.P.S.* 206 (1980) 67–9.

15 – The five exceptions: Lysias frag. 38. 1–4 (*Against Aeschines the Socratic*), a loan from a banker to start a perfumery; [Dem.] XL 52, a loan from a banker to purchase a mining concession; Xenophon, *Memorabilia* II 7, a loan to set up a destitute family as cloth makers; Dem. XXXVII (passim), a loan to purchase a mill to process silver ore; *horos* No. 3 in Finley (1952), a loan to purchase a piece of land (with a possible parallel in *Arch. Delt.* 17 (1961–2) *Khronika* 35 No. 4).

16 – Paul Cartledge rightly reminds me that in reality, consumption credit is also typical of modern capitalism, without being one of its *differentia*. This point is hardly ever acknowledged in conventional models of the capitalist economy. A glance at any textbook of neo-classical economics will help to verify this point. In a work of over 850 pages, Samuelson has half a page on consumption loans: *Economics* (New York, 1970) 579; most of the standard texts have nothing at all. Because economists tend to take it for granted that 'credit' means 'productive credit', it is difficult to find adequate definitions of different types of credit transaction.

17 – Finley (1951) 87, (1973) 141. The idea is discussed in greater detail by de Ste Croix (1974) 42–3, who sees maritime loans as the closest approximation to proper insurance known from the classical world.

18 – The source of this material on medieval marine insurance is F. E. de Roover, 'Early examples of marine insurance', *Journal of Economic History* 5 (1945) 172–200.

19 – III 1–12. For a fuller summary of the speech from a different angle, see Finley (1951) 68–9.

20 – The most striking parallel is given by Marshall, describing lenders to costermongers in late nineteenth-century London: A. Marshall, *Principles of economics* (London, 1922) 589.

21 – The passages are collected in J. Korver, *De Terminologie van het credietwezen in het Grieksch* (Amsterdam, 1934) 20–5.

22 – Hasebroek (1933) 7–10, 36–7. Worth a separate mention is the statement of the plaintiff (Chrysippus) in the Demosthenic speech *Against Phormio* [XXXV] 51: The resources required by those who engage in trade come not from those who borrow, but from those who lend; and neither ship nor shipowner nor passenger can put to sea, if you take away the part contributed by those who lend.

Taken at face value, this passage would be conclusive evidence that every trader was forced to borrow in order to cover the costs of his voyage. Against this interpretation, de Ste. Croix points out – in support of the insurance theory – that this is an *ex parte* statement made by a litigant who is himself a lender. Chrysippus is trying to persuade the jury that it is in their own interests to decide the case in his favour, against the borrower: (1974) 43. Of course, Chrysippus is exaggerating traders' dependence on credit, but it would be pointless for him to weaken his case by making a claim that was blatantly untrue.

23 – With the exception of Isocrates XVII, all the relevant speeches are from the Demosthenic corpus: XXXVI, XLV, [XLVI], [XLIX], [LII].

24 – Bogaert (1968) 370 n.391. Demonstration of the non-involvement of bankers in maritime loans: Bogaert (1965); unconvincing counter-arguments by Erxleben (1974) 490–4 and Thompson (1979) 233–7.

25 – Isaeus XI 42–3; Aeschines I 97; Dem. XXVII 9. The evidence of the *horoi* also supports the idea of widespread casual money-lending by citizens. So far as I am aware, no creditor appears more than once on over 200 *horoi*.

26 On the size and nature of the estate: Davies, (1971) 152–4. Amongst the doubtful cases I omit from this category are the philosopher Zeno of Citium, who was rumoured to have more than 1,000 talents lent out in maritime loans (Diogenes Laertius VII 13); also Demo, the speaker in Dem. XXXII.

27 – Disregarding the transaction in [Dem.] XLIX 12, which is not a proper loan. For a summary of the Pantaenetos case: Finley (1951) 32–5.

28 – Roman evidence: de Ste Croix (1974) 55–6; medieval: C. B. Hoover, 'The sea loan in Genoa in the twelfth century', *The Quarterly Journal of Economics* 40 (1926) 495–529.

5 – CLAUDE MOSSÉ: The 'World of the *Emporium*' in the private speeches of Demosthenes

1 – Erxleben (1974) 460–520; Gluskina (1974) 111–38; Pecirkà (1976) 5–30.

2 – Davies (1971) 418.

3 – I should explain what I mean by 'circles of leadership' more fully. Athens was a democracy and, furthermore, a direct democracy. A 'political personnel' nevertheless existed, even if a popular vote could at any moment remove one or other of its members. This 'professionalism' becomes more marked in the fourth century, as the role of the orators becomes more important. Now, so far as we can tell, all the men who in effect controlled the affairs of the city appear to have been well-to-do.

4 – The litigant in *Against Theocrines* ([Dem.] LVIII) refers to a decree proposed by a certain Moerocles, which protected the *emporoi* and the *naukleroi* against any slanderous attacks (§§ 10, 53). This Moerocles may have been the opponent of Eubulus, mentioned in the speech *On the Embassy* 293, a man who appears to have been a supporter of Demosthenes at that time. In all probability, the only purpose of this decree was to ensure supplies for the city and it did not imply any agreement reached between any particular party and the world of the merchants. In this respect the remark of the litigant in *Against Zenothemis* ([Dem.] XXXII), when he refers to Demosthenes' refusal to ensure his defence because thenceforward he would be taken up with public affairs (§§ 31–2) is revealing.

6 – D. J. THOMPSON (CRAWFORD): Nile grain transport under the ptolemies

1 – E.g. *W. Chrest*. 442. 10–11 (late second century BC). For full details of editions of papyri referred to in this article see E. G. Turner, *Greek Papyri: An Introduction* (Oxford, 1968).

2 – See Rostowzew (1906); Hohlwein (1938); Boerner (1939); Préaux (1939) 137–53; Welles (1964); Meyer-Termeer (1978) and F. Heichelheim, 'Sitos', *R.E.* Suppl. 6 (1935) 819–92.

3 – See A. Calderini, Thesauroi – *ricerche di topografia e di storia della pubblica amministrazzione nell' Egitto greco-romano.* Studi della Scuola Papirologica 4 III (Milan, 1924).

4 – In the main *P. Petrie* II–III; *P. Tebt*. I, III, IV; *B.G.U.* VIII, for the Arsinoite and Herakleopolite nomes; Reekmans and van 't Dack (1952) publish a corn archive from Upper Egypt covering the provisionment of troops in Syene in 163 BC; Packman (1968).

5 – *P. Mich. Zen*. 17.4 (257 BC); *P. Petrie* II 20 iv. 4 = III 36 b iv (218 BC), royal dock; *U.P.Z.* 149 = *W. Chrest*. 30. 11–18 (third century BC): S. R. K. Glanville, 'Records of a royal dockyard of the time of Tuthmosis III: Papyrus British Museum 10056', *Z.A.S.* 66 (1932) 105–21; 68 (1932) 7–41 for the fifteenth century. Naucratis was a similar centre: *P.S.I.* 533. 16 (third century BC); *B.G.U.* 1744. 11 (64–63 BC); cf. 1746. 12.

6 – E.g. *P. Lond.* VII 1940. 1–13 (257 BC), wheat and barley.

7 – *P. Tebt*. 856. 85–9 (*c*.171 BC)

8 – *P. Hib*. 39. 15; *S.B.* 8754. 14–15; *B.G.U.* 1742. 14–16; 1743. 11–13; cf. Zilliacus (1939); U. Wilcken, 'Urkunden-Referat III', *A.P.F.* 13 (1939) 223–5.

9 – *P. Lond.* VII 1940. 62 (257 BC).

10 – *W. Chrest*. 442; cf. *P. Hib*. 38 (252–251 BC); *Bodleian corn archive* (n.4) 10 (163 BC).

11 – Hauben (1978).

12 – For this use of the genitive cf. *B.G.U.* 1741.9 (63 BC).

13 *P. Petrie* III 107 (226–225 BC), carrying passengers, salt, wine, wheat, beans, fish, bags, charcoal, fleeces, tiles, private possessions, sacred goods of Souchos and measuring ropes for the dykes.

14 – For references see Hauben (1978) 99–101.

15 – *P. Tebt*. 1035 (157 BC); *P. Lille* 22 (155 BC); 23 = *W. Chrest*. 189 (155 BC); *P. Sorb. inv.* 110 a = W. Clarysse, 'Notes on the use of the iota subscript in the third century BC', *C.E.* 51 (1976) 156 (147 BC).

16 – By Theoxenos, a prominent Alexandrian, *P. Tebt*. 1034. 15.

17 – *P. Petrie* III 107 (226–225 BC); cf. Hauben (1971); W. Clarysse and H. Hauben, 'New remarks on the skippers of *P. Petrie* III 107', *A.P.F.* 24–5 (1976) 85–90.

18 – *P. Hib*. 110. 21–33 (*c*.270 BC) Hiera Nesos to Alexandria including clerical charges at all stages, tolls (76 dr.) and protection charges (14 dr.); *P. Lond.* VII 1940. 53 (257 BC) 12 dr. for 100 artabas of grain from Syron Kome in the Gynaikopolite nome to Alexandria; *P. Cairo Zen*. 59669 (mid third century BC) 10 dr. for 150 artabas of wheat from the Fayum to Alexandria; 59320 (249 BC); 59753 (mid third century BC); *P.S.I.* 332 (257 BC) 300 artabas of garlic from Alexandria to Kerke; *P. Cornell* 3 (mid third century BC) freightage charge, Memphite inspection tax and

tolls, clerical, labour and measuring charges, 3½ obols per artaba (58½ copper dr. per 100 artabas) possibly from Memphis to Alexandria. The rates of transport on the Fayum canals (including tax) seem relatively high, *P. Petrie* III 107 d i. 17, 22, 29 (226–225 BC), charcoal at 8 dr. per 100 art. for c. 25 km; *U.P.Z.* 149 = *W. Chrest.* 30. 11–18 (late third century BC), some unofficial but necessary expenses.

19 – On the date see Wilcken (1939) 223.

20 – On the date see Hauben (1971a) 273.

21 – For improved readings see Wilcken (1939). There is difficulty in construing the Greek at this point. The supplement of line 17, depending on *B.G.U.* 1743. 13, implies that the load of grain is the object of *parakomisai*, whereas in *S.B.* 8754. 16 'instructions' stand as object.

22 – H. Ranke, 'Istar als Heilgöttin in Aegypten', *Studies presented to F.Ll. Griffith* (London, 1932) 412–18.

23 – *P.S.I.* 531. 1.

24 – See J. J. Jannsen, *Two ancient Egyptian ship's logs* (Leiden, 1961) 34, 73 for the thirteenth century; N. Aimé-Giron, *Textes araméens d'Egypte* (Le Caire, 1931) nos. 5–73 with R. A. Bowman, 'An Aramaic journal page', *Am. Journ. Sem. Lang. and Lit.* 58 (1941) 302–13 for Aramaic evidence. *P.S.I.* 488. 10 (258–257 BC) Syro-Persikon dyke; *P. Louvre* E 3266. 5 Q (197 BC) = F. de Cenival, 'Un acte de renonciation consécutif à un partage de revenus liturgiques Memphites (*P. Louvre* E 3266)', *B.I.F.A.O.* 71 (1972) 11–65.

25 – *W. Chrest.* 443. 3–4 (AD 15); *P. Oxy.* 276. 8–10 (AD 77); 749 (fourth century AD).

26 – *P. Lille* 25. 5, 64 (third century BC) *machimos; P. Cairo Zen.* 59753. 72–3 (third century BC) *rhabdephoroi; U.P.Z.* 149. 8–10 (third century BC); *P. Ryl.* 576. 1–2 (246–222 BC) *phulakites epiplous; P. Tebt.* 824. 9 (171 BC?) *phulakites;* 1035. 1–2 (second century BC) *phulakites epiplous; S.B.* 8754. 12–13 (77 BC) *phulakitai* who are cleruchs, cf. 20 *machairophoroi* and *epiploi*.

27 – *U.P.Z.* 110. 22–3 (164 BC) *phulakides* with *naukleromachimoi; P. Tebt.* 5 = *C. Ord. Ptol.* 53. 46 (118 BC).

28 – Cf. *B.G.U.* 1743. 9–10 (63 BC), 8 cleruch-guards for a load of 1,800 artabas.

29 – *S.B.* 8754. 15 (77 BC); *B.G.U.* 1742. 16–17; 1743. 12–13 (63 BC).

30 – *S.B.* 8754. 16–19 (77 BC).

31 – *P. Tebt.* 825 a–c (176 BC?), *puros agorastos*.

32 – Cf. *P.S.I.* 594, mullet, tunny, venison and other foodstuffs brought upstream.

33 – *P. Cairo Zen.* 59031 (December 258 BC), aboard a grain barge.

34 – *P. Cairo Zen.* 59217. 3 (254 BC); *P. Mich. Zen.* 60. 3 (248 or 247 BC) to Memphis. See also the Bodleian corn archive (note 4).

35 – *P. Cairo Zen.* 59488, cheap strigils, in Memphis; 59250 and 59823, wax prices.

36 – From the Ptolemaic period: *Abu(denos), akation, achor* or *akor, baioielupiou, baris, thalamegos, Kasiotikon, keles, kerkouros, kerkouroskaphe, kontoton, kubaia, kubaidion, lembos, paktotos, ploiarion, ploion, prosagogis, skaphe, skenagogos, huperetikon, phaselion, phulakis;* cf. Merzagora (1929); Casson (1971) 157–68.

37 – *Kerkouros* capacities, in artabas, are recorded as follows with actual cargoes in brackets when known: 1000: *B.G.U.* 1933; 1200: *B.G.U.* 1933; (1500): *P. Strassb.* 113; ? *P. Petrie* II 48 = III 116. 1–10; 2000 (2000): *P. Stras.* 562–3 = Clarysse (1976), 185–6; (2750): *P. Tebt.* 1034; 3000 (332 1/2): *P. Tebt.* 824; (4800): *W. Chrest.* 441; 5000: *P. Tebt.* 856. 194; (5556): *P. Tebt.* 823; 9000: *P. Tebt.* 856. 129, 188; 10,000: *W. Chrest.*

442: *P. Tebt.* 856. 93 with 202, 97, 116, 124, 126, 186, 191, 205, 206; 11,000: *P. Tebt.* 856. 103 with 114, 107, 109, 125; *P. Tebt.* 825; 12,000: *P. Tebt.* 856. 6, 99, 118, 187; 16,000: *P. Tebt.* 856. 127; 18,000: *P. Tebt.* 856. 112.

38 – *Hist. nat* XVIII 66, 20 5/6 Roman pounds (6.812 kg) to a modius.

39 – Fraser (1972) I 91; II 171–2.

40 – C. Clark and M. Haswell, *The economics of subsistence agriculture*, 4th ed. (London, 1970) 62.

41 – F.A.O., *Nutritional studies 15: Calorie requirements*, (Rome, 1957) 43.

42 – Clark and Haswell (n.40) 58. But ancient milling techniques may not have achieved this extraction rate.

43 – Reekmans (1966) 18–19 with Duncan-Jones (1979) 366.

44 – D. Bonneau, 'Ptolémais Hormou dans la documentation papyrologique', *C.E.* 54 (1979) 310–26.

45 – *B.G.U.* 1760. 23 (51–50 BC).

46 – *O.G.I.S.* 56. 13–18 (239–8 BC).

47 – *P. Petrie* II 20 ii. 8–9 = III 36 b; *P. Tebt.* 825 a. 13–14, b. 11–12 (176 BC?).

48 – *P. Strassb.* II 93 = Clarysse (1976), 192; cf. *P. Tebt.* 813. 4 (8 Dec. 186 BC).

49 – Other examples: *P.S.I.* 332. 9–10 (257 BC), a boat in the harbour of Alexandria for imported garlic; *P. Petrie* II 20 iv. 5, 14 = III 36 b iv, a *lembos* taken for fodder (?) for elephants now needed for corn.

7 – CHR. GOUDINEAU: Marseilles, Rome and Gaul

1 – I cite, among the 300 or so studies relevant to this subject, only a few of the more important: M. Clerc, *Massalia* 2 vols. (Marseilles, 1927–9), F. Benoit, *Recherches sur l'hellénisation du Midi de la Gaule* (Aix-en-Provence, 1965), Villard (1960), Baratier (1973), Clavel (1977). Morel (1966) (1975) are valuable.

2 – Note that Plutarch does not say (*Solon* IV) that Marseilles was founded *for commerce* only.

3 – M. Clerc and F. Benoit have listed all the texts, the latter adding to the traditional data hypotheses partly suggested by his excellent knowledge of regional economies in the Middle Ages and in modern times. It is hard to be up-to-date in this area because of the delayed publication of major archaeological excavations, starting with those of the Bourse at Marseilles itself. This is why unpublished data is discussed in a way that is sometimes imprecise – from necessity.

4 – See among others, on exactly this type of problem, Lepore (1970) 19–20: 'enthusiasm for recent discoveries from excavations has led to excessive faith in archaeological evidence'.

5 – By two texts only – which are derived from Posidonius: Strabo III 2.9 and Diodorus V 38.4. No other passage cites Marseilles. Strabo V 1.12 on precious metals apparently refers to the period later than the conquest.

6 – The transport of corn referred to by Demosthenes *Zenoth.* between Syracuse and Athens can with difficulty be attributed to Gaul. For skins, the only text which makes allusion is Strabo III 5.11 à propos of the inhabitants of the Cassiterides who 'give their metals and skins in exchange for pottery, salt and bronze objects to the merchants', but Marseilles is not mentioned.

7 – There again the argument is by analogy: Diodorus V 26.3 mentions the

exchange of a Gallic slave for an amphora of wine, but he only talks of Italian merchants. It is by reference to Athenaeus IV 152c (who gives his source, Posidonius) that we can extend this traffic to the benefit of the Massaliotes since the wine 'imported to the Celts is imported from Italy and the *chora* of the Massaliotes'. A *graffito* from Olbia is worthy of note: 'Greetings. I shall send you a letter about the slaves'.

8 – It is never attested for the direction Gaul to Mediterranean, only for south to north (cf. n.6). However, Strabo IV 1.6–7 lays stress on the saline marshes of the south, and Benoit (1965) 195–8, recalls the importance of salt in the Massaliote economy at different periods. Note that Agathe (Agde) and Olbia are in direct proximity to the areas of production.

9 – The only passage making allusion to a trade is that which we have quoted, n.5. It must be further noted that he says not one word of Massaliote traders, but confines himself to referring to the arrival point of tin: 'it is transported from the British Isles to Marseilles'. It is also characteristic of almost all the texts to give no nationality to merchants, with the exception of Diodorus V 26.3 (Italians); in V 22, à propos of tin, Diodorus speaks of 'foreign merchants'. The text of Polybius cited by Strabo IV 2.1 ('When Scipio, recalling the extraordinary stories of Pytheas, asked them about Britain, none of the Massaliotes who had joined his side could tell him anything satisfactory') is almost always interpreted as showing the 'secrecy' with which the ancients like to envelop commercial journeys and exchanges. It seems wiser to me to take the passage literally.

10 – Cf. n.7 giving the *only* obvious text: Athenaeus IV 152c. All the other references are the object of more or less strained interpretations: is it wine in Athenaeus IV 152d and 154c? Does it come from Marseilles?

11 – Note nevertheless that this 'ceremonial' is attested above all for the early periods (sixth-fifth century BC), and that the objects which it brings together are largely metallic and, often, of Etruscan origin.

12 – Nothing new has been recorded to the north of Lyon since the lists given by F. Benoit mentioning Vix ((1965) 186), Château-sur-Salins ((1965) 183), Montmirey-la-Ville, Montmorot and Savoyeux ((1965) 186), all excavations largely of Halstatt material.

13 – Recent excavations have demonstrated the almost exclusive presence of Massaliote (or imported) material in the possessions of Marseilles. If this phenomenon is not in itself surprising (there is evidence for it in other Greek colonies), the feeble penetration of these same pots into native sites very close by leads us to wonder about the importance of pottery in commercial relations at this period.

14 – On the 'grey' pottery, see Ch. Arcelin, *La céramique grise monochrome en Provence*, in press. On 'pseudo-ionienne' there are numerous articles, e.g. recently, M. Py, 'La céramique grecque de la Vaunage et sa signification', *Cah. Lig. Préh. Arch.* 20 (1971) 5–153.

15 – The statistics are given in M. Bats, 'Bols hellénistiques à reliefs d'Olbia', *Rev. arch. Narb.* 12 (1979) 163–4. Contrary to Clavel (1977) 55 ('pottery . . . with a very wide distribution') the rarity of this production must be stressed.

16 – J.-P. Morel, 'Etudes de céramique campanienne I. L'atelier des petites estampilles,' *M.E.F.R.* 81 (1969) 59–117; M. Bats, 'La céramique à vernis noir d'Olbia en Ligurie: Vases de l'atelier des petites estampilles,' *Rev. arch. Narb.* 9

(1976) 63–80; M. Py, 'Notes sur l'évolution des céramiques à vernis noir des oppida languedociens de Roque de Viou et de Nages (Gard, France)', *M.E.F.R.* 88 (1976) 545–606. etc.

17 – See the very useful study in a new periodical, *Archéologie en Languedoc* 1 (1978) entirely devoted to work done on Campanian pottery. There are numerous articles on southern Gaul and also on imports into the interior of Gaul: cf. the synthesis of J.-P. Morel, 149–68.

18 – Villard (1960) 128ff., and the study, with some reservations, of H. Gallet de Santerre, 'La diffusion de la céramique attique aux Ve et IVe s. av. J.-C.' *Rev. arch. Narb.* 10 (1977) 33–57.

19 – *Archéologie en Languedoc* (n.17) passim.

20 – Such an assertion is perhaps still unwise: certain French archaeologists are involved in violent polemic with specialists in this pottery, and chronological estimates can vary by more than a century. Let us accept nevertheless this assertion of J.-P Morel (n.17, 157): 'For a long time Campanian A was thought to be pottery of the third and second centuries . . . This dating is absolutely false . . . Campanian A is a pottery of the second and first centuries.' The well-documented evidence is above all from Languedoc. We must not forget that various arguments suggest that Languedoc might have passed, more or less formally, under the control of Rome from the first half of the second century BC; cf. Chr. Goudineau in Nicolet (1978), 686–7.

21 – I am very grateful to Michel Py for having supplied this information.

22 – R. Lequément, B. Liou, 'Les épaves de la côte de Transalpine', *Cah. lig. préh. arch.* 24 (1975) 76–82.

23 – See A. Tchernia in this volume, ch. 8. In the event it is less a question of 'multiplication' than of a prodigious leap ahead which has *no equivalent* in the traditional settlements of the south of Gaul.

24 – Recent and unpublished discoveries at Marseilles itself. On other excavations in the south, notably at Fréjus, amphorae called 'gauloises' with flat bases, which contained wine from Narbonensis under the Empire, are of the characteristic Massaliote fabric. There was no interruption therefore.

25 – VII 1.7 or XI 2.12, but this is not true for Elea (VI 1.1), a Phocaean foundation.

26 – IV 1.5: 'later, however, their valour enabled them to take in some of the surrounding plains, thanks to the same military strength by which they founded their cities, I mean their stronghold cities'.

27 – Texts in Nicolet (1978) 684–93.

28 – Nicolet (1978) 684, for a summary of the question.

29 – G. Barruol, *Les peuples pré-romains du sud-est de la Gaule* (Paris, 1969) 221–30.

30 – Cf. E. Lepore (1970) 41–54: the 'crisis' described by Villard (1960) for the end of the fifth century BC and the start of the fourth corresponds to a structural change. Marseilles passes from an *emporion* controlled by a few rich families to a more open type of city, a true 'colonial' *polis*. On the archaeological front, the analyses of Villard have been disproved by Gallet de Santerre (cf. n.18). This does not affect Lepore's analysis.

31 – The events of 154 BC are generally underestimated. The text of Polybius XXXIII 8 is nevertheless clear: 'The Massaliotes had long since been subjected to the attacks of the Ligures. They were now *hemmed in at home*, while Antipolis and Nikaia were even besieged'. Must we imagine that Marseilles could not intervene

because a barbarian fleet prevented all exit? It seems unlikely. However, Marseilles had complained to Rome, in 181, of the activity of Ligurian pirates, and Strabo IV 6.3 especially makes it clear that not only Ligurians but also the Salyans (so those nearest to Marseilles) had made their law prevail 'by *sea* as by *land*'.

32 – The majority of analysts allow themselves to be boxed into a series of contradictions. The problem should be posed clearly. One possibility is that Marseilles, an insignificant city having control only of a few comptoirs, found itself at the mercy of savage and cruel barbarians on the move. But then how can the 900 'Massaliote men' – around a certain Craton – in the capital of the Salyans (Diodorus XXXIV 23) be explained? That group should represent at least a quarter of the population of the 'town'. Again how could Charmolaus (Strabo III 4.17) acquire possessions among the Ligurians, if all that the victories of 154 and then 124–123 brought was a small coastal strip of land (Strabo IV 1.5)? If, alternatively, Marseilles was a powerful city with a very extensive *chora*, it goes without saying that not only the threats which weighed on her but especially the descriptions of the pretended 'Arvernian empire' are only myths, or at least exaggerations. These fit oddly with an expansionist explanation, above all if Languedoc was even informally under the control of Rome as we have said (cf. n.20).

33 – E.g. the precise meaning of *para tois anthropois*, the reference of *autois eti toutois* and *charientes*; (Greeks or barbarians?).

34 – A bronze hand in the Cabinet des Médailles at Paris is inscribed: *sumbolon pros Ouelaunious* (the Velaunii were a people of the Alpes-Maritimes).

35 – None of which can be dated before the Roman conquest. Cf. P.-M. Duval, 'Les inscriptions gallo-grecques trouvées en France', *Actes du Colloque sur les influences helléniques en Gaule* (Dijon, 1958) 63–9; M. Lejeune, 'Inscriptions lapidaires de Narbonnaise', *Etudes celtiques* 12 (1968–71) 21–83 and 'Textes Gallo-grecs' *Études celtiques* 15 (1976–8) 105–37.

36 – His *origo* (Justin XLIII 5.11) was the city of the Vocontii (*a Vocontiis origine ducere*), his grandfather had received the citizenship from Pompey at the time of the war against Sertorius. He himself wrote in Greek around the start of the Christian era.

37 – M. Clavel, *Béziers et son territoire dans l'antiquité* (Paris, 1970) 310–12.

38 – J. Jannoray, *Ensérune, contribution à l'étude des civilisations préromaines de la Gaule mériodionale* (Paris, 1955) 262–3.

39 – See, for example, M. Py, *L'oppidum des Castels à Nages* (Gard) (*Gallia* Suppl. 35 (1978) 150–3.

40 – Cf., apart from Justin XLIII 5, Cicero, *Off.* II 8.28 *Pro Font.* I 3, *Phil.* VIII 6.18, Amm. Marc. XV 11, Val. Max. II 6.7, etc.

41 – Strabo uses identical terms for three cities: Marseilles, Rhodes and Cyzicus (cf. XIV 2.5: 'here as at Massalia, as at Cyzicus, all works of naval construction, manufacture of machines of war, arms depots and establishments of the same kind, are the object of particular care'). Neither Rhodes nor Cyzicus kept such an arsenal to resist the barbarians, even if, on occasions, its defensive value was evident (for Cyzicus, against Mithridates). That said, we must also avoid all naivety vis-à-vis the pretended 'weakness' of Marseilles and the 'rescuing' of Rome: the campaigns against the Allobroges and Arverni were unleashed not by these last – who sought an understanding – but by Rome herself (Appian, *Celt.*

XII). But whatever part Roman and Massaliote imperialism played, the basic problem remains: did a town of military engineers (*architecti*) accumulate the engines of war (*arma tormentaque*: Caesar, *B.C.* II 22) solely for her own use? *Even after the Roman conquest* of 124, warlike acts are attested *between peoples of the south*. Posidonius describes the custom of the 'têtes coupées' (Strabo IV 4.5) and this is documented archaeologically towards 50 BC in an *oppidum* near to Marseilles (la Cloche). Did the quarrels between major peoples of the interior of Gaul (Sequani, Arverni, Aedui) not offer even more possibilities?

42 – For example a site such as Teste-Nègre (unpublished) – equally near to Marseilles – destroyed in 180–160. At Entremont itself, bullets have been found at two successive levels: unless the context is the two successive campaigns of 124 and 123 (with a total remaking of the streets in a few months?), and if, following the current interpretation, we exclude occupation later than 123, what can they relate to? There remains equally the maritime domination of the Salyans (n.31).

8 – ANDRÉ TCHERNIA: Italian wine in Gaul at the end of the Republic

* This article is intended as a response to Sir Moses Finley's plea for 'more specification, more qualification, where possible quantification of such otherwise misleading vague phrases as "intensive exchange" . . .' (*The ancient economy* (1973) 33). It has profited greatly from the comments made by audiences in Cambridge and in Aix. I should like in particular to thank all the archaeologists who have been so good as to provide me, either in conversation or in writing, with complementary information on the diffusion of Dr. 1 amphorae, namely Mm. Barruol, Domergue, Ferdière, Galliou, Labrousse, Py, Rancoule, Roman, Sanquer, Sablayrolles, Vaussanvin, Vidal.

All the dates given are BC, unless otherwise indicated.

1 – Ampurias: J.-M. Nolla Brufau, 'Una produccio caracteristica, las amforas DB', *Cypsela* 2 (1977) 222–4; for Toulouse, of the inscriptions published in *Gallia* 38, 2 (1980) 486 in the form *C MARIO/ L AVR OLI* and *M VTT / M . . . CAEC . . . O*, the former quite certainly represents the names of the consuls *C. Marius* and *L. Aurelius Orestes*.

2 – Py (1978) 251 and 325–6; information communicated to me by H. Vaussanvin.

3 – Peacock (1971) 172; Nash (1976) 116; Nash (1978) 112 and 321–8; Panella (1981) 56–7.

4 – Cited in L. Bonnamour 'Le port gaulois et gallo-romain de Châlon', *Mémoires Soc. d'Hist. et d'Arch. de Châlon* 45 (1975) 63–5.

5 – J.-G. Bulliot, *Fouilles de Mont Beuvray de 1867 à 1895* (Autun, 1899) passim.

6 – Guillaume du Catel, *Mémoires de l'histoire du Languedoc* (Toulouse, 1633) 128.

7 – Abbé Audibert, *Dissertation sur les origines de Toulouse* (Avignon and Toulouse, 1764) 3.

8 – Hédan and Vernhet (1975) 74; R. Gourdiole, 'Exploitations métallurgiques antiques dans la Haute vallée de l'Orb', *Fédération historique du Languedoc* . . . (1977) 69–87; Barruol et Gourdiole (1980).

9 – I shall elsewhere produce a more extended analysis of the documentation which is completed and corroborated by the more fragmentary evidence that can be adduced for other regions.

10 – M. Beltràn Lloris, *Las anforas romanas en España* (Saragossa, 1970) fig. 99.
11 – C. Domergue, 'La mine antique de Diogenes El Real (Ciudad Real)' *Mél. Casa Velasquez* III (1967) 39.
12 – See the maps based on the study of the diffusion of amphora stamps dating from the first century AD in A. Tchernia, 'Amphores et marques d'amphores de Bétique à Pompéi et à Stabies', *M.E.F.R.* 76 (1964) 419–49 at 428, and D. Colls, R. Etienne, R. Lequément, B. Liou, F. Mayet, 'L'épave Port-Vendres II et le commerce de la Bétique à l'époque de Claude', *Archeonautica* 1 (1977) 136–8.
13 – Review of M. H. Callender, *Roman Amphorae* (London, 1965) in *Germania* 45 (1967) 179.
14 – R. Lequément, B. Liou, 'Les épaves de la côte de Transalpine', *Cah. Lig. préh. arch.* 24 (1975) 76–82.
15 – A. Carandini, 'Il vigneto e la villa del fondo di Settefinestre nel Cosano: un caso di produzione per il mercato transmarino', in d'Arms/Kopff (1980) 1–11.
16 – Figures of M. Kirkbride James, *Studies in the Medieval wine trade* (Oxford, 1971), conveniently collected in Ch. Higounet (ed.), *Histoire de l'Aquitaine. Documents* (Toulouse, 1973) 130.
17 – Ch. Higounet, *Annales Cisalpines d'histoire sociale*, series I. 3 (1972) 51.
18 – R. W. Davies, 'The Roman military diet', *Britannia* 2 (1971) 124. There is no reason for translating *acetum* as 'sour wine': what it means is vinegar; J. André, *L'alimentation et la cuisine à Rome* (Paris, 1961) 175.
19 – J. Harmand, *L'armée et le soldat à Rome de 107 à 50 av. n. è.* (Paris, 1967) 190.
20 – Athenaeus IV 36. 152c; Cicero, *De Rep.* III 9.16; Diodorus V 26. 2–3; Caesar, *B.G.* II 15, IV 2.6: the reason why it is remarkable that the Nervii and the Suevi prohibit wine is that other peoples are certainly importing it.
21 – Cf. Rancoule (1980) 88.
22 – Polybius II 19.4; XI 3.1; Livy V 33.3 and 44.6; Dionysus Hal. XIV 8.12; Plutarch *Camillus* XV 2; Appian, *Celt.* VII; Polyaenus VIII 25.1.
23 – Cl. Feuvrier-Prévotat, 'Echanges et sociétés en Gaule indépendante: à propos d'un texte de Poseidonios d'Apamée', *Ktema* 3 (1978) 242–59.
24 – Posidonius in Athenaeus IV 40. 154a–c. This text has been explained by M. Mauss, 'Sur un texte de Posidonius, le suicide contre-prestation suprême', *R.C.* 42 (1925) 324–8 = *Oeuvres* III (Paris, 1969) 52–7.
25 – Athenaeus IV 37. On the importance of largesse for the Gauls (*liberalitas, largiri*) cf. Caesar *B.G.* I 18.3–4.
26 – J. Renaud, 'Notes sur l'oppidum d'Essalois (Loire)', *Ogam* 14 (1962) 60; J.-P. Preynat, 'L'oppidum d'Essalois', *Ogam* 14 (1962) 287–314; R. Périchon, 'L'âge du fer en Forez', *Actes du 98è Congrès Soc. Sav. St Etienne 1973* (Paris 1975) 285.
27 – See n.8 and G. Rancoule and Y. Solier, 'Les mines antiques des Corbières audoises', *Fédération historique du Languedoc* (1977) 24–39; G. Rancoule and L. Rigaud, 'La fosse à amphores N° 38 de Lacombe, commune de Lastours (Aude)', *Bull. Soc. d'Et. Sc. de l'Aude* 78 (1978) 27–33; R. Sablayrolles, 'Intérêt et problèmes de l'études des ferriers antiques: l'exemple de la Montagne Noire', *Mines et fonderies* (1980); C. Dubois and J. E. Guilbaut, 'Mines de cuivre antiques dans le Séronais (Pyrénées ariégeoises)', *Mines et fonderies* (1980).
28 – Strabo V 1.12 for metal. The other sources will be examined in the text.
29 – See n.30 and G. Rancoule and L. Guiraud, 'Fond de cabane gaulois dans le secteur minier de Lastours (Aude)', *Bull. Soc. d'Et. Sc. de l'Aude* 79 (1979) 33–8.

30 – See, for bibliography for the mines, in particular J. Ramin (1974), where maps, references to the texts and to the earlier bibliography can be found.
31 – F. Laubenheimer-Leenhardt, *Recherches sur les lingots de cuivre et de plomb d'époque romaine dans les régions de Languedoc-Roussillon et de Provence-Corse, Rev. Arch. Narb.* Suppl. 3 (Paris, 1973) 129.
32 – Barruol and Gourdiole (1980) give an account of the important discoveries in the mines of the upper valley of the Orb of tessera inscribed *Soc(ietas) Arg(entaria) Rut(enorum). S(ocietas) R(utenensis).* The authors conclude that these mines were the property of the Ruteni or had been ceded to this people. The Roman legal form suggests that this may have been a mixed society: cf. Strabo IV 6.12.
33 – B. M. Henry, 'Le bassin inférieur de la Loire et la Méditerranée du VIIIè s. au Ier s. av. J.C.', *Bull. du Centre de Recherches et d'Ens. de l'Ant. Angers*, 3 (1977–8) 65–7. Galliou (1982) 15: four or five amphorae, each representing possibly one wreck.
34 – R. Dion, 'Transport de l'étain des îles britanniques à Marseille à travers la Gaule préromaine', *Actes du 93è Congrès des Soc. Sav., Tours, 1968* (Paris, 1970) 423–38.
35 – Polybius XII 4.8; Varro *R.R.* III 2.9–11; Strabo. V 3.1.
36 – Livy *Per.* 96; Appian *B.C.* I 14.116: 10,000; Orosius V 24.
37 – W. L. Westermann, *The slave systems of Greek and Roman antiquity* (Philadelphia, 1955) 66.
38 – Crawford ((1977) 123) suggests an annual replacement rate of 5 per cent, but W. V. Harris, 'Towards a study of the Roman slave trade', in d'Arms/Kopff (1980) 118 goes higher.
39 – E. Lapore, 'Sul carattere economico-sociale di Ercolano', *P.P.* 145 (1955) 437 following the *Tabulae Herculanenses*.
40 – Polybius IV 38.4–5; Strabo V 1.8 and XI 2.3.
41 – Zenobius, s.v. (*Corpus paroemiogr. graec.*); Pollux VII 14. I am indebted to M. I. Finley who brought these texts to my attention.
42 – Fr. Villard, *La céramique grecque de Marseille* (Paris, 1960) 158.
43 – Tenney Frank, *E.S.A.R.* I (Baltimore, 1933) 173 and E. Badian, *Roman Imperialism in the late Republic* (Oxford, 1968) 19f., 68, have already suggested that Cicero's interpretation should be discounted, but their idea of a protectionist policy favouring Marseilles wine does not fit this period, which is precisely the time when the Marseilles amphorae are disappearing from the *oppida* and being replaced by amphorae from Italy. The idea put forward recently by J. Paterson ('Transalpinae gentes: Cicero, *De Rep.* III 16', *C.Q.* 28 (1978) 452–8), who suggests that the victims of the prohibition were the Transalpine peoples installed in 186 close to the future site of Aquileia, cannot be accepted, among other reasons because olives cannot be grown in this region. There is no new information of any importance in the latest article to appear on the subject: B. Van Rinsveld, 'Cicero *De Republica* III 9.15–16: origine, date et but de l'interdiction de planter des vignes et des oliviers en Gaule transalpine' *Latomus* 40 (1981) 280–91.
44 – Cf. M. Clavel-Lévêque, 'Pour une problématique des conditions économiques de l'implantation romaine dans le Midi gaulois', *Cah. Lig. préh. arch.* 24 (1975) 55 and A. Daubigney (1981).
45 – Crawford (1977), to which this article owes much.
46 – P. Vilar, 'Le temps des hidalgos' and P. Chaunu, 'L'empire du soleil éternel' in *L'Espagne au temps de Phillipe II* (Paris, 1965) 68 and 101 respectively.

47 – Finley (1980) 128.
48 – J.-L. Fiches, 'Processus d'urbanisation indigènes dans la région de Nîmes (VIIè – Ier s. av. n. è.)', *D.H.A.* 5 (1979) 47.
49 – Rancoule (1980) 129; G. Rancoule and L. Rigaud, 'La fosse à amphores N° 38 de Lacombe, commune de Lastours (Aude)', *Bull. Soc. d'Et. Sc. de l'Aude* 78 (1978) 33.
50 – Chr. Goudineau, 'La romanisation des institutions en Transalpine', *Cah. Lig. préh. arch.* 24 (1975) 26–34.
51 – This article had already been completed when J.-P. Morel, 'Le commerce étrusque en France, en Espagne et en Afrique' in *L'Etruria mineraria, Atti del XII convegno di studi etruschi e italici, 16–20 June 1979*, Florence (1981) 463–508, appeared. On the subject of the Gallic demand for wine, and the importance of metal from the Cévennes and the Corbières as an exchange commodity, our studies seem to me to be mutually supportive, despite the fact that they focus upon exchanges five centuries apart.

9 – GIUSEPPE PUCCI: Pottery and trade in the Roman period

*I presented an earlier version of this paper to the seminar on May 26th 1980, and to a smaller group, consisting of P. Cartledge, P. Garnsey, K. Hopkins, D. Rathbone and C. R. Whittaker, on June 4th. I am most grateful to friends and critics (I was lucky enough to find both in the same persons).

I should like to thank in particular M. I. Finley, who proposed me that year as Leverhulme Visiting Fellow at Darwin College, though I shall hardly acquit myself of the debt of friendship which I have contracted with him since.

In preparing this paper I especially profited from the works of A. Carandini, D. Manacorda, C. Panella, C. Pavolini, A. Ricci, in particular Carandini (1979a) and (1979b). Also important are d'Arms/Kopff (1980) and Giardina/Schiavone (1981). The latter contains articles by scholars belonging – like the writer – to the Gruppo di studio di Antichistica, Istituto Gramsci. For the first part of my paper I broadly utilized the essay by C. Ginzburg, 'Spie. Radici di un paradigma indiziario' in A. Gargani (ed.), *Crisi della Ragione* (Torino, 1979) 57–106, esp. 82ff.

1 – Cf. M. Torelli, *D.d.A.* 7 (1973) 321 (à propos of F. Heichelheim).
2 – Cf. M. Détienne, J. P. Vernant, *Les ruses de l'intelligence. La mètis des Grecs*, (Paris, 1974).
3 – Ginzburg's essay stimulated in Italy an interesting debate on these problems. See A. Carandini, 'Quando l'indizio va contro il metodo', *Q.S.* 11 (1980) 3–12; M. Vegetti, 'La ragione e le spie', *Q.S.* 11 (1980) 13–18; A. Canfora, 'Il paradigma venatorio', *Q.S.* 14 (1981) 161–8; L. Borzacchini, E. De Benedictis, C. De Marzo, G. F. Lanzara, V. D. Pesce, 'Contro-spie: indizi di un paradigma inesistente', *Q.S.* 14 (1981) 169–85.
4 – See M. I. Finley, 'Slavery and the Historians', *Histoire sociale-Social History* 12 (1979) 255.
5 – Finley (1973) 180 n.24. The quotation is from Nicholas Georgescu-Roegen. My italics.
6 – F. Villard, *La céramique grecque de Marseille (VIe-IVe siècle). Essai d'histoire économique*. Bibl. Ec. Fr. d'Athènes et de Rome 195 (Paris, 1960).

7 – T. B. Webster, *Potter and patron in classical Athens* (London, 1972) esp. 8.

8 – See N. McKendrick, 'Josiah Wedgwood: An eighteenth-century entrepreneur in salesmanship and marketing', *E.H.R.* 12 (1960) 428ff. Cf. also G. Pucci, 'Elgin o della manifattura', *D.d.A.* 8–9 (1974–5) esp. 478–87.

9 – Unless the primary cargo was of small dimensions and high value. See R. Lequement, B. Liou, *Cah. Lig. Préhist. Arch.* 24 (1975) 81.

10 – See the discussion in P. A. Gianfrotta, P. Pomey, *Archeologia subacquea* (Milano, 1980) 170ff.

11 – I have suggested ('Cumanae testae', *P.P.* 164 (1975) 368ff.), an identification of 'Pompeian Red Ware' with a Cuman production known from the literary sources. See also Ch. Goudineau, 'Notes sur la céramique à engobe interne rouge-pompéien (Pompejanisch-roten Platten)', *M.E.F.R.* 82 (1970) 159–86, and D. P. S. Peacock, 'Pompeian Red Ware', in D. P. S. Peacock (ed.), *Pottery and early commerce* (London, 1977) 147–62.

12 – See S. Tortorella, 'Ceramica di produzione africana e rinventimenti archeologici sottomarini della media e tarda età repubblicana: analisi dei dati e dei contributi reciproci', *M.E.F.R.* 93 (1981) 337ff.

13 – Cf. A. Carandini, 'Riflessioni su E. Sereni, *Capitalismo e mercato nazionale in Italia*', *D.d.A.* 7 (1973) 324–9 and Finley (1973) 22ff.

14 – I am compelled by the friendly tyranny of the editors to reduce this part of my paper to a list of up-to-date synthetic literature. On black-glazed pottery see J.-P. Morel, 'La céramique campanienne: acquis et problèmes', *Céramiques hellénistiques et romaines, Annales littéraires de l'Université de Besançon* 242 (1980) (henceforth = *Céramiques*) 85–122 and 'La produzione della ceramica campana: aspetti economici e sociali', Giardina/Schiavone (1981) 81–98. On thin-walled pottery see F. Mayet, 'Les céramiques à parois fines: état de la question', *Céramiques* 201–30, and A. Ricci, 'I vasi potori a pareti sottili', Giardina/Schiavone (1981) 23–138. On Roman lamps see C. Pavolini, 'Le lucerne nell' Italia romana', Giardina/Schiavone (1981) 139–86; 'Una produzione italica di lucerne: le Vogelkopflampen ad ansa trasversale', *Bull. Com.* 85 (1976–7) 45–134. On amphorae see Panella (1981), but also 'Annotazioni in margine alle stratigrafie delle Terme ostiensi del Nuotatore', *Recherches sur les amphores romaines*. Coll. Ec. Fr. Rome 10 (1972) 69–106; C. Panella, A. Carandini, in *Ostia* III 2, *Studi Miscellanei* 21 (Roma, 1973) esp. 659–96; C. Panella, 'Anfore tripolitane a Pompei', *L'instrumentum domesticum di Ercolano e Pompei nella prima età imperiale*, Quaderni di cultura materiale 1 (Roma, 1977) 135–50; Manacorda (1981); 'Anfore spagnole a Pompei', *L'instrumentum domesticum* (1977) 121–34; 'The ager cosanus and the production of the amphorae of Sestius: new evidence and a reassessment', *J.R.S.* 68 (1978) 122–31; Tchernia (1980). On Italian sigillata see G. Pucci, 'La produzione della ceramica aretina. Note sull' industria nella prima età imperiale romana', *D.d.A* 7 (1973) 255–93; Delplace (1978); F. Favory, 'Le monde des potiers gallo-romains', *Les dossiers de l'archéologie* 6 (1974) 90–102; Ch. Goudineau, 'La céramique arétine', *Céramiques*; Goudineau (1974); Pucci (1977); Pucci (1980); M. T. Marabini Moevs, 'New evidence for an absolute chronology of decorated late Italian sigillata', *A.J.A.* 84 (1980) 319–27; Pucci (1981).

15 – See also Carandini (1979b) 219–21.

16 – Hopkins (1980) 101–25. Cf. Carandini (1979b) 235–7.

17 – See A. Carandini, 'Roma imperialistica: un caso di sviluppo precapitalistico',

in d'Arms/Kopff (1980) 11–20 and Id., 'Sviluppo e crisi delle manifatture rurali e urbane', Giardina/Schiavone (1981) 249–60.

18 – See Manacorda (1980) esp. 177–82, and the evidence gathered in K. Painter (ed.), *Roman villas in Italy, recent excavations and researches*, British Museum Occasional Papers 24 (London, 1980) and A. Giardina, A. Schiavone (ed.), *Società romana e produzione schiavistica, I, L'Italia: insediamenti e forme economiche* (Bari, 1981).

19 – Pucci (1980) 142–5; Pucci (1981) 75–7.

10 – PETER GARNSEY: Grain for Rome

1 – I am aware that other cereals, barley in particular, were needed for animals in Rome (they must have been numerous), and to some extent for slaves.

2 – The literature on Rome's food needs is extensive. I cite here only K. J. Beloch, *Die Bevölkerung der griechisch-römischen Welt* (Leipzig, 1886); U. Kahrstedt, 'Über die Bevölkerung Roms', in L. Friedländer, *Darstellung aus der Sittengeschichte Roms*, ed. 10, IV (Leipzig, 1921), 11–21; d'Escurac (1976) 166ff.; Hopkins (1978a) 96–9; Rickman (1980) 8ff.; Casson (1980).

3. – Cf. d'Escurac (1976) 174 (but see below, n.5). Beloch (1886) 411–2, does not give a figure for total consumption. His discussion at one point (411) implies a figure of 24 million modii, at another (412) one of 28 million modii. Hopkins (1978) 96–9 is similarly inexplicit, but his conjectured population figure (800,000–1 million) and consumption rate (200 kg per person year) produce a figure in the range of 24–30 million modii. But he rightly regards 200 kg as a high figure, cf. 3n. (160 kg, mid-eighteenth century Madrid).

4 – Casson (1980), with bibl.

5 – As Beloch (n.2) 411 pointed out briefly long ago. Unlike d'Escurac (1976) and Gallotta (1975), I remain unconvinced by the attempt of G. Ch.-Picard in 'Néron et le blé d'Afrique', *Cah. Tun.* 14 (1956) 163–73, to reconcile the Epitome and Josephus by positing a pronounced fall in Egyptian exports to Rome after the age of Augustus.

6 – 'Moriens septem annorum canonem, ita ut cotidiana septuaginta quinque milia modium expendi possent reliquit'. The difficulty lies in *canonem* which implies that the grain for issue was all *tribute* grain. On the Lucan scholiast, I summarize a communication from Dr Roland Mayer: The collection of Weber (vol. III (Leipzig 1831) 53) from which the item derives is classed by Schanz-Hosius, *Gesch. der Lat. Lit.* as 'unbrauchbar . . . ohne Sichtung'. Usener and Endt omitted the item, evidently considering that it had no good claim to be late antique. Certainly the remarks immediately following, on Milo's trial, show our scholiast to be capable of gross error. All in all, any point of fact that he cites needs corroboration by an external source.

7 – On this point at least, I follow Meiggs (1973) 472-3 in his critique of Casson (1954).

8 – C. R. Whittaker's (unpublished) estimate, perhaps over-generous (but conservative in comparison with that of Ch.-Picard), is that N. African production of grain after an Augustan expansion reached a level of ca. 60–70 million modii. This would have yielded the state something in the range of 10–18 million modii in tax and rent, depending on the rate of levy. Republican evidence is thin. See Plut.

Caes. LV (Africa Nova); Livy XLIII 6.13, cf. 11 (territories of Cirta and Carthage, respectively).

9 – In the time of Justinian (Just., *Ed.* XIII 8), Egypt sent to Constantinople 8 million artabae annually, or 36 million modii. See R. P. Duncan-Jones, 'The Choenix, the Artaba and the Modius', *Z.P.E.* 21 (1976) 43–52.

10 – Of AD 39. Recent brief discussion in Casson (1980) 26ff., whose arguments against the state control of Egyptian grain, however, I find very forced.

11 – Recently restated by Rickman (1980), 64–5, the view appears to originate in Th. Mommsen's interpretation of Varro *R.R.* 2 pr. See *R.G.* III[6] 507.

12 – In this paper for reasons of space I ignore the chain from shipper to miller to baker.

13 – Badian (1972); Nicolet (1966) 318–55; Nicolet, *Rome et la conquête du monde méditerranéen. 1. Les structures de l'Italie romaine* (Paris, 1977) 260–9; Nicolet, 'Deux remarques sur l'organisation des sociétés de publicains à la fin de la République romaine', H. van Effenterre (ed.), *Points de vue sur la fiscalité antique* (Paris, 1979) 69–93.

14 – Livy XXI 63: 300 amphorae. In effect, senators could not own boats of ca. 15 tons capable of carrying ca. 2,250 modii of wheat. On tonnage and capacity of Roman ships see Pomey/Tchernia (1978).

15 – See also Cic. *ad Fam.* XIII 79; XIII 35; and J. d'Arms, '*C.I.L.* X 1792: A municipal notable of the Augustan age', *H.S.C.Ph.* 76 (1972) 207–16.

16 – Banking is normally, and credibly, assumed to have been the major enterprise of Italian *negotiatores* abroad. Cicero is rarely precise about the activities of *negotiatores*, a term best translated by the equally non-descriptive 'businessmen'. See Rougé (1966) 274ff.; Nicolet (1966) 357–86.

17 – The main discussions are by Rougé (1966) 233ff.; 274ff; Baldacci (1967); Palma (1975); d'Escurac (1976) 204ff.; Rickman (1980) 72ff.

18 – Suet. *Claud.* XVIII 3–4 and 19; Gaius *Inst.* I 32c; *Dig.* III 6 (Ulp.). See Pomey/Tchernia (1978) 237–43.

19 – The terminological problems are comprehensively discussed by Rougé (1966). It is not a central concern of this paper to follow developments in the meaning of *negotiator* or to distinguish precisely, insofar as this can be done, between *negotiator* and *mercator*, *navicularius* and *naucleros*.

20 – E.g. *C.I.L.* XIV 161 = *I.L.S.* 1427; *C.I.L.* XIV 303; XIV 4142 = *I.L.S.* 6140; with Meiggs (1973) 277ff.

21 – M. Christol, 'Remarques sur les naviculaires d'Arles', *Latomus* 30 (1971) 643–63.

22 – See Appendix.

23 – See e.g. *C.Th.* XIII 5.14, AD 371. In general, Jones (1966) 827–30.

24 – The main recent contributions are by Baldacci (1967); Meiggs (1973) 298–310; d'Escurac (1976) ch. 11; Rickman (1980) 27ff.; 87ff.; Casson (1980).

25 – I intend to discuss this matter elsewhere. The main text is Cic. *de domo* XI.

26 – See Dio LV 26.2–3; Tac. *Ann.* II 87; VI 13; XV 39; Suet. *Aug.* XLII; *Claud.* XVIII–XIX; Pliny *Pan.* XXIXff. The evidence for official wheat-prices is collected in Duncan-Jones (1976) 247–9.

27 – The case for considerable regular intervention in the market by the prefect of the corn supply has been put by d'Escurac (1976) 260ff.

28 – The opposite is suggested (for the late Republic) by Cicero, who puts official

compensation at HS 3–4 per modius and market prices at HS 2–3, in Sicily. See Duncan-Jones (1976) 249 for refs.

29 – See Baldacci (1967) 277ff.; 284; d'Escurac (1976) 260.

30 – See, most recently, d'Escurac (1977); d'Arms (1981).

11 – H. W. PLEKET: Urban elites and business in the Greek part of the Roman Empire

1 – H. W. Pleket, 'Afscheid van Rostovtzeff', *Lampas* 8 (1975) 267–84; d'Arms (1977).

2 – Finley (1973) 60. The low status of 'businessmen' leads to the conclusion that business was insignificant and the economic structure primitive. Naturally, other institutional weaknesses in the Greco-Roman world are adduced as well, as proof of the primitiveness of the economy, e.g. the underdevelopment and small scale of the operations of banking, the absence of anything like joint ownership in shipping, etc. In this essay we do not discuss these aspects. For banking see Veyne (1979) 279–80; for shipping etc. Rougé (1980) 296–300 (similarities between Roman maritime *societates* and commercial associations of the Middle Ages); for commercial banking operations of some size, see the Murecine tablets in L. Casson (1980) 33 and 26–9 (bankers and debtors are linked to Pompeian and Puteolean upper class families as freedmen).

3 – See the discussion of Lis/Soly (1979) 11ff., from which the quotation is taken. As to 'commercial bourgeoisie', Lis/Soly note a predominance of merchants rather than entrepreneurs/mastercraftsmen. Finley is influenced by the Weberian Ideal-Types of consumer (ancient) city and producer (medieval) city. Cf. Finley (1977).

4 – Veyne (1976) 135. That is the period in which de Tocqueville's famous dictum 'il faut faire des affaires mais non être dans les affaires' no longer reflect the generally accepted value-system. Incidentally, on the basis of A. J. Mayer's *The Persistence of the Old Regime* (New York, 1981), one is tempted to conclude that pre-industrial structures and mentalities lingered on even longer than the 19th century. Cf. Pleket, *Mnemosyne* 29 (1976) 211; G. Chaussinand-Nogaret 'Aux origines de la revolution: noblesse et bourgeoisie', *Annales E.S.C.* 30 (1975) 265ff.; C. Lucas, 'Nobles, bourgeois and the French revolution', *Past and Present* 60 (1973) 84ff.

5 – *C.Th.* XIII 1.5; cf. Ruggini (1961) 134, nn.366–7.

6 – *C.Th.* XIII 1.8; 1. 10–13; Cf. Ruggini (1961) 127–8 n.344; also P. A. Brunt, *J.R.S.* 71 (1981) 166.

7 – Hopkins (1978) (1980).

8 – Ward Perkins (1980). Hopkins' position on taxes in kind: cf. in the same sense P. A. Brunt, *J.R.S.* 71 (1981) 161–2.

9 – For Sombart, cf. Veyne (1976) 119, 129–30.

10 – Certainly for the later period in pre-industrial Europe there is plenty of evidence for investment in landed estate by the urban bourgeoisie and indirect involvement of noble landed proprietors in urban economies. For the latter, cf. e.g. D. Cannadine, *Lords and landlords, the aristocracy and the towns 1774–1907* (Leicester, 1980). Cf. d'Arms (1981) 94 n.96 quoting Braudel ('the social takeover of the countryside by the money of the towns').

11 – Cf. d'Arms (1981) 128 n.23 for a Roman parallel: well-to-do freedmen (Augustales) conceptualized as 'les bourgeoisies urbaines'. Naturally the problem remains how far successful freedmen became independent of their masters; cf. d'Arms (1981) 103 n.30, 142–6, with n.110.

12 – For the conception of 'Gelegenheitshandel', see Veyne (1976) 121, 124, and Veyne (1979): one is not a full-time professional merchant; nor is commercial profit-making the only object; the latter is typical of a professional.

13 – Veyne (1976) 125 n.157. Cf. *Die Inschriften von Ephesos* V no. 1487 (Hadrian and the shipper Philokyrios).

14 – *Dig.* L 7.5.5; with P. Garnsey, 'Aspects of the decline of the urban aristocracy in the Empire', *A.N.R.W.* II 1 (1974) 229–52, at 232.

15 – *S.E.G.* XXVII 828 (Roman Empire).

16 – L. Robert, *B.C.H.* 102 (1978) 422–6. As we shall see below, it is by no means certain that all these *naukleroi* were independent shipowners who traded with their own goods. *Naukleroi* could be agents, working for landed aristocrats.

17 – Cf. Pleket in *Mnemosyne* 29 (1976) 217 n.4. See d'Arms (1981) esp. 168 n.91 for the suggestion that patrons may have played the role of economic 'masterminds' behind the fragmentation of small producers (and, I would add, of small traders).

18 – L. C. Ruggini, 'La vita associativa nelle città dell' Oriente greco: tradizioni locali e influenze romane', in *Assimilation et Résistance à la culture gréco-romaine dans le monde ancien. Travaux du VIe Congrès Intern. d'Etudes Classiques.* (Paris, 1976) 481 n.67.

19 – L. Robert, *Opera Minora Selecta* I 542–8.

20 – Veyne (1979) 275n. 46, on *Tetrabiblos* IV 2; cf. also Ruggini (1961) 202, 631.

21 – Rougé (1966) 254–5; cf. Finley (1973) 58. Lucian in Loeb, vol. VI, p. 444 (§ 14).

22 – Brunt (1973) 12.

23 – *I.G.* XII 8. 581, with L. Robert, *Études Anatoliennes* (1937) 245 n.2. Robert speaks about a 'société d'armateurs et négociants' but that seems a rather audacious inference from the fact that the Heracles on record in this inscription was owned by two or three *emporoi*. Admittedly, the latter were not slaves, but the possibility cannot be ignored that they were indebted to powerful members of the elite; cf. below, n.26.

24 – For the involvement of the upper class in banking (and for that matter in overseas commerce) via slaves and freedmen, see Veyne (1979) 279–80; also Veyne (1981) 258–9; cf. nn.2, 26, 33.

25 – Veyne (1979) 277 n.51; cf. also Veyne (1976) 124 n.154.

26 – For the difference between a *professional* banker (which the professor was not) and a wealthy elite-member who lends money to friends for political purposes and to business people via middlemen (slaves, freedmen) cf. the discussion between Finley (1973) and Frederiksen (1975) 167–8; cf. also nn. 2, 24, 33.

27 – See d'Arms (1977) 177 n.67; d'Arms (1981) 158 n.38; cf. Frederiksen (1975) 166 ('. . . owning and financing of ships was often undertaken without the person acting as *naukleros* or *magister* . . .').

28 – Philostratus, *V.S.* p. 266 (Loeb). The ships are *holkades* ('. . . les navires de gros transport par excellence', Vélissaropoulos (1980) 59). Cf. d'Arms (1981) 159, 164–5.

29 – Cf. J. Rougé, 'Ports et escales dans l'empire tardif', *Settimane Spoleto* 25 (1978) I 67–128, at 124. Cf. also d'Arms (1981) 85.
30 – Cf. Vélissaropoulos (1980) 52; services of *naukleroi* hired in Hellenistic Egypt. Rougé (1966) 230–55, tries to show that in the course of the Roman imperial period *naukleros* came to mean *magister navis*, i.e. the agent-representative of the shipowner; since I am not certain that he proved his point, I do not use his support. Vélissaropoulos (55) is doubtful whether an inference to the Greek world is justified: I am more confident than she.
31 – Cf. also Jones (1964) 866–7 (shipowners not navigating their own ships; great landowners owning ships).
32 – For the points that follow see W. Brulez, 'De scheepvaartwinst in de nieuwe tijden', *Tijdschrift voor Geschiedenis* 72 (1979) 1–19, at 11, 8, 6.
33 – Quoted by Ruggini (1961) 202 n.631.
34 – Jones (1964) 866–7; for 4th century BC Athens, L. Casson, 'The Athenian Upper-class and New Comedy', *T.A.P.A.* 106 (1976) 29–59, esp. 43–5.
35 – *O.G.I.S.* 524; cf. Harris (1980) 127, 131.
36 – The precise hierarchy, if any, of Greek urban magistracies is unclear. For the aedileship-*agoronomia* as an office of some status, see Apul., *Met.* I 24; cf. F. Millar, *J.R.S.* 71 (1981) 69.
37 – C. P. Jones (1978) 345–6 n.40; for the list, see 351 n.60.
38 – *Dig.* L 2. 12; cf. R. Macmullen, *Roman social relations 50 BC to AD 284* (New Haven, 1974), 99.
39 – See Jones (1964) 870.
40 – Cf. Casson in d'Arms/Kopff (1980) 26–9. *Pace* Casson, C. Sulpicius Cinnamus was C. Sulpicius Faustus' freedman. See J. G. Wolf 'Aus dem neuen pompejanischen Urkundenfund: Der Seefrachtvertrag des Menelaos', *Freiburger Universitätsblätter* 65 (1979) 23–36, esp. 27–8. The freedman C. Novius Eunus, a large-scale dealer in foodstuffs, is undoubtedly related to the family of the Novii. Another grain-dealer is P. Annius Seleucus, connected with the Pompeian and/or Puteolean Annii; cf. P. Castren, *Ordo Populusque Pompeianus. Polity and Society in Roman Pompeii* (Rome, 1975) 135 (and 226–7, 496–7 on the Sulpicii and Novii); d'Arms (1974) 107–8, 122.
41 – Judeich, *Altertümer von Hierapolis* (1898), *Die Inschriften*, no.156; cf. Cichorius' commentary on p. 54–5; or is he a second choice? cf. n.38.
42 – Cichorius (n.41). Note that in Italian Aquinum the upper class family of the Barronii possessed dye-works; cf. d'Arms (1977) 177 n.62.
43 – J. and L. Roberts, *B.E.* (1971) no. 647; cf., later, Aurelius Psates from Panopolis, Egypt, owning four houses and sons employing assistants. See Jones (1964) 865.
44 – Cf. M. M. Postan in *Cambridge Economic History of Europe* II 168ff: most merchants were 'small fry'; even in the later Middle Ages English landlords dabbled in the wool trade.
45 – See d'Arms (1974) 110 on the Cnaeii Haii of Puteoli; cf. d'Arms (1981) 49ff. on Vestorius, who introduced the production of special colouring dyes. H. v. Petrikovits, *Z.P.E.* 43 (1981) 286, pointed out that purple-dying was about the only craft for which 'Fachbücher' have been written; most other craftsmen were illiterate. For a possible relation between urban elite and purple-dying cf. note 42, above.

46 – Jones (1974) 362; Jones (1964) 861–2.

47 – Lis/Soly (1979) 11–14 (1000–1300 AD), 36–7 (1350–1450 AD: merchants dominating the increasing rural production of textiles), 63–6 (1450–1630 AD: predominance of merchants, who used the putting-out system, and of small production-units), 105–6 (1630–1750: merchants controlling putting-out system; small percentage of the merchants really important).

48 – Lis/Soly (1979) 11; cf. also *Cambridge Economic History of Europe*, II 369–77.

49 – As to the Western part of the Empire, I refer to Drinkwater (1977–8), who suggests that the Secundinii from Trier were wealthy and socially important cloth-merchants, forerunners of their later medieval colleagues. See also J. F. Drinkwater, 'Money rents and food-renders in Gallic funerary reliefs' in A. King, M. Henig, *The Roman West in the third century, B.A.R.* 109 (1981) 215–33. (It is fair to add that Drinkwater follows Jones in admitting that the decurional elite was a landowning elite and that the wealthiest merchants do not seem to have formed part of the ruling group: in his view what prevented merchants 'from transforming comfortable fortunes into great ones' was the absence of significant state borrowing). Trier and the area of the Treviri and Nervii was renowned for its wool; cf. Diocletian's Edict 19, 44 and 66; 22, 21; so there is reason to suppose that the Secundinii specialized in luxury textiles. One is tempted to see a parallel in *C.I.L.* III 5800 from Augsburg, recording the erection of a temple by the textile merchants for themselves and for a father (?) and son; one of them was *eques Romanus* and member of the town-council. Schlippschuh (1974) 40 assumes that this urban dignitary was himself a member of the guild of *negotiatores*. Cf. also *C.I.L.* XIII 2010 mentioning a textile merchant, buried in Lyon and called *IIII vir*. Cf., for N. Italian businessmen in public office, Garnsey (1976). The presence of wealthy freedmen among the *negotiatores* shows that being a cloth merchant could be rewarding and create the wealth on the basis of which descendants could rise to urban elite status. It is important to distinguish between the great textile centres and the average town which produced for its own consumption. Pompeii, despite W. D. Moeller (*The Wool Trade of Ancient Pompeii*, Leiden (1976)), is not known to have been a major, exporting textile centre. If structures comparable to those of the later pre-industrial European textile-cities existed at all in the Roman Empire, they are likely to have occurred in the great weaving towns.

50 – For slaves as *negotiatores* cf. Pavis d'Escurac (1977) 345–7; Veyne (1981) 257–8, n.62. Schlippschuh (1974) 164 incorrectly maintains that slaves did not act as independent *negotiatores*; cf. also Ruggini (1961) passim for the use of 'straw-men' in the grain-trade in Italy.

51 – Cf. J. K. Evans, 'Wheat production and its social consequences in the Roman world', *C.Q.* 31 (1981) 428–42, at 429 n.6, who stresses the inadequacy even of maritime transport during famines.

52 – Wörrle (1971) 333–7; Casson in d'Arms/Kopff (1980) 23–5.

53 – Casson in d'Arms/Kopff (1980) 21, 24, 29; Rickman (1980) 72.

54 – *C.I.L.* XIV 4142 (*I.L.S.* 6140) and 4620; cf. Rickman (1980) 142.

55 – For the latter cf. e.g. Ruggini (1978), the table at the end (after p. 92) nos. 1, 4, 5 and 8 (the latter being a *nauta* who also was *duovir bis* of Vienna: a parallel to a *naukleros* being a member of the town-council of Nicomedia). Cf. text to n.15.

56 – Cf. nn.2 and 40. concerning the Murecine archive.

57 – Lis/Soly (1979) 61.

58 – The late Roman lady Melania is an obvious parallel (one domain had 60 hamlets, with a total of 24,000 slaves). Cf. Finley (1980) 122.
59 – Cf. the review by N. Purcell of two recent monographs in *J.R.S.* 71 (1981) 214–15. The Roman upper-class landowners made money from the *figlinae* in their estates by letting contracts for the making of bricks to another individual who did the job through his own dependents. Previously it was thought that the *figlinae*-owners used slaves and freedmen for that purpose. Purcell argues that the latter system reflected 'great capitalist interests' whereas the *locatio-conductio* scheme 'drives out the spectre of capitalist industrialism'. In my view in both cases the term 'industrialism' is out of place, since the production-units were invariably small. But I fail to see why the contract system is less capitalistic than the slave-system; the former coupled a regular flow of income with the smallest possible trouble about management. The leasing of a pottery in Egyptian Oxyrhynchus (cf. *J.R.S.* 71 (1981) 87–98) provides a nice parallel. It is not certain that the slave and freedman system would have produced larger profits. For a recent attempt to show that in agriculture to run an estate by slave labour alone was far from profitable see D. W. Rathbone, 'The development of agriculture in the "Ager Cosanus" during the Roman Republic: Problems of evidence and interpretation', *J.R.S.* 71 (1981) 10–23.
60 – Cf. nn. 2, 24, 26, 33.

12 – ANDREA CARANDINI: Pottery and the African economy

1 – The text of this article is an English version (for which I am indebted to my friend Henry Hurst) of my introduction to African Pottery published in the *Atlante delle Forme Ceramiche, I Ceramica fine romana del medio e tardo impero nel bacino mediterraneo (Enciclopedia dell' Arte Antica*, Rome, 1982). The Atlas contains a full bibliography on the topic. Here the main works of reference, in addition to those provided in the text and notes, are: J. Deneauve, *Lampes de Carthage* (Paris, 1967); A. Ennabli, *Lampes chrétiennes de Tunisie* (Paris, 1976).
2 – We call 'terra sigillata africana' the assemblage of wares that Lamboglia defined as 'terra sigillata chiara' A, C, D (excluding B whose origin has been established as Gallia Narbonensis) and that Hayes has more recently termed 'African Red-Slip Ware'. Hayes suggests that it would be advisable to distinguish the pottery with a high surface polish of the early Empire (Red-Gloss Terra Sigillata) from that with a less shiny surface of the middle and late Empire (Fine Red-Slip Wares).

We have nevertheless preferred to retain the term 'terra sigillata' for the great majority of the fine table wares of the middle and late Empire, both for reasons of terminological uniformity (to avoid alarming 'humanist' archaeologists with excessive complications) and for strictly technical reasons (thinking, for example, of the high surface polish and somewhat purified clays of some products of Byzacena).
3 – Waagé (1933); see Appendix for the terminology used.
4 – Cf. Carandini (1976) 45ff.
5 – See *Ostia* III, form LIX_2 (n.13).
6 – See *Ostia* I–IV, discussed in note 13.
7 – A. Carandini, *D.d.A.* 7 (1973) 312–29.

8 – See A. Carandini, 'Ricerche sui problemi dell'ultima pitture tardo-antice sul bacino del Mediterraneo meridionale', *Archeologia Classice* (1962) 210ff. and 'Appunti sulle composizione del mosaico detto della "grande collia" rinvenuto nell'ambulocro della villa del Casale a Piazza Armerina' *D.d.A.* 4–5 (1970/71) 120.

9 – A. Carandini, *D.d.A* 1 (1966) 93.

10 – Carandini (1979b), A. Carandini and S. Settis, *Schiavi e padroni nell'Etruria romana* (Roma, 1979).

11 – J. Kolendo, *Le colonat en Afrique sous le haut-empire* (Paris, 1979); Whittaker (1978).

12 – F. Favory, 'Le monde des potiers gallo-romains', *Les dossiers de l'archéologie* 6 (1974) 90–102.

13 – *Ostia I–IV, Studi Miscellanei* nos. 13, 16, 21, 23, reviewed by G. E. Rickman in *J.R.S.* 71 (1981) 215ff. in a typically British way, in which an aversion to generalization is linked to a veneration for 'continuity'. Thus, an excavation must content itself with being 'careful', and late antique Italian amphorae for wine 'must have' existed, even if they did not.

13 – C. R. WHITTAKER: Late Roman trade and traders

1 – References and comments in Laurent (1932).

2 – Baynes (1929), for instance, argued that Vandal pirates created the crucial decline in Mediterranean trade, but recent excavations at Carthage and in Tunisia are against him; see now Fulford (1980).

3 – Lyon (1972) 72; Pounds (1974) 72–3.

4 – Laurent (1938); cf. Latouche (1961) 121–2.

5 – *M.G.H.*, LL, V. 314ff., no. 37.

6. – The latter is confirmed by the Capitulary *de villis* of Charlemagne, *M.G.H.*, LL, II 1. 82–91, no. 32. Section 30 deals with goods *ad opus nostrum* or those to be sent to the army (*in hostem*); section 8 discusses a steward (*iudex*) purchasing wine for the royal estate.

7 – Laurent (1938) 238–91, with refs.

8 – Van Werveke (1923) 656; cf. also Van Werveke (1925), for similar abbey ownership of saltings and olive farms.

9 – J.-M. Pardessus, *Diplomata, chartae, epistolae, leges ad res Gallo-Francicas spectantia* (Paris, 1843–9) n. 230, p. 207; the while will is a good example of the massive property transactions of the Church by this time.

10 – *M.G.H.*, S.S.R.M., III. 315–16, ch. 22; cf. Doehaerd (1978) 4 (although with incorrect ref.).

11 – *Polyptique de l'abbé Irminion*, B. E. C. Guérard (ed.) (Paris, 1844) II 334–5.

12 – Duby (1968) 46; J. Richards, *Consul of God. The life and times of Gregory the Great* (London, 1980) 138.

13 – Laurent (1938) 294.

14 – Cf. Lambrechts (1949) attacking Piganiol (1947) for just such an ideological distortion.

15 – Grierson (1959) (1961).

16 – Sawyer (1977).

17 – Hodges (1977) esp. 200.

18 – Renfrew (1975).

19 – Polanyi, Mimeo no. 1.13 quoted in Dalton (1975) 91; cf. Finley (1973) 34 for his general argument about the absence of a single ancient economy.
20 – Duby (1968) 42; Pirenne (1969) 46.
21 – Hodges (1977) 199.
22 – Pounds (1974) 77.
23 – Cf. J. M. Wallace-Hadrill, *The Barbarian West* (London, 1966) 9: 'The Franks may well have misunderstood and failed to use much of what they found of government and administration in Gaul but they certainly brought no alternative with them.'
24 – Jullian (1926) 194–5 notes that the imperial dye-works at Toulon or Narbonne (*N.D.* (Oc.) XI 72–3), or the armour production at Argentan (*N.D.* (Oc.) IX 31), were located at places known for their skills in their earlier Empire.
25 – Wipszycka (1966) 2 notes this point for Egypt; Wild (1977) 30 and (1970) 53 believes in something like factories in the later Empire, but admits there is no archaeological evidence yet.
26 – Rougé (1966) 480–3, points out that requisitioning was always possible in the earlier Empire.
27 – As Palma (1975) 30 argues.
28 – Ruggini (1961) is the only attempt I know.
29 – Martindale, *P.L.R.E.* 'Aetius 1' thinks the legislation related to *C.J.* I 2.4 and hence refers to Church staff.
30 – C. Verlinden, *L'esclavage dans l'Empire mediéval I* (Brugge, 1955) 672–7.
31 – Cf. Rougé (1966) 313 for Jews in commerce in general.
32 – Richards (n.12) 89 with references.
33 – I believe Jones (1974) Ch. XVII, and (1964) 804 exaggerates the extent of gold rents in view of references to false measures of corn used by Church agents in Sicily and to *horrea ecclesiae* (Greg. *Epp.* I 42, XIII 47), although I admit that the Church may have also purchased corn from its own tenants, as in Greg. *Ep.* I 70.
34 – The Greek life of John is in *Anal. Boll.* 45 (1927) 19–73, esp. sections 23 and 26; cf. Jones (1964) 866–7.
35 – e.g. *Conc. Carthag.* I, canon 6; *Conc. Hippo*, canon 15; *Conc. Arles* II, canon 14.
36 – Jones (1974) 347.
37 – Richards (n.12) 89.
38 – Compare Amm. Marc. XXIX 5.13 – *fundi in modum urbis* – and Auson. *Ep.* XXVI 42 using the term *oppidum* of his villa at Lucaniac, with the celebrated second century AD description of African estates by Fronto.
39 – Auson. *Parent.* 8: the importance of *ruris cultus*; Sidon. *Ep.* II 14: the reward for *industria* is full storehouses.
40 – Olymp. fr. 44; this gold was 'apart from the corn and the wine and all other goods', which might also be sold off, says the author.
41 – Jullian (1926) 361, with references.
42 – R. de Maeyer, *De Romeinische villas in België* (Antwerp, 1937) 309 lists at least twenty-two major villas out of 129 which certainly continued after the third century invasions, despite the vulnerability of this region compared to Aquitania.
43 – Comments and references in C. R. Whittaker, 'Rural labour in three Roman provinces' in P. Garnsey (ed.), *Non-slave labour in the Greco-Roman world*, *P.C.P.S.* Suppl. 6 (1980) 81.

44 – Jullian (1926) 142 believed many *mansiones* for storage were on private estates, the origin of the word 'maison'.
45 – Jullian (1926) 165–6.
46 – J. H. W. G. Liebeschuetz, 'Money, economy and taxation in kind in Syria in the 4th century AD,' *Rh.M.* 104 (1961) 251 rightly notes this was not normal commerce.
47 – Liebeschuetz (1972) 46.
48 – See, for instance, the list of property-owners submitted to the PPO Oriens for selection into the *corpus* of *navicularii*, noted in *C.Th.* XIII 5.14 (371).
49 – Patlagean (1977) 342–4.
50 – Jones (1964) 465, 847, 871 estimates the lustral revenue at no more than 5 per cent of the total, and compares maximum known sums of merchant capital with the huge gold annual incomes from senatorial estates.
51 – Finley (1980) 139–40; see my comments in *Opus* 1 (1982) 171–9.
52 – Whittaker (1980).
53 – Février (1980) redresses the balance in Gaul; cf. Patlagean (1977), esp. 232, for the East.
54 – L. Friedländer, *Darstellungen aus der Sittengeschichte Roms* (8th ed. Leipzig, 1922) I 378, points out that the term 'Syrian', like that of 'Lombard' later, had become an occupational rather than an ethnic label.
55 – Rougé (1966) 313.
56 – Patlagean (1977) 425.
57 – Wipszycka (1965) 94; E. R. Hardy, *The large estates of Byzantine Egypt* (New York, 1931) 122–9.
58 – P.-A. Février, 'Les sarcophages d'Arles', *Congr. Arch. de France 1976* (Paris, 1979) 317–59 and (1980) 477.
59 – Whittaker (1978), recently challenged by E. Lo Cascio in *Opus* 1 (1982) 147–59; but see Finley's comments in the same journal on the inadmissibility of the free labour-market model used by Lo Çascio.
60 – R. Agache, 'La campagne à l'époque romain dans les grands plaines du Nord de la France', *A.N.R.W.* II 4 (1975) 658–713.
61 – A. Mócsy, *Pannonia and Upper Moesia* (London, 1974) 319; see Carandini's contribution to this volume and Ph. Leveau, 'Études de l'évolution d'un paysage agraire d'époque romaine', *Quad. di Storia* 13 (1981) 167–85, esp. 173 for changes in Africa.
62 – *M.A.M.A.* III 200–788, discussed in detail by Patlagean (1977) 159–63.
63 – Jullian (1926) 137.
64 – J. Matthews, *Western aristocracies and the imperial court AD 364–425* (Oxford, 1975) 27–31.
65 – Jones (1974); Richards (n.12) 127, with references.
66 – Jones (1964) 415–6; Cl. Lepelley, 'Déclin ou stabilité de l'agriculture africaine au Bas-Empire' *Ant. Afr.* 1 (1967) 135–44.
67 – Manacorda (1976/7); Zevi/Tchernia (1969); *Ostia IV* (1977) 189–93.
68 – Gren (1941) esp. 141–6.
69 – F. Millar, 'The privata from Diocletian to Theodosius' in *Imperial revenue, expenditure and monetary policy in the fourth century AD*, C. E. King (ed.), *B.A.R.* Suppl. 76 (Oxford, 1980) 132.
70 – Duby (1968) 345.

71 – J. Goody, 'Economy and feudalism', *Ec.H.R.* 22 (1969) 393–405 makes this point in comparing the differences between African and European long-distance trade.
72 – Pounds (1974) 73; Mócsy (n.61) 320; Jellema (1955).
73 – Hedeager (1977) 202.
74 – Cf. the remarks by Fixot (1980) 525.
75 – Lambrechts (1939).
76 – The distinction is made clear in Philos. *V.S.* II 21 where we are told of Proclus of Naucratis, a rich propertied emigré from Egypt, in Athens: 'He used to receive from Egypt regular supplies . . . which he would sell to those who traded such things . . . *not seeking for profits or usury but being content with the principal*'.
77 – Slaves *qui praepositi essent negotii exercendi causa, velut qui ad emendum locandum conducendum praepositi essent*, *Dig.* XXXII 65. C. Fufius Cirta was a *negotiator, qui rei frumentariae iussu Caesaris praeerat*, Caes. *B.G.* VII 3.1.
78 – Middleton (1979).
79 – Schlippschuh (1974) 16. Oddly enough it is Rostovtzeff (1957) 166 who, despite his multitude of examples of commercial traders and entrepreneurs, ends up by concluding that the main merchants of Trier, Lyon and Arles 'were mostly agents of the imperial government'.
80 – Goudineau (1980) 376 also notes the limited distribution of freedmen seviri Augustales, who were closely associated with trade.

Bibliography

Andreau, J. (1977). 'M. I. Finley, la banque antique et l'économie moderne', *Ann. sc. norm. sup. Pisa* 7: 1130–52.

Ashmole, B. (1970). 'Aegean marble: science and common sense', *A.B.S.A.* 65: 1–2.

Austin, M. M. (1970). *Greece and Egypt in the archaic age*, P.C.P.S. Supp. 2.

– Vidal-Naquet, P. (1977). *Economic and social history of ancient Greece. An introduction*. London.

Badian, E. (1972). *Publicans and Sinners*. Oxford.

Baldacci, P. (1967). 'Negotiatores e Mercatores Frumentarii nel Periodo Imperiale', *R.I.L.* 101: 273–91.

Baratier, E. (ed.) (1973). *Histoire de Marseille*. Paris.

Barruol. G., Gourdiole, R. (1980). 'Les mines antiques de la haute vallée de l'Orb (Hérault)', *Mines et fonderies antiques*.

Baynes, N. (1929) 'M. Pirenne and the unity of the Mediterranean world' (part of a review of F. Lot, *La fin du monde antique et le début du moyen âge* (Paris, 1927). *J.R.S.* 19: 230–5.

Boardman, J. (1980). *The Greeks overseas. Their early colonies and trade*. 3rd ed. London.

Boerner, E. (1939). *Der staatliche Korntransport im griechisch-römischen Aegypten*. diss. Hamburg.

Bogaert, R. (1965). 'Banquiers, courtiers et prêts maritimes à Athènes et à Alexandrie', *Chronique d'Egypte* 40: 140–56.

– (1968). *Banques et banquiers dans les cités grecques*. Leiden.

Bohn, O. (1923). 'Die ältesten römischen Amphoren in Gallien', *Germania* 7: 8–16.

Brashinsky, I. B. (1980). *Greek imports on the Lower Don in the C5th to the C3rd BC* (in Russian). Leningrad.

Bravo, B. (1974). 'Une lettre sur plomb de Berezan: colonisation et modes de contrat dans le Pont', *D.H.A* 1: 111–87.

– (1977). 'Remarques sur les assises sociales, les formes d'organisation et la terminologie du commerce maritime grec à l'époque archaïque', *D.H.A.* 3: 1–59.

Brunt, P. A. (1973). 'Aspects of the social thought of Dio Chrysostom and of the Stoics', *P.C.P.S.* 19: 9–34.

Buchner, G. (1970). 'Mostra degli scavi di Pithecusa', *D.d.A.* 3: 85–101.

Burford, A. M. (1960). 'Heavy transport in classical antiquity', *Ec.H.R.* n.s. 13: 1–18.

– (1969). *The Greek temple-builders at Epidauros*. Liverpool.

Carandini, A. (1970). 'Produzione agricola e produzione ceramica nell' Africa

dietà imperiale. Appunti sull' economia della Zeugitana e della Byzacena', *Studi Miscellanei* 15: 95–124.
– (1976). 'Studio di una forma ceramica africana: un esempio di "selezione artigianale"', *Studi Miscellanei* 22: 45–56.
– (1979a). *Archeologia e cultura materiale*, 2nd ed. Bari.
– (1979b). *L'anatomia della scimmia. La formazione economica della società prima del Capitale*. Turin.
Casson, L. (1971). *Ships and seamanship in the ancient world*. Princeton.
– (1980). 'The role of the state in Rome's grain trade', in d'Arms/Kopff (1980) 21–33.
Clavel, M. (1977). *Marseille grecque, la dynamique d'un impérialisme marchand*. Paris.
Clemente, G. (1974). *I Romani nella Gallia meridionale (II°–I° sec. a.C.)*. Bologna.
Cook, R. M. (1959). 'Die Bedeutung der bemalten Keramik für den griechischen Handel', *J.d.I.* 74: 114–23.
Crawford, M. H. (1977). 'Republican denarii in Romania: The suppression of piracy and the slave-trade', *J.R.S.* 67: 117–24.
D'Arms, J. H. (1974). 'Puteoli in the second century of the Roman Empire: a social and economic study,' *J.R.S.* 64: 104–24.
– (1977). 'M. I. Rostovtzeff and M. I. Finley: the status of traders in the Roman World', in *Ancient and Modern: Essays in honor of G. F. Else*, J. H. D'Arms, J. W. Eadie (ed.) 159–80. Ann Arbor.
– (1981). *Commerce and Social Standing in Ancient Rome*. Cambridge, Mass.
– Kopff, E. C. (1980). *The Seaborne commerce of Ancient Rome*. M.A.A.R. 36. Rome.
D'Escurac. See Pavis d'Escurac.
Dalton, G. (1975). 'Karl Polanyi's analysis of long-distance trade and his wider paradigm' in Sabloff, J. A., Lamberg-Karlovsky, C. C. (1975) 63–132.
Daubigney, A. (1979). 'Reconnaissance des formes de la dépendance gauloise', *D.H.A.* 5: 145–90.
– (1981). 'Relations marchandes méditerranéennes et procès des rapports de dépendance (*Magu*-et ambactes) en Gaule protohistorique' in *Colloquio internazionale su forme di contatto e processi di trasformazione nelle società antiche, Cortone, 24–30 mai 1981*.
Davies, J. K. (1971). *Athenian Propertied Families 600–300 B.C.* Oxford.
Delplace, Ch. (1978). 'Les potiers dans la société et l'économie de l'Italie et de la Gaule au 1er siècle av. at au 1er ap. J.-C.', *Ktema* 3: 55–76.
Doehaerd, R. (1978). *The early middle ages in the West: economy and society*. North Holland.
Drinkwater, J. F. (1977–1978). 'Die Secundinier von Igel und die Woll- und Textil-industrie in Gallia Belgica: Fragen und Hypothesen', *Trierer Zeitschrift* 40–41: 107–25.
Duby, G. (1968). *Rural economy and country life in the medieval West*. London.
– (ed.) (1980). *Histoire de la France urbaine. I. La ville antique des origines au IXè siècle*. Paris.
Duncan-Jones, R. P. (1974). *The Economy of the Roman Empire*. Cambridge.
– (1976). 'The price of wheat in Roman Egypt under the Principate', *Chiron* 6: 241–62.
– (1979). 'Variations in Egyptian grain-measure', *Chiron* 9: 347–75.
Earle, T. K., Ericson, J. E. (ed.) (1977). *Exchange Systems in Prehistory*. New York.

Erxleben, E. (1974). 'Die Rolle der Bevölkerungsklassen im Aussenhandel Athens im 4 Jahrhundert v.u.Z.', in *Hellenische Poleis*, Welskopf, E. C. (ed.) I. 460–520. Berlin.

Fédération historique du Languedoc méditerranéen et du Roussillon (1977). *Mines et mineurs en Languedoc-Roussillon et régions voisines de l'Antiquité à nos jours*. Montpellier.

Février, P.-A. (1980). In Duby, G. (1980).

Finley, M. I. (1935). 'Emporos, Naukleros and Kapelos. Prolegomena to the study of Athenian Trade', *C.Ph.* 30: 320–36.

– (1952). *Studies in land and credit in ancient Athens*, New Brunswick.

– (1953). 'Land, debt and the man of property in classical Athens', *Pol. Sc. Qu.* 68: 249–68. Reprinted in Finley (1981b) 62–76.

– (1962). 'The Black Sea and Danubian regions and the slave trade in Antiquity', *Klio* 40: 51–9. Reprinted in Finley (1981b) 167–75.

– (1965). 'Classical Greece', *Deuxième conférence internationale d'histoire économique, Aix-en-Provence 1962. I. Trade and Politics in the ancient world.* 11–35. Paris. Reprinted New York 1979.

– (1970). 'Metals in the ancient world', *J.R.S.A.* 118: 597–607.

– (1973). *The ancient economy*. London and Berkeley.

– (1977). 'The ancient city: from Fustel de Coulanges to Max Weber and beyond', *C.S.S.H.* 19: 305–27. Reprinted in Finley (1981b) 3–23.

– (ed.) (1979). *The Bücher-Meyer controversy*. New York.

– (1980). *Ancient slavery and modern ideology*. London.

– (1981a). *Early Greece: the bronze and archaic ages*. 2nd ed. London.

– (1981b). *Economy and Society in ancient Greece*, Shaw B. D., Saller, R. P. (ed.). London.

Fixot, M. (1980). In Duby, G. (1980).

Fraser, P. M. (1972). *Ptolemaic Alexandria*. Oxford.

Frederiksen, M. W. (1975). 'Theory, evidence and the ancient economy', *J.R.S.* 65: 164–71. Review-discussion of Finley (1973).

Fulford, M. G. (1980). 'Carthage: overseas trade and the political economy, c. AD 400–700', *Reading Medieval Studies* 6: 68–80

Galliou, P. (1982) *Les amphores tardo-républicaines découvertes dans l'ouest de la France et les importations de vin italien à la fin de l'Age de Fer. Fasc. I du Corpus des amphores découvertes dans l'ouest de la France, dir. Sanquer, R., Archéologie en Bretagne*, Suppl. 4, Brest.

Gallotta, B. (1975). 'L'Africa e i rifornimenti di cereali all'Italia durante il principato di Nerone', *R.I.L.* 109: 28–46.

Garlan, Y. (1979). 'Koukos. Données nouvelles pour une nouvelle interprétation des timbres amphoriques thasiens', *Thasiaca* (B.C.H. Suppl. 5) 213–68.

Garnsey, P. (1976). 'Economy and society of Mediolanum under the Principate', *P.B.S.R.* 44: 13–27.

– (1981). 'Independent freedmen and the economy of Roman Italy under the Principate', *Klio* 63: 359–71.

Gauthier, Ph. (1972). *Symbola. Les étrangers et la justice dans les cités grecques*. Nancy.

– (1976). *Un commentaire historique des Poroi de Xénophon*. Paris.

– (1981). 'De Lysias à Aristote (Ath. Pol. 51–4): le commerce du grain à Athènes et les fonctions de sitophylaques', *R.H.D.F.E.* 59: 5–28.

Germann, K., Holzmann, G., and Winckler, F. J. (1980). 'Determination of marble provenance: limits of isotopic analysis', *Archaeometry* 22: 99–106.

Giardina, A., and Schiavone, A. (1981). *Società romana e produzione schiavistica.* II *Merci mercati e scambi nel Mediterraneo*, Rome/Bari.

Glodariu, I. (1976). *Dacian trade with the Hellenistic and Roman world.* B.A.R. Suppl. 8. Oxford.

Gluskina, L. M. (1974). 'Studien zu den sozial-ökonomischen Verhältnissen in Attika im 4 Jahr. v.u.Z.' *Eirene* 12: 111–38.

Gomme, A. W. (1937). 'Traders and manufacturers in Greece', in *Essays in Greek history and literature*, 42–66. Oxford.

Goudineau, Ch. (1974). 'La céramique dans l'économie de la Gaule', *Les Dossiers de l'archéologie*, 6: 103–9.

– (1978). 'La Gaule transalpine' in Nicolet (1978) 679–99.

– (1980). In Duby, G. (1980).

Grace, V. (1979). *Amphoras and the ancient wine trade.* Rev. ed. Princeton.

Gren, E. (1941). *Kleinasien und der Ostbalkan in der wirtschaftslichen Entwicklung der römischen Kaiserzeit.* Uppsala/Leipzig.

Grierson, P. (1959). 'Commerce in the Dark Ages: a critique of the evidence', *Trans. Roy. Hist. Soc.* 9: 123–40.

– (1961). La fonction sociale de la monnaie en Angleterre au VIIe – VIIIe siècles', *Sett. Stud. Cent. Ital. Stud. Med.* 8: 341–62.

Harris, W. V. (1980). 'Towards a study of the Roman slave trade' in d'Arms/Kopff (1980) 117–40.

Hasebroek, J. (1920). 'Zum griechischen Bankwesen der klassischen Zeit', *Hermes* 55: 113–73.

– (1931). *Griechische Wirtschafts- und Gesellschaftsgeschichte.* Tübingen.

– (1933). *Trade and politics in ancient Greece.* London.

Hauben, H. (1971). 'An annotated list of Ptolemaic naukleroi with a discussion of *B.G.U.* X 1933', *Z.P.E.* 8: 259–75.

– (1978). 'Nouvelles remarques sur les nauclères d'Egypt à l'époque des Lagides', *Z.P.E.* 28: 99–107.

– (1979). 'Le transport fluvial en Egypte ptolémaique. Les bateaux du roi et de la reine', *Pap. Brux.* 19: 68–77.

Hayes, J. W. (1972) *Late Roman Pottery.* London.

Hédan, E., Vernhet, A. (1975). 'Note sur le cuivre et ses alliages au 1er s. av. J.-C. chez les Rutènes et les Gabales', *Actes du 98è congrès nat. des soc. sav., St.-Etienne, 1973*, 71–8. Paris.

Hedeager, L. (1977). 'A quantitative analysis of Roman imports in Europe north of the *limes* (0–400 AD)' in Kristiansen, K., Palaudan-Müller, C. (ed.), *New directions in Scandinavian Archaeology*, 191–216. Lyngby.

Hodges, R. (1977). 'Trade and urban origins in Dark Age England', *B.R.O.B.* 27: 191–215.

Hohlwein, N. (1938). 'Le blé d'Egypte', *Etudes de Papyrologie* 4: 33–120.

Hopkins, K. (1978a). *Conquerors and Slaves.* Cambridge.

– (1978b). 'Economic growth and towns in classical antiquity' in *Towns in Societies*, Abrams, P., Wrigley, E. A. (ed.) 35–79. Cambridge.

– (1980). 'Taxes and Trade in the Roman Empire', *J.R.S.* 70: 101–25.

Humphreys, S. C. (1978). *Anthropology and the Greeks.* London.

Isager, S., Hansen, M. H. (1975). *Aspects of Athenian society in the fourth century B.C.* Odense.

Jantzen, U. (1972). *Samos* VIII: *Ägyptische und örientalische Bronzen aus dem Heraion.* Bonn.

Jellema, D. (1955). 'Frisian trade in the Dark Ages', *Speculum* 30: 15–36.

Johnston, A. W. (1979). *Trademarks on Greek vases.* Warminster.

Jones, A. H. M. (1964). *The Later Roman Empire, 284–602.* 3 vols. Oxford.

– (1974). *The Roman Economy*, Brunt, P. A. (ed.) Oxford.

Jones, C. P. (1978). 'A Syrian in Lyon', *A.J.P.* 99: 336–53.

Jullian, C. (1926). *Histoire de la Gaule.* Vol. VIII. Paris.

Kahrstedt, U. (1921). 'Über die Bevölkerung Roms', in Friedländer L. *Darstellungen aus der Sittengeschichte Roms*, ed. 10, vol. 4. 11–21. Leipzig.

Knorringa, H. (1926). *Emporos. Data on trade and traders in Greek literature from Homer to Aristotle.* Amsterdam.

Labrousse, M. (1958). 'Exploitation d'or et d'argent dans le Rouergue et l'Albigeois', *Fédération historique du Languedoc méditerranéen et du Roussillon, Congrès de Rodez, 14–16 juin 1958: Rouergue et confins*, 91–106. Rodez.

– (1968). *Toulouse antique.* Paris.

Lamboglia, N. (1958). 'Nuove osservazioni sulla terra sigillata chiara (Tipi A e B)', *Riv. St. Lig.* 24: 257–330.

– (1963). 'Nuove osservazioni sulla terra sigillata chiara. II. La sigillata chiara C', *Riv. St. Lig.* 29: 145–212.

Lambrechts, P. (1939). 'Les thèses de Henri Pirennes sur la fin du monde antique et les débuts du Moyen-Age', *Byzantion* 14: 513–36.

– (1949). 'Le problème du dirigisme d'état au IVe siècle: à propos de quelques publications nouvelles', *A.C.* 18: 109–26.

Landels, J. G. (1978). *Engineering in the ancient world.* London.

Latouche, R. (1961). *The birth of Western economy.* London.

Laurent, H. (1932). 'Les travaux de M. Henri Pirenne', *Byzantion* 7: 495–509.

– (1938). 'Marchands du palais et marchands d'abbayes', *R.H.* 183: 281–97.

Lazzarini, L., Moschini, G., Stievano, B. M. (1980). 'A contribution to the identification of Italian, Greek and Anatolian marbles through a petrological study and the evaluation of Ca/Sr ratio', *Archaeometry* 22: 173–82.

Lepore, E. (1970). 'Strutture della colonizzazione Focea in Occidente', *Parola del Passato* 25: 19–54.

Liebeschuetz, J. H. W. G. (1972). *Antioch. City and imperial administration in the later Roman Empire.* Oxford.

Lis, C., Soly, H. (1979). *Poverty and capitalism in pre-industrial Europe.* Hassocks.

Lyon, B. (1972). *The origin of the Middle Ages: Pirenne's challenge to Gibbon.* New York.

Manacorda, D. (1976/7). 'Testimonianze sulla produzione e il consumo dell' olio tripolitano nel III secolo', D.d.A. 9–10: 542–601.

– (1980). 'L'ager cosanus tra tarda repubblica e impero: forme di produzione e assetto della proprietà' in d'Arms/Kopff (1980) 173–84.

– (1981). 'Produzione agricola, produzione ceramica e proprietari nell'ager cosanus nel I a.C.', in Giardina, A., Schiavone, A. (1981) 55–80.

Meiggs, R. (1973). *Roman Ostia*, 2nd ed. Oxford.

Mele, A. (1979). *Il commercio greco arcaico. Prexis ed emporie.* Naples.

Merzagora, M. (1929). 'La navigazione in Egitto nell'età greco-romana', *Aegyptus* 10: 105–48.

Meyer-Termeer, A. J. M. (1978). *Die Haftung der Schiffer im griechischen und römischen Recht*. Zutphen.

Middleton, P. (1979). 'Army supply in Roman Gaul' in *Invasion and Response: The case of Roman Britain*. Burnham, B. C., Johnson, H. B., (ed.) *B.A.R.* Suppl. 73: 81–97.

Mines et fonderies antiques de la Gaule (1980). Table ronde du C.N.R.S. (Toulouse 21–22 Nov. 1980). Toulouse.

Morel, J.-P. (1966). 'Les Phocéens en occident: certitudes et hypothèses', *Parola del Passato* 21: 378–420.

Morel, J.-P. (1975). 'L'expansion phocéenne en occident: dix années de recherches (1966–75)', *B.C.H.* 99: 853–96.

Morrison, J. S., Williams, R. T. (1968). *Greek oared ships*. Cambridge.

Mossé, C. (1972). 'La vie économique d'Athènes au IVème siècle. Crise ou renouveau', *Praelectiones Patavinae*: 135–44.

Nash, D. (1976). 'The growth of urban society in France' in Cunliffe, B., Rowley, T. (ed.) *Oppida: the beginnings of urbanization in Barbarian Europe*, B.A.R. Suppl. 2: 95–133. Oxford.

– (1978). *Settlement and coinage in central Gaul c.200–c.50 B.C. B.A.R.* Suppl. 39.2 Oxford.

Nicolet, Cl. (1966). *L'ordre equestre à l'époque republicaine (312–43 av. J.-C.).* Paris.

– (ed.) (1978). *Rome et la création du monde méditerranéen. II. La genèse de l'empire.* Paris.

Packman, Z. M. (1968). *The taxes in grain in Ptolemaic Egypt*, American Studies in Papyrology 4. New Haven.

Palma, A. (1975). 'L'evoluzione del navicolariato tra il I ed. il III sec. d. C.', *A.A.N.* 86: 7–13.

Panella, Cl. (1981). 'Merci destinate al commercio transmarino. Il vino: la distribuzione e i mercata', in Giardina, A., Schiavone, A., (1981).

Patlagean, E. (1977). *Pauvrété économique et pauvrété sociale à Byzance, 4è – 7è siècles*. Paris.

Pavis d'Escurac, H. (1976). *La Préfecture de l'annone: service administratif impérial d'Auguste à Constantin*. Rome.

– (1977). 'Aristocratie sénatoriale et profits commerciaux', *Ktema* 2: 339–55.

Peacock, D. P. S. (1971). 'Roman amphorae in pre-Roman Britain' in Jesson, M., Hill, D., (ed.), *The Iron Age and its hill-forts: studies presented to Sir Mortimer Wheeler*: 161–8. Southampton.

Pecirkà, J. (1976). 'The crisis of the Athenian Polis', *Eirene* 14: 5–30.

Piganiol, A. (1947). 'L'économie dirigée dans l'empire romain au IVe siècle', *Scientia* 81: 95–100.

Pirenne, H. (1969). *Medieval cities. Their origins and the revival of trade*. Princeton.

Polany, K. (1957). *Trade and market in the early empires: economies in history and theory*. Polanyi, K., Arensberg, C., Pearson, H. W. (ed.) Chicago.

– (1968). *Primitive, archaic and modern economies: Essays of Karl Polanyi*, Dalton, G. (ed.) New York.

– (1977). *The human livelihood*, Pearson, H. W. (ed.) New York.

Pomey, P., Tchernia, A. (1978). 'Le tonnage maximum des navires de commerce romains', *Archaeonautica* 2: 233–51.

Pounds, N. J. G. (1974). *An economic history of medieval Europe*. London.

Préaux, Cl. (1939) *L'économie royale des Lagides*. Brussels.

Pucci, G. (1977). 'Le sigillate italiche, galliche e orientali', in *L'instrumentum domesticum di Ercolano e Pompei nella prima età imperiale. Quaderni di Cultura Materiale* I: 9–22. Rome.

– (1980). 'Le officine ceramiche tardo-italiche', in *Céramiques hellénistiques et romaines. Annales littéraires de l'Université de Besançon* 242: 135–53.

– (1981). 'La ceramica italica (terra sigillata)', in Giardina, A., Schiavone, A. (1981) 99–122. Bari.

Ramin, J. (1974). 'L'espace économique en Gaule. Les documents historiques concernant les mines', in *Mélanges Roger Dion, Caesarodunum* IX bis, Chevallier R. (ed.): 417–37. Paris.

Rancoule, G. (1980). *La Lagaste, agglomération gauloise du Bassin de l'Aude*, Atacina, 10. Carcassonne.

– Guilaine, J. (1979). 'La fin de l'Age du Fer et les débuts de la romanisation dans les Corbières occidentales' in Guilaine. J. (ed.) *L'Abri Jean Cros*: 439–46. Toulouse.

Reekmans, T. (1966). *La sitométrie dans les archives de Zénon*. Brussels.

– van 't Dack, E. (1952). 'A Bodleian archive on corn transport', *C.E.* 27: 149–95.

Renfrew, A. C. (1975). 'Trade as action at a distance', in Sabloff, J. A., Lamberg-Karlovsky, C. C. (1975) 3–59.

– (1977). 'Production and exchange in early state societies. The evidence of pottery', in *Pottery and early commerce: characterization and trade in Roman and later ceramics*, Peacock, D. P. S. (ed.): 1–20. London.

– Peacey, J. Springer (1968). 'Aegean marble: a petrological study', *A.B.S.A.* 63: 45–66.

Rickman, G. (1980). *The corn supply of ancient Rome*. Oxford.

Rostowzew, M. (1906). 'Kornerhebung und -transport im griechisch-römischen Ägypten', *A.P.F.* 3: 201–24.

Rostovtzeff, M. (1941). *Social and economic history of the Hellenistic world* (S.E.H.H.W.) Oxford.

– (1957). *Social and economic history of the Roman Empire* (S.E.H.R.E.) (2nd ed.) Oxford.

Rougé J. (1966). *Recherches sur l'organisation du commerce maritime en Méditerranée sous l'empire romain*. Paris.

– (1980). 'Prêt et société maritimes dans le monde romain', in d'Arms/Kopff (1980) 291–303.

Ruggini, L. C. (1961). *Economia e società nell'Italia annonaria. Rapporti fra agricolturae commercio dal IV al VI s. d. C.* Milan.

– (1978). 'Les structures de la société et de l'économie Lyonnaises au IIe siècle, par rapport à la politique locale et impériale', in *Les Martyrs de Lyon (177). Coll. Intern. du C.N.R.S.* 575: 65–92.

Sabloff, J. A., Lamberg-Karlovsky, C. C. (ed.) (1975). *Ancient civilization and trade*. Albuquerque.

Ste. Croix, G. E. M. de (1974). 'Ancient Greek and Roman maritime loans', in Edey, H., Yamey, B. S. (ed.) *Essays in honour of W. T. Baxter*: 41–59. London.

Salomonson, J. W. (1962). 'Late Roman earthenware with relief decoration found in Northern Africa and Egypt', *Oudheidkundige Mededelingen uit het Rijksmuseum van Oudheiden te Leiden* (= *O.M.R.L.*) 43: 53–95.
– (1968). 'Etude sur le céramique romaine d'Afrique sigilée claire et céramique commune de Henchir el Ouiba (Raqqado) en Tunisie centrale', *Bulletin van de Vereniging tot bevordering der kennis van de antieke beschaving.* (= *B.A.Besch.*) 43: 80–145.
– (1969). 'Spätrömische rote Tonware mit Reliefverzierung aus Nordafrikanischen Werkstätten', *B. A. Besch.* 44: 4–109.
Sawyer, P. H. (1977). 'Kings and merchants', in *Early medieval kingship*, Sawyer, P. H., Wood, I. (ed.) 139–58. Leeds.
Schippschuh, O. (1974). *Die Händler im römischen Kaiserreich in Gallien, Germanien und den Donauprovinzen Rätien, Noricum und Pannonien.* Amsterdam.
Shelov, D. B. (1972). *Tanais and the lower Don in the C3rd to C1st B.C.* (in Russian). Moscow.
Shelov, D. B. (1975). *Pottery stamps from Tanais, C3rd to C1st B.C.* (in Russian). Moscow.
Sijpesteijn, P. J. (1978). 'Three new Ptolemaic documents on transportation of grain', *C.E.* 53: 107–16.
Snodgrass, A. M. (1980). *Archaic Greece: the age of experiment.* London.
Starr, C. G. (1977). *The economic and social growth of early Greece, 800–500 BC.* New York.
Tchernia, A. (1980). 'Quelques remarques sur le commerce du vin et les amphores' in d'Arms/Kopff (1980) 305–12.
Thompson, W. E. (1979). A view of Athenian banking', *M.H.* 36: 224–41.
Uenze, O. (1958). *Frührömische Amphoren als Zeitmarken im Spätlatène.* Marburg.
Vallet, G., Villard F. (1963). 'Céramique grecque et histoire économique', in Courbin P. (ed.) *Etudes archéologiques. Recueil de travaux.* 205–17. Paris.
Van Werveke, H. (1923). 'Comment les établissements religieux belges se procuraient-ils du vin au haut moyen age?', *R.B.Ph.* 2: 643–62.
– (1925). 'Les propriétés excentriques des églises au haut moyen âge', *R.B.Ph.* 4: 136–41.
Vaussanvin, H. (1979). 'A propos des amphores découvertes à Cersot', *Bull. Soc. des Amis des Arts et des Sciences de Tournus*, 78: 101–27.
Vélissaropoulos, J. (1980). *Les nauclères grecs. Recherches sur les institutions maritimes en Grèce et dans l'Orient hellénisé.* Geneva.
Veyne, P. (1976). *Le Pain et le Cirque.* Paris.
– (1979). 'Mythe et Réalité de l'autarcie à Rome, *R.E.A.* 81: 261–81.
– (1981). 'Suicide, fisc, esclavage, capital et droit romain', *Latomus* 40: 217–68.
Vidal-Naquet, P. (1965). 'Economie et société dans la Grèce ancienne: L'oeuvre de Moses Finley', *Archives Européennes de Sociologie* 6: 111–48.
Waagé, F. O. (1933). 'Excavations in the Athenian Agora. The Roman and Byzantine Pottery', *Hesperia* 2: 279–328.
Walter, H., Vierneisel, K. (1959). 'Heraion von Samos: die Funde der Kampagnen 1958 und 1959', *A.M.* 74: 10–34.
Ward-Perkins, J. B. (1980). 'Nicomedia and the marble trade', *P.B.S.R.* 48: 23–70.
Welles, C. B. (1964). 'On the collection of revenues in grain in Ptolemaic Egypt', *Festschrift Oertel*: 7–16. Bonn.

Whitehead, D. (1977). *The ideology of the Athenian metic*. P.C.P.S. Suppl. 4.
Whittaker, C. R. (1978). 'Land and labour in North Africa', *Klio* 60: 331–62.
– (1980). 'Inflation and the economy in the fourth century AD.', in *Imperial revenue, expenditure and monetary policy in the fourth century A.D.* King, C. E. (ed.) *B.A.R.* Suppl. 76: 1–22. Oxford.
Wild, J. P. (1970). *Textile manufacture in the northern Roman provinces*. Cambridge.
– (1977). *Textiles from Vindolanda, 1973–75*. (Vindolanda III). Hexham.
Will, E. (1954). 'Trois quarts de siècle de recherches sur l'économie grecque antique', *Annales E.S.C.* 9: 7–22.
– (1956). 'Archéologie et histoire économique. Problèmes et méthodes. Etude de quelques cas particuliers', *Etudes d'Arch.* 1: 147–66.
– (1965). 'La Grèce archaïque', *Deuxième conférence internationale d'histoire économique, Aix-en-Provence 1962. I. Trade and Politics in the ancient world*: 41–96, 107–15. Paris. Reprinted New York 1979.
Wipszycka, E. (1965). *L'industrie textile dans l'Egypte romaine*. Warsaw.
– (1966). 'Das textilhandwerk und der Staat', *Archiv f. Papyrusforschung* 18: 1–22.
Wörrle, M. (1971). 'Ägyptisches Getreide für Ephesos', *Chiron* 1: 325–40.
Wycherley, R. E. (1973). 'Pentelethen', *A.B.S.A.* 68: 349–53.
Zevi, F., Tchernia, A. (1969). 'Amphores de Byzacène au Bas-Empire', *Ant. Afr.* 3: 173–214.
Zilliacus, H. (1939). 'Neue Ptolemäertexte zum Korntransport und Saatdarlehen', *Aegyptus* 19: 59–76.

Contributors

KEITH HOPKINS is Professor of Sociology at Brunel University, Uxbridge, England.

PAUL CARTLEDGE is University Lecturer in Ancient History, and Fellow of Clare College, Cambridge.

A. M. SNODGRASS is Laurence Professor of Classical Archaeology in the University of Cambridge.

YVON GARLAN is Professor of Ancient History, Université de Haute-Bretagne, Rennes.

PAUL MILLETT is Lecturer in Ancient History in the University of Leicester.

CLAUDE MOSSÉ is Professor of the History of Antiquity, University of Paris.

D. J. THOMPSON (CRAWFORD) is Fellow and Senior Tutor at Girton College, Cambridge.

CHRISTIAN GOUDINEAU is Professor of Archaeology, University of Provence, Aix.

ANDRÉ TCHERNIA is at the Centre Camille Jullian, Centre National de la Recherche Scientifique, and the University of Provence, Aix.

GIUSEPPE PUCCI is Professor of Classical Archaeology, University of Siena.

PETER GARNSEY is University Lecturer in Ancient History and Fellow of Jesus College, Cambridge.

H. W. PLEKET is Professor of Ancient History and Epigraphy, University of Leiden.

ANDREA CARANDINI is Professor of Classical Archaeology, University of Pisa.

C. R. WHITTAKER is University Lecturer in Ancient History, and Fellow of Churchill College, Cambridge.

Translators

ASSIA HURST translated the articles by Yvon Garlan and Christian Goudineau; HENRY HURST that by Andrea Carandini; and JANET LLOYD those by André Tchernia and Claude Mossé.

General Index

Index Locorum

Index Locorum

How important was trade in the economies of ancient Greece and Rome? What was the status of traders? Modern archaeologists have discovered massive evidence that goods in the ancient world were exchanged, but how many of the excavated statues and wine-jars had been traded? Some were probably gifts, others were votive offerings; many undoubtedly were containers for taxes in kind. They had never been items of trade. The frequent modern assumption that trade dominated ancient exchange needs careful examination.

In ancient communities, wealth was invested mostly in agriculture. High status depended upon ownership of land, political activity and conspicuous consumption. Merchants generally played no role in ruling élites. Commerce had no overt impact on politics. Ancient civilizations flourished, without benefit of the wealthy merchants who figure so largely in the economic history of post-mediaeval Europe.

This book contains fourteen contributions by leading scholars from five countries. Their interests range over more than a thousand years, from Archaic Greece to the Later Roman Empire. Their disagreements reflect the difficulties of conceptualising, understanding and interpreting the surviving evidence. Their lively debates and this volume's title also reflect the seminal influence of Sir Moses Finley's book, *The Ancient Economy* (California, 1973).